LEAVING CERTIFICATE

LESS STRESS MORE SUCCESS

English Revision
Higher Level

Martin Kieran and Frances Rocks

g GILL EDUCATION

Gill Education
Hume Avenue
Park West
Dublin 12
www.gilleducation.ie

Gill Education is an imprint of M.H. Gill & Co.

ISBN 978 071 719029 4

Design by Liz White Designs
Print origination by Carole Lynch

The paper used in this book is made from the wood pulp of managed forests.
For every tree felled, at least one tree is planted, thereby renewing natural resources.

For permission to reproduce photographs, the authors and publisher gratefully
acknowledge the following:

© Alamy: 8, 21, 89, 90, 102, 114, 125, 134, 149, 156, 161, 199, 205, 213, 223, 228;
© Bloomsbury Publishing Plc: 28R; © Doubleday Ireland: 18; © Faber and Faber Ltd: 111;
© Getty Images: 5, 24, 25; © iStock/Getty Premium: 10, 13, 67, 73, 81, 86, 152, 202;
© Johan Persson/ArenaPAL: 143; © Penguin Random House: 28L; © RTÉ Archives: 221, 226.

The authors and publisher have made every effort to trace all copyright holders,
but if any have been inadvertently overlooked we would be pleased to make the
necessary arrangement at the first opportunity.

CONTENTS

Introduction

● Recognising and understand the different genres of language use in the examination.

Language genres

To prepare for Leaving Certificate Higher Level English, you are expected to be familiar with these five broad language genres.

Informative writing

Found in newspapers, reports, etc.

- Factual, direct, using verifiable data
- Clearly organised, accessible language

Argumentative writing

Found in newspapers, discussions, etc.

- Logical, using valid evidence
- Reasonable, rational language

Persuasive writing

Found in speeches, opinion pieces, debates, etc.

- Presents a strong view or opinion
- Emphatic, often emotional language

There is no single exclusive style of writing. Different language **genres usually overlap**. Persuasive writing, for example, is similar to argument and often includes elements of informative language.

Narrative writing

Found in novels, plays, films, etc.

- Story-telling based on plot, characterisation and conflict
- Fictional language, structured and atmospheric

Aesthetic writing

Found in poetry, short stories, diaries, etc.

- Appeals to our appreciation of beauty
- Poetic imaginative language, often using rich imagery

English (Higher Level) Paper 1 Overview

English (Higher Level) Paper 1 overview

Paper 1 accounts for 200 marks (half the overall examination total).
You are required to:

- choose one of the three texts in **Section A** (50 marks – 45–50 minutes)
- choose one question from **Section B**. However, you cannot answer the Section B question that accompanied the Section A text you have chosen (50 marks – 40 minutes)
- answer one question from **Composing** (100 marks – 75 minutes).

> The time limit for Paper 1 is
> **2 hours and 50 minutes.**

- Read the questions carefully to discover the various tasks in each question.
- All parts of the tasks need to be addressed in order to achieve a high mark.
- Plan your answer before you begin your response.

1 Paper 1: Comprehending A

> **aims**
> - Understanding the different types of 'Comprehending' questions (information retrieval, personal opinion and style).
> - Developing the thinking and writing skills that are essential for successful answers.

Comprehending A at a glance

The total mark awarded for Paper 1 is 200 (half the overall total for the exam). This includes 100 for Section 1 (Comprehending) and 100 for Section 2 (Composing). The Comprehending A section (worth 50 marks) tests your ability to read, understand, analyse and respond to a particular text. This section consists of three parts.

exam focus

Choose **one** of the three Comprehending A texts and allocate your time carefully:
- Reading the text – allow about **6–8** minutes
- Answering part (i) – allow **10–12** minutes
- Answering part (ii) – allow **10–12** minutes
- Answering part (iii) – allow **15–18** minutes

Parts (i) and (ii)

Parts (i) and (ii) are each worth 15 marks. In these two questions, you might be asked **to summarise** (in your own words) **or give your opinion on key aspects of the text.**
Possible questions include:

- Your impressions of places, settings and atmospheres.
- An outline of the writer's own views.
- Your observations about a character, relationship or ideas in the text.

exam focus

Three short paragraphs (based on three relevant, supported points) should be sufficient for an answer to part (i) or (ii). Focused, succinct answers are required.

- Compare or comment on visual images.
- The overall impact of the text (or particular parts of the text).
- Responding personally to the text.

Part (iii)

Part (iii) is worth 20 marks and often refers to the writer's style. Allow about 15–18 minutes to write three or four succinct paragraphs based on three relevant, supported points – and aim for at least 200 words.

Read the questions first, identifying the specific type of question (information retrieval, personal opinion, style or a mixture of these). Keep this in mind as you read through the extract.

Responding to Comprehending A questions

It's essential to **study the wording** of questions carefully before you begin writing. Highlight the key words in the question, so that you are clear about the task.

Outline	Briefly describe only the main points or facts about something.
Comment on	Give a critical, analytical response on subject matter and/or style of writing.
Explain	Clarify by giving details and/or reasons.
Discuss	Examine and distinguish the positive and negative points of something or someone.
Identify	Find one or more examples.
Evaluate	Consider something carefully and decide how significant/insignificant it is.
Define	Specify exactly what something means.
Analyse	Consider and question closely in order to explain.
Illustrate	Show by giving more information or examples to explain or prove something.
Compare and contrast	Examine similarities and differences. You may also be asked to refer to some of the prescribed texts studied for Paper 2.
Develop your own point of view	Support the points you make through further – and more detailed – discussion, using suitable reference.

Neat, legible handwriting will help to make a positive impression on examiners. Corrections should be made by simply drawing a line through the mistake.

Being scared isn't easy – but it's fun!

When she's not stuck at her desk, the best-selling thriller writer, Patricia Cornwell, is a scuba diver and helicopter pilot.

I'm always scared when I learn a new sport but my number one rule in life is that I will not be ruled by fear. If I'm afraid of something I'm going to figure out a way to deal with it. Since I was a little kid I've loved fast, powerful machines but the truth is I find all my hobbies – scuba diving, helicopter flying and motorcycling – nerve-racking. I'm terrified.

During my scuba diving training, the dive master made me sit on the bottom of the bay and take my mask off, then put it back on. I could not do it. The water went rushing up my nose. I thought I was going to drown; I started to bolt up to the surface and he grabbed my ankles to hold me down. It was just an awful experience.

Even now when I dive, I hope the weather gets bad so I don't have to go. I get into the water and have to settle for a minute because my heart starts racing. But you cannot dive if you get hyped up – you have to calm down. And when you do, you might have the dive trip of your life.

The first time I flew a helicopter solo, my knees were knocking together – literally – I had to start singing to myself. Then all of a sudden it was like, 'Oh my God, this is the most fun thing I have ever done. I am flying, I'm alone and it's just me doing this.'

The most frightened I have ever been was flying a helicopter. We were north of Florida, and we got caught in weather we weren't expecting – an unpredictable storm was moving in. We got trapped in fog, flying at 100-something feet in a wooded area, and couldn't see. It was raining like a monsoon and I really thought this was going to be it; any minute we were going to hit a power line and come down. It was terrifying. Just when we thought it was hopeless, all of a sudden this little grass strip opened up under us and we landed.

If I hadn't learned to deal with fear, I would have been crippled by it. If you don't confront your fear, it wins. Which is why I'm a totally different person since I took up my extreme hobbies. It's made me more confident, bolder, keener to try other things.

You don't need to do what I do – unfortunately it's expensive to fly a helicopter. But you could do a helicopter tour and enjoy the ride. Scuba diving is more accessible. You can go out on a charter boat with a group of people and down you go.

It's as simple as this: if an opportunity presents itself, don't walk away from it. If someone says it might be cool to learn to snorkel, or ride a motorcycle, and you light up like a Christmas tree when they say it, don't argue yourself out of it. Take the next step. And don't let anyone tell you that you can't do something. Everything I do is stuff I was told I couldn't do.

A lot of people enjoy fear as pleasure. It's delicious that you can get so close to the dragon that you can feel its warm breath, but you're not going to get burned. That's an empowering experience.

All this makes you feel more alive because you are taking power and control over a world that is random and difficult. And the more you do with boldness and confidence, the more you get out of life. That's what we should do while we're here. Don't just exist – do something!

Question A

(i) Based on your reading of the above extract, what do you learn about Patricia Cornwell's attitude to fear?   **(15 marks)**

Prompt!

It's natural to feel scared.

- Fear can be seen as a challenge.
- It's important to confront fear.
- Fear can even be exhilarating.
- Overcoming fear is empowering, and gives us a great sense of achievement.

Sample answer

Patricia Cornwell has changed her attitude towards fear over the years. She is honest in admitting that she has often been fearful in the past, but says that she 'will not be ruled by fear'. While her extreme sports hobbies, such as scuba diving, excite and scare her, she has always succeeded in conquering fear.

Allow about 10–12 minutes and aim for three focused, supported points in short paragraphs.

The famous author is a very positive person who encourages everyone to face up to what terrifies them: 'If I hadn't learned to deal with fear, I would have been crippled by it'. From personal experience, she believes that she has become a 'totally different person' by taking up extreme hobbies, including helicopter flying and motorcycling.

Cornwell obviously gets great pleasure from taking part in such 'nerve-racking' sports. Her enthusiasm for life is evident throughout the extract. It's interesting that she conquers her fears by taking on challenging sports that make her feel confident and 'more alive'. Her concluding tone is particularly enthusiastic ('Don't just exist – do something!') and makes it clear that she is totally convinced about the many benefits of overcoming fear.

EXAMINER'S COMMENT

- Succinct, well-organised response is directly focused throughout.
- Three distinct, relevant points are aptly supported by reference and quotation.
- Discussion ranges over the entire extract.
- Controlled economical language use. Clear expression, e.g. 'succeeded in conquering fear', 'concluding tone is particularly enthusiastic'.

MARKS AWARDED: $\frac{15}{15}$

Realistic time management is an essential part of successful answering. For the Comprehending A 15-mark questions, allow about 10–12 minutes and aim for three relevant points, supported by suitable evidence. Do not fall into the trap of over-writing, as this is likely to leave you short of time for the other questions.

Running away

Waris is a young girl, living with her family in the desert in Somalia, in Africa. She decides to run away from home to avoid an arranged marriage.

A slight sound awoke me, and when I opened my eyes, I was staring into the face of a lion. Riveted awake, my eyes stretched wide – very wide – as if to expand enough to contain the animal in front of me. I tried to stand up, but I hadn't eaten for several days, so my weak legs wobbled and folded beneath me. Collapsing, I slumped back against the tree where I had been resting, sheltered from the African desert sun that becomes so merciless at noon. I quietly leaned my head back, closed my eyes, and felt the rough bark of the tree pressing into my skull. The lion was so near I could smell his musty scent in the hot air. I spoke to God: 'It's the end for me, my God. Please take me now'.

My long journey across the desert had come to an end. I had no protection, no weapon. Nor the strength to run. I knew I couldn't beat the lion up the tree, because with their 10 strong claws, lions are excellent climbers. By the time I got half way up – boom – one swipe and I'd be gone. Without any fear, I opened my eyes again and said to the lion, 'Come and get me. I'm ready for you'.

He was a beautiful male with a mane of golden hair and a long tail switching back and forth to flick the flies away. He was five or six years old, young and healthy. I knew he could crush me instantly; he was the king. All my life I'd watched those paws take down wildebeest and zebras weighing hundreds of pounds more than me.

Waris Dirie

The lion stared at me and slowly blinked his honey-coloured eyes. My brown eyes stared back, locked on his. 'Go on. Take me now.' He looked at me again, then looked away. He licked his lips and sat down on his haunches. Then the lion rose and paced back and forth in front of me elegantly. Finally, he turned and walked away.

Question A

(i) Outline, in your own words, Waris's thoughts and feelings in the above extract.

(15 marks)

Allow about 10–12 minutes and aim for three focused, supported points in short paragraphs.

key point

Autobiographical texts include memoirs and diaries.

- They are personal records of past experiences.
- These texts often describe people and places in detail.
- They are written in the first person.
- They usually have a reflective or nostalgic (sentimental) tone.

Sample answer

Waris is acutely aware of the great danger she faces. She is so weak, however, that all she can think of is how close she is to the lion, 'I could smell his musty scent in the hot air'. This physical sense of the wild animal's presence is intense. Waris is also convinced that she will be killed and prays to God, 'Please take me now.'

Although exhausted, the young girl takes a moment to consider the possibility of escape, but is realistic enough to accept that she has neither the energy nor speed to run away to safety, 'I knew I couldn't beat the lion up the tree'. Her past experience of lions confirms her worst fears, 'I knew he could crush me instantly'.

Waris strikes me as being remarkably courageous. Even though she believes that she will soon die, Waris can still admire the lion, 'a beautiful male with a mane of golden hair'. She is highly observant and is able to describe close-up details of this stunning creature. As she stares at the lion's 'honey-coloured eyes', it is evident that she feels very much at one with nature.

EXAMINER'S COMMENT

- Clearly focused concise points ('aware', 'realistic', 'courageous') tackle the question directly.
- Uses relevant supportive quotations, well-integrated into commentary.
- Impressive expression – fluent, varied and controlled.
- A confident, successful response.

MARKS AWARDED: $\frac{15}{15}$

Some Comprehending A questions might ask you to deal with both content and style (sometimes including visual images). Re-read your answer to check that you have covered all the key elements in the question.

Parents, rise up!

Read carefully the online article written by Liat Hughes Joshi and answer the question that follows.

Nothing sums up modern parenting more than slogan T-shirts. You know, the ones that say 'Daddy's Princess' or 'No. 1 Child'. Parents fifty years ago may have loved and adored their children, but they would never have proclaimed it to the world. And certainly never to their child. There was a strict difference between the generations, with children – for the most part – knowing their place. Today's children are placed on pedestals and they know it. No wonder we're seeing more anti-social, selfish and bad behaviour than ever before.

I recall trying to leave a café recently. In front of the doorway, two young children were playing on the floor, their parents smiling indulgently at them. Not wanting to push past, I waited for the children to move aside or for the parents to tell them what to do. Nothing happened. I waited and waited until, frustrated, I had to ask them to move away. No big deal? Perhaps not. But recently in another café the table next to mine was mobbed by teenagers, throwing food and screeching at the top of their voices. It was dreadful and their seemingly irresponsible parents stood by and did nothing. I could go on.

How many of us have been frustrated by children who push, shout over their parents, won't accept bedtimes, never say please or thank you and scowl when given a present which doesn't meet their demands? Too many modern children – while at times loveable – are becoming bad-mannered, self-centred and utterly without the social skills they'll need in adulthood.

There's no doubt that treating children as individuals and enjoying their company is helping us to develop young people with stronger self-esteem. But we have to find a balance before we create an entire generation of selfish brats who are unable

to function in the real world. Take helping around the house. Why don't many modern children clear the table and wash up? Why don't they earn pocket money by washing the car? Yes, children have a lot of homework these days, but learning the discipline of doing household chores matters too.

We also have to stop entertaining children so much. Stop the constant ferrying around, the endless hobbies and extra classes. Not only are we becoming worn out, but we're not allowing children to learn the essential life skill of managing boredom. Getting tougher isn't about teaching needless etiquette. I don't want to sit opposite a child eating with their mouths hanging open, but I'm quite relaxed about whether they're holding their knife and fork the right way. Equally, I don't want to sit frustrated as teenagers (and young children) stare at their tablets or smart phones when I'm trying to have a conversation. I like the fact that we respect our children more these days. But that respect has to cut both ways.

Stand firm. Not meeting expectations can mean no pocket money or less screen time. Remind unhelpful children that neglecting to do tasks could result in a 'No' the next time they need a lift. It's fine for teenagers to text and message each other, but make sure their online socialising is balanced with plenty of face-to-face interaction. Look at what makes him or her tick: is it watching TV, gaming with friends? Identify what they want and offer it as a reward.

As parents, we have three main responsibilities: to keep our children safe, to make them happy, and to prepare them to be well-functioning, content adults. But, if we carry on as we are, we're in real danger of creating a generation of self-centred brats. To stop that, we need to take back the tiaras and put an end to the tantrums!

Question A

(i) How does the writer try to persuade readers that children and teenagers are 'spoilt'? (15 marks)

Prompt!

- What persuasive techniques are used? (See checklist on page 17.)
- Does the opening make an immediate impact?
- Is the writer's tone effective?
- Are the arguments valid and convincing?
- Any persuasive examples or illustrations?
- Does the writer affect the reader's responses?

Sample answer 1

I don't agree that the writer Liat Hughes Joshi is persuasive. In fact, she seems to just totally hate young people and is one-sided for no good reason. Except actually prejudice.

Allow about 10–12 minutes and aim for three focused, supported points in short paragraphs.

What is so wrong with praising young kids today and buying them T-shirts? We live in the modern world and old people in their forties are no longer in tune and not with reality half the time. I never see teenagers throwing food at people. This is totally prejudice. This writer of the extract has issues with young people. Some of us live in the country and actually depend on lifts from parents.

She tries to be a persuasive writer but only ends up looking ridiculous because she is so totally negative. Everything she says is against teenagers as if they never work. Many of my friends have jobs at weekends and I have had a summer job last year to pay for a holiday. This writer uses insulting language about brats and this is totally out of order.

I think a lot of the time she is trying to get attention by such insults in which there is no truth. I don't agree that children and teenagers are spoilt and that this is actually persuasive language at all.

MARKS AWARDED: $\frac{8}{15}$

Improving the answer:

- Sample answer 1 would gain marks if there were greater focus on the question (by discussing the writer's arguments).
- Develop points, e.g. about the writer's generalising and subjective views.
- Avoid drifting into personal opinion.
- Refer to the text by commenting on key points and quotations.
- Language needs to be more carefully managed. Overuse of 'and', 'actually' and 'total'.

Sample answer 2

The writer expresses very strong personal views from the start – but seems to be generalising about how parents spoil their children. However, the emphatic opening sentence grabs the reader's attention. This is followed up by an effective visual image of T-shirt slogans, such as 'Daddy's Princess' – something that will be familiar to many people.

Liat Hughes Joshi builds her argument by appealing to traditional parenting values when children knew 'their place' and contrasting them with today's young people who, she asserts, are 'placed on pedestals'. She supports her strong views with several anecdotes of her own experiences in cafés where parents apparently ignored their children as they misbehaved. Hughes then appeals to the reader's good sense by arguing that there needs to be a sensible balance, so that children develop responsibly, equipped with the 'social skills they'll need in adulthood'.

By using the inclusive personal pronoun, the writer invites us to agree with her views: 'We also have to stop entertaining children'. She gives many examples of self-indulgent teenage behaviour and suggests that parents use rewards to improve how young people can improve their manners in an atmosphere of mutual respect. The article is rounded off effectively by offering parents a choice between well-functioning, content adults and 'self-centred brats'.

EXAMINER'S COMMENT

- Clearly focused, top-grade response that never strays from the question of the writer's persuasive techniques.
- Organised points in paragraphs supported effectively with apt reference and quotation.
- Ranges over the full extract in discussing persuasive arguments.
- Impressive expression (e.g. 'emphatic opening', 'traditional parenting values', 'atmosphere of mutual respect').

MARKS AWARDED: $\frac{15}{15}$

The Red Door

Read the extract below from *The Red Door* by Iain Crichton Smith and then answer the question that follows.

As he stared at the door he felt strange flutterings within him. First of all the door had been painted very lovingly so that it shone with a deep inward shine such as one might find in pictures. And indeed it looked like a picture against the rest of the house which wasn't at all modern but on the contrary was old and intertwined with all sorts of rusty pipes like snakes.

He went back from the door and looked at it from a distance as people in art galleries have to do when studying an oil painting. The more he regarded it the more he liked it. It certainly stood out against the drab landscape as if it were a work of art. On the other hand the more he looked at it the more it seemed to express something in himself which had been deeply buried for years. After a while there was something boring about green and as for blue it wouldn't have suited the door at all. Blue would have been too blatant in a cold way. And anyway the sky was already blue.

But mixed with his satisfaction he felt what could only be described as puzzlement, a slight deviation from the normal as if his head were spinning and he were going round in circles. What would the neighbours say about it, he wondered. Never in the history of the village had there been a red door before. For that matter he couldn't remember seeing even a blue door himself, though he had heard of the existence of one.

The morning was breaking all over the village as he looked. Blue smoke was ascending from chimneys, a cock was crowing, belligerent and heraldic, its red claws sunk into the earth, its metallic breast oriental and strange. There was a dew all about him and lying on the fences ahead of him. He recognised that the village would wake to a new morning, for the red door would gather attention to itself.

And he thought to himself, 'I have always sought to hide among other people. I agree to whatever anybody tells me to do. If they think I should go to church, I go to church. If they want me to cut peats for them, I do. I have never,' he thought with wonder, 'been myself.' He looked down at his grey fisherman's jersey and his wellingtons and he thought, 'I have always worn these things because everybody else does. I have never had the courage to wear what I wanted to wear, for example a coloured waistcoat and a coloured jacket.'

The red door stood out against the whiteness of the frost and the glimmerings of snow. It seemed to be saying something to him, to be asking him a question. Perhaps it was pleading with him not to destroy it. Perhaps it was saying, 'I don't want to be green. There must be a place somewhere for me as myself. I wish to be red. What is wrong with red anyway?' The door seemed to him to have its own courage.

Wine of course was red and so was blood. He drank none of the former and only saw the latter when he cut himself while repairing a fence or working with wood when a nail would prick his finger.

But really was he happy? That was the question. When he considered it carefully he knew that he wasn't. He didn't like eating alone, he didn't like sitting in the house alone, he didn't like having none who belonged to him, to whom he could tell his secret thoughts, for example that such and such was a mean devil and that that other one was an ungrateful rat.

He had to keep a perpetually smiling face to the world, that was his trouble. But the red door didn't do that. It was foreign and confident. It seemed to be saying what it was, not what it thought others expected it to say. On the other hand, he didn't like wellingtons and a fisherman's jersey. He hated them in fact: they had no elegance.

Now Mary had elegance. Though she was a bit odd, she had elegance. It was true that the villagers didn't understand her but that was because she read many books, her father having been a teacher. And on the other hand she made no concessions to anybody. She seemed to be saying, 'You can take me or leave me.' She never gossiped. She was proud and distant. She had a world of her own.

Question A

(ii) In the above text, Iain Crichton Smith describes a scene where an individual is in conflict with conforming to what society expects. With reference to one of the comparative texts you have studied for this year's Leaving Cert course, identify a scene or situation where a central character is in conflict with conforming to what society expects. Describe the scene and the nature of the conflict, and your own response to the incident. (20 marks)

Prompt!

- Choose a scene or situation where a character is in conflict with how his society functions.
- Describe the scene.
- Identify the nature of the conflict with society.
- Explain your own thoughts and feelings about this event.

Sample answer 1 (basic grade)

I have chosen the scene where Gar meets the boys, his friends. When the boys come in to visit Gar they are loud and noisy. They want to talk about the local match and drinking and getting girls. Gar is in conflict with all that. He wants to talk about his leaving Ballybeg to go to Philadelphia. Only the youngest Joe tries to talk about that but he is stopped by Ned. They want to boast about what they are going to do. They don't want to know about Gar. Whenever the conversation is about girls, all the boys join in and laugh. Private gives the true version of Ned's false story. After that, Ned boasts about 'picking up a couple of women' at the dance, but it's all talk. There is more conflict when Ned throws a belt to Gar as a present and then they all go off. Joe stays behind to tell Gar about how his mother says he can leave when the trees planted beside the house grow big. Gar tells him to go and join the others and Gar is left alone.

MARKS AWARDED: $\frac{8}{20}$

Improving the answer:

- Name text and author (*Philadelphia, Here I Come!* by Brian Friel). Focus on Gar's objections to rural Irish life.
- Discuss aspects of Ballybeg society that are evident in this scene.
- Is it free or oppressive? Are young people happy?
- Use more detailed reference and quotation to support opinions expressed.
- Do you relate to Gar's attitude? Give your personal response to the event.
- Using paragraphs would clarify the different tasks required by the question.

Sample answer 2 (top grade)

Brian Friel's play, *Philadelphia, Here I Come!*, contains a revealing scene where Gar meets up with his Ballybeg friends. The 'boys' have been asked by Madge the housekeeper to visit Gar at home on the night before he emigrates. Gar was longing for recognition from them of this crucial occasion in his life. Yet they are reluctant to acknowledge his leaving and Gar 'becomes apart from the others'.

Gar tries to refer to his departure indirectly, 'Lads, when you're out lining up on the pitch, you can think of me, because I'll be thinking of you'. But the conversation is immediately steered away by the others into loud macho talk. 'Who's the blondie thing I seen last Sunday?' Rural Irish patriarchy in the 1960s is reflected in Ned's comment about 'two wee Greenock pieces'. His description of women, of course, is all bluster and self-delusion. He exaggerates his success with girls to impress others and be as masculine as possible. In a sense, this is what Gar wants to escape from. Young men in Ballybeg are expected to be macho and to put on a brave act – no matter how false it is.

Gar is in conflict with the restricted life he is expected to live. Apart from Joe, the 'boys' refuse to mention his departure because it would force them to face up to their own restricted dependent lives. Ned and the others are poor and have little to look forward to. Any relationships with girls are imagined. Gar now objectively sees them as 'louts, ignorant louts, and you've always known it'. But he retains a fond memory of the times they shared, 'there was fun and there was laughter'.

This short scene made me feel sad that the young men of this small rural village found it impossible to communicate their real feelings towards each other. It's pitiful to think of anyone retreating into fantasy and macho boasting. Gar's admission that he would retain the memory of their shared times together as 'precious, precious gold' struck me as heart-breaking. He seems to have a love-hate relationship with his community. Yet despite wanting to escape Ballybeg's restrictions, he could not fully break the suffocating barrier of the accepted masculine norm of 'uneasy silence'.

EXAMINER'S COMMENT

- Impressive top-grade response tackling all aspects of the question.
- Sustained critical arguments engaging closely with Gar's conflict.
- Organised points, well-supported with suitable reference.
- Some quotes slightly inaccurate.
- Expression is generally clear and varied (e.g. 'all bluster and self-delusion', 'Irish patriarchy', 'accepted masculine norm').

MARKS AWARDED: $\frac{18}{20}$

Writing about style

Style is **the way written language is used** to suit the specific context, purpose, or audience. Vocabulary, syntax (the order of words) and sentence fluency – all contribute to the particular style of a piece of writing.

The writer's **unique voice** is another essential element of style. It can be personal or formal, authoritative or reflective, objective or passionate, serious or humorous, etc.

Once you start reading a text, you will soon notice how a writer is using language. A **pattern** may emerge where a particular technique is evident. For example, the style might be highly descriptive (lots of adjectives and details).

Checklist: style features used to engage readers

Narrative writing

- ○ First-person narration, interior monologue creates empathy
- ○ Strong characterisation connects readers to the story
- ○ Dialogue reveals character and conflict

- Use of tension, plot twists, absorb audiences
- Careful observation of setting, skilfully created mood add credibility

Aesthetic writing

- Descriptive details and dynamic verbs increase the reader's involvement
- Poetic techniques: personification, similes, repetition, rhythm enrich the re
experience
- Sound effects: alliteration, assonance, onomatopoeia, heighten the reader's
engagement

Informative writing

- Reference to historical background lends credibility
- Use of data, statistics, examples add authority
- Factual, accessible language aids reader's understanding
- Logical, organised structure impresses
- Use of contrast and similarity aids comprehension

Personal writing

- Anecdotal, personal approach creates empathy between writer and reader
- Emotional language affects readers
- Humour lightens the message, strengthens the bond between writer and reader
- Sense of audience affects reader's response

Persuasive writing

- Rhetorical devices, such as repetition and questions attract attention
- Inclusive/superlative language reinforces the message
- Emphatic, emotional verbs move readers

Descriptive writing

- Vivid sensory details paint pictures that appeal to the reader's senses
- Precise, colourful adjectives can help create mood and atmosphere
- Personification (giving human qualities to inanimate objects) can add interest and
drama, e.g. 'A fierce wind howled'

key
point

There is **no single exclusive style** of writing.
Different styles usually overlap. Personal writing,
for example, often includes anecdotes, detailed
description and elements of informative language.

Nothing on Earth

Read this opening section of Conor O'Callaghan's novel, *Nothing on Earth*, and answer the question on style that follows.

'Strange, beautiful and quietly terrifying'
DONAL RYAN

Conor O'Callaghan

Nothing on Earth

It was around about then the door started banging. The wood shook with the banging. So did the letterbox's brass-plated inward flap. Even the cutlery in its open drawer, the delft drying on its drainer, seemed to tremble a fraction. It was a time when nobody called. Early evening, the hottest August in living memory.

On the other side, on a doorstep in the middle of nowhere, stood a story everybody already knew. And the form that story took, as they say, on the evening in question? Breathless skin-and-bone, a girl of twelve or thereabouts. Her tummy, her breastbone, the edges of her rib, were all visible. She looked like one who had neither eaten proper food nor inhaled fresh air for years. Her teeth were yellow, her nails uncut and filthy. Her skin was sunburned, except for those white lines that had been covered by straps. It was also marked in places, her skin was: scratches, creases, streaks of dirt, and words.

There were actual words scrawled round her skin, dozens in blue, frayed at the edges, blurred by sweat and largely illegible. The more blurred ones resembled bruises. The more intact were like little darns meant to mend those points where the fabric of her flesh had worn threadbare. The words were not confined to her hands and wrists either. They were scattered all over her, and they were hard not to stare at.

'Come in.'

She was wearing fluffy panda slippers, a pair of light grey tracksuit bottoms smeared with black dust and food stains, and a man's bomber jacket that was easily five sizes too baggy. She was wearing, also, an odd shade of lipstick: a red-brown that hadn't been applied with any great care and served only to accentuate her air of wildness. Her hair was wavy jet black and quite long, halfway down her spine. But it had not, by the look of it, been washed for several weeks. Nor was her face particularly clean. Her eyes had black around them: liner, sure, but a lack of sleep as well. Their irises were a bottle green. Like emerald.

Question A

(iii) Do you agree that elements of descriptive and aesthetic language are used effectively to engage the reader in the above passage? Give reasons for your answer, supporting your views with reference to the text.   (20 marks)

Prompt!

- What descriptive details are effective?
- Is the portrayal of the girl intriguing?
- Does the author make effective use of colour?
- Is there an engaging poetic or aesthetic style?
- Any interesting personification or metaphorical writing?
- How does the writer create a mysterious atmosphere?

Sample answer 1

This passage is very descriptive. Someone is standing in a hall-way and the young girl bangs on the front door. She is in a desperate way. Not eating or taking care in the sun. Also, she's wearing slippers and a tracksuit and there is marks all over her skin. The girl is wearing lipstick even though she is only about 12 and her hair isnt even washed.

Allow about 15–18 minutes and aim for three focused, supported points in short paragraphs.

There are description sentences throughout the text passage and these are seen in the way she is knocking at the front door and looking thin. Her teeth are yellow and her nails are filthy and not cut. The girl's whole skin is sun-burnt and she has streaks of dirt and words on her skin as well. This passage is aesthetic in which the girl might have a story everybody would be wanting to know about.

The young girl of 12 in the extract hasnt been sleeping and might be homeless by all accounts. Her story is not a very happy one and she isn't cared for properly but actually desperate and in need of emergency help.

MARKS AWARDED: $\frac{8}{20}$

Sample answer 2

The precise details introduce us to a disturbing scene. There is a sense of a flashback as it seems the house is haunted – the wood 'shook' and the delft 'seemed to tremble'. The writer personifies these objects, as if they were ghosts. Even the weather adds to the oppressive atmosphere – 'the hottest August in living memory'.

The remaining paragraphs feel equally edgy. O'Callaghan slowly builds up a picture of the unnamed girl, suggesting that she has a troubled story to tell. He focuses on her physical appearance – 'skin and bones', covered in 'scratches, creases, streaks of dirt, and words'. The language is poetic at times, rich in metaphor, e.g. 'the fabric of her flesh had worn threadbare'.

The writing also has a cinematic quality. This unexpected encounter between strangers is recorded in a series of close-ups as though a camera was telling the story through colourful images. We see the girl's 'yellow teeth', 'red-brown' lipstick and 'jet black' hair. This highlights her weird appearance.

Overall, this is a powerful and imaginative introduction to a novel, inviting us to find out more about this odd character. The writing is both descriptive and aesthetic. Its slow pace and exact description have a hypnotic impact. The author captures moments vividly to create a very uneasy atmosphere. I wanted to know more about what had happened to this girl.

EXAMINER'S COMMENT

- Focused top-grade response that addresses all aspects of the question.
- Unlike the first sample answer, organised points are supported effectively with suitable reference and quotation.
- Ranges over the full extract in discussing both descriptive and aesthetic language.
- Clear, varied expression (e.g. 'sense of a flashback', 'cinematic quality', 'hypnotic impact').

MARKS AWARDED: $\frac{20}{20}$

Resistance

Read the following extract from Owen Sheers's novel, *Resistance*, and answer the question on style that follows.

The snow came to the valley the same way the men had left it; suddenly, silently and overnight. When Sarah pulled back her curtains the next morning the day was still half dark, washed out in greys and blues. The only light shining into the room was from an undulating seam of white pressed against the lower panes of the window; a miniature range of bright hills, their contours bisected by the glass. She looked at it, her eyes still grainy with sleep, confused. There had been no warning, no sign this would happen. On going to bed she'd been able to see the stars but now the sky and the world beneath it were obscured. There was a wind too, wild about the house. She looked out at the branches of the trees. She could just see them, black behind the still-falling snow. Yesterday they'd been upright, motionless, but now they were all swept the same way like iron filings drawn to a magnet, bowing under the wind that pressed upon them.

The day was no lighter by the time Sarah was out in the yard, clumsy and heavy under layers of jackets and coats, a woollen scarf wrapped about her head, a sack over her shoulders. She fumbled with the dogs' chains, her fingers thick under gloves. Taking Tom's crook and a spade from the shed she began walking down to the lower field where she and Maggie had herded the lambing ewes just weeks before. She was walking against the wind. The snow caught in her eyelashes, melting her vision. With each step her leg sunk up to the knee. When she pulled her boots back out again she tinged her own footholes with red-brown mud, like the edging of blood around a punctured bandage.

The world had turned white, the twigs of the hedges fleshed out with inches of snow balanced along their upper sides. With every step forwards she had to push herself against the crook, up and on, walking within her own sphere of mist, the rest of the valley extinguished. The dogs went before her, leaping through the snow like salmon against the current of a stream. Despite the wind Sarah was soon sweating under her heavy clothes. Her breath came hard and fast as she cursed Tom for leaving her like this, quietly at first but then louder, letting the wind snatch the damning of her husband from her mouth.

Owen Sheers

When she reached the field she knew immediately that at least a third of the flock was missing. Those that were left had bunched together at the far end where the snow was shallower. At the other end the wind had swept a massive drift over the height of the hedge. Fresh snow spun off its edge, sculpting a delicate curl like the blank page of an open book suspended in the breeze between turning and falling. That was where the other ewes would have been lying. Against the hedge, trying to find some shelter. And they were still there somewhere, trapped under the weight of drifted snow.

Sarah waded through the field and began poking her crook into the drift. She'd only ever known this happen once, and even then Tom had got to the ewes before they'd been completely covered. With William in the valley and Maggie's radio, they'd never been taken unawares by the weather. Sarah didn't know if she'd find the ewes alive or dead. Or even if she'd find them at all.

Question A

(iii) Based on your reading of the above extract, do you agree that Owen Sheers's descriptive writing is rich in language and imagery?   (20 marks)

Prompt!

- What examples of a poetic style (metaphors, similes, etc.) are used?
- Where are vivid, cinematic details evident?
- Are contrasting colours used effectively?
- Does Sheers use imagery that appeals to various senses?
- Is the portrayal of Sarah intriguing? Why?
- What kind of atmosphere does the writer create?

Sample answer

This is a very atmospheric description of a remote country area after an unexpected snowfall. The author focuses on the overcast early morning scene, by referring to the 'half dark, washed out in greys and blues'. The trees are 'black behind the still-falling snow'. The colours highlight this transformed landscape.

Sarah's clothes are described in detail 'under layers of jackets and coats'. She wears 'a sack over her shoulders', woollen gloves and a scarf. The fact that she is 'sweating under her heavy clothes' adds realism to the description. In the freezing cold, she 'fumbled with the dogs' chains'. Such details give a very convincing picture of the harsh landscape.

Sheers uses vivid similes throughout the piece. For example, the branches are weighed down and have a curved shape 'like iron filings drawn to a magnet'. The dogs 'leap like salmon', suggesting the energy needed to get through the thick snow. Mud stuck to Sarah's boots is 'like the edging of blood around a punctured bandage'. All these rich comparisons have a strong visual impact and make the wintry scene come alive.

We get a very credible sense of the journey as Sarah makes her way to check on the sheep. The author succeeds in making us feel the sensation of her efforts as she trudges along, 'each step her leg sunk up to the knee' as she 'waded' through the heavy snow. Owen Sheers really brings readers into this hostile landscape where 'the world had turned white.'

key point

EXAMINER'S COMMENT

- Clear, organised points focused throughout on the descriptive qualities of the writing.

- Descriptive writing appeals to the senses (sight, smell, sound, touch and taste).

- Characters and places should feel real. Vivid, descriptive writing usually portrays a person, place, or object in a way that helps us visualise the subject.

- Excellent use of supportive quotation and reference.
- Ranges over the full extract in discussing both descriptive language and rich imagery.
- Impressive expression (e.g. 'atmospheric description', 'strong visual impact', 'hostile landscape').
- Top-grade response that addresses the question with confidence.

MARKS AWARDED: $\frac{20}{20}$

Visual literacy questions

Visual texts (photographs, book covers, images, posters, paintings, screenshots, graphics, etc.) are usually included as part of the Comprehending A questions.

Visual literacy is the ability to understand, interpret, decode, question and find meaning from information presented in the form of images.

You might be asked to:

- write a description of an image or series of images
- analyse and interpret images and their effectiveness
- compare two or more visuals
- comment on the impact visual images make on you
- write an introduction to a group of images
- relate the visual imagery to the accompanying written text
- suggest alternative images to illustrate a text effectively.

key point

Since meaning can be communicated effectively through the visual medium (illustrations, cartoons, posters, photographs, etc.), images can therefore be 'read'.

How to study visual images

Consider the purpose:

Is the image's purpose to inform? Persuade? Entertain? Educate? Shock?

Examine the subject matter:

Who or what is the subject of the visual? What details are included?

Comment on visual features:

Check out colours, contrasts and symbols. Do they enhance the picture's message?

Assess the tone or atmosphere:

Does the image create a particular mood? Or tell a story? Convey a message?

Think about the impact on the viewer:

How is the picture composed? What is in the foreground? What is the effect of the image?

Study the most striking visual elements:

What strikes you most about an image at first glance? It could be the mix of settings, characters, their expressions, use of light and shadow, camera angles, etc.

Colours can be important in visual images. They affect the way we feel about the picture.

- Red is often dramatic, suggesting power or danger.
- Vivid yellow and orange can signify happiness and wellbeing.
- Blue suggests calm or unhappiness.
- Green is connected with nature and jealousy.
- Black and white could suggest a picture from the past, encouraging you to look at specific features, such as shape and texture.

Responding to visual literacy questions

Compare the two war images below, addressing the following: setting and atmosphere, the visual qualities of the images, and the impact both images have on you.   (20 marks)

Allow about 15–18 minutes and aim for at least three focused points. The notes above will be helpful in responding to the question.

Image 1: A Syrian man waters herbs on the roof of his damaged building in the Syrian rebel-held town of Arbin, on the outskirts of the capital, Damascus.

Image 2: An Iraqi policeman uses a helmet on a stick to try and draw fire from an Islamic State sniper in an attempt to make him reveal his position during the battle to recapture West Mosul.

Sample answer

Both images depict different views of dramatic war scenes. Almost all of Image 1 shows a desolate wasteland, dominated by crumbling bomb-damaged buildings. There is an eerie atmosphere of shocking devastation. For as far as I can see, windows and doors are blown out. Only the bare skeleton of the abandoned structure remains. Vertical columns sticking up into the air suggest that the bombs destroyed the building before construction was completed.

Image 2 highlights another haunting reality of modern-day warfare, focusing on a lone soldier in full military uniform who is directly engaged in battle. As in the first photograph, I was aware of a powerful sense that death is close at hand. Concentration is etched on the soldier's face as he raises a helmet above the wall that is protecting him from the enemy. Look-out holes have been made in the walls of the bombed-out building where he hides. The signs of conflict and decay are everywhere. On the ground around him are crumpled blankets, rifles and spent bullet shells.

In both images, debris and rubble litter the war-torn scene. There is no sign of the families and homes that once existed here. Instead, collapsed concrete floors seem dangerously close to toppling altogether. For me, what stands out most in the first image is the surreal scene on one rooftop where a civilian waters plants in a makeshift garden allotment. The green grass contrasts with the surrounding grey ruins. This unexpected detail is a powerful symbol of human resilience and the desire for a return to normal life despite the tragic conflict.

When answering visual literacy questions, treat the images as texts.

- 'Read' the image. What do you notice?
- Describe what you see and mention specific details that are interesting.

EXAMINER'S COMMENT

- Succinct critical points supported effectively with suitable reference to both images.
- Impressive detailed examination of the visual qualities and symbolism.
- Convincing personal response ('For as far as I can see', 'I was aware of').
- Clear expression (e.g. 'eerie atmosphere', 'haunting reality', 'symbol of human resilience').
- Excellent comparative response that addresses all aspects of the question.

MARKS AWARDED: $\frac{20}{20}$

Let the Great World Spin

The narrator of this passage is looking back on his childhood.

One of the many things my brother, Corrigan, and I loved about our mother was that she was a fine musician. She kept a small radio on top of the piano in the living room of our house in Dublin and on Sunday afternoons, after scanning through whatever radio stations we could find, she raised the lid of the piano, spread her dress out at the wooden stool and tried to follow the piece of music from memory.

Our mother played with a natural touch, even though she suffered from a hand which she had broken many times. We never knew the origin of the break; it was something left in silence. When she finished playing, she would lightly rub the back of her wrist. After all these years I can still sit in the museum of those afternoons and recall the light spilling across the carpet. At times our mother put her arms around us both, and then guided our hands so we could clang down hard on the piano keys.

It is not fashionable anymore, I suppose, to have a regard for one's mother in the way my brother and I had then, in the mid-1950s, when the noise outside the window was mostly wind and sea. One looks for the chink in the armour such as the leg of the piano stool shorter than the other or the sadness that would detach us from her, but the truth is we enjoyed each other, all three of us, and never so evidently as those Sundays when the rain fell grey over Dublin and the squalls blew against the window.

Our father, a physicist, had left us years before. A cheque, postmarked in London, arrived through the letter box once a week. Never a note, just a cheque, which spun in the air as it fell. We ran to bring it to our mother. She slipped the envelope under a flowerpot on the kitchen windowsill and the next day it was gone.

Nothing was ever said.

The only other sign of our father was a wardrobe full of old suits in our mother's bedroom. Our mother found us one afternoon, dressed in his grey suits with the sleeves rolled up and the trousers held up by elastic bands. We were marching round when she came in and froze in the doorway, the room so quiet we could hear the radiator tick.

'Well,' she said, as she knelt on the ground in front of us. Her face spread out in a grin that seemed to pain her. 'Come here.' She kissed us both on the cheek. 'Now run along.' We slipped out of our father's old clothes and left them in a puddle on the floor. Later that night we heard the clang of the coat hangers as she hung the suits.

Over the years there were the usual tantrums and bloody noses and our mother had to deal with the whispers of the neighbours, sometimes even the attentions of the local widowers but for the most part things stretched comfortably in front of us.

Corrigan and I shared a bedroom and I don't know how it happened but he, the younger one by two years, took control of the top bunk. He slept on his stomach, reciting his prayers. I knew the Catholic hit parade – the Our Father, the Hail Mary – but that was all. I was a raw, quiet child, and God was already a bore to me. I kicked the bottom of Corrigan's bed and he fell silent, but then started up again. Sometimes I woke and he was alongside me, arm draped over my shoulder, his chest rising and falling as he whispered his prayers. I'd turn on him. 'Shut up, Corr.'

My brother was light-skinned, dark-haired, blue-eyed. He was the type of child everyone smiled at. He could look at you and draw you out. People fell for him. On the street, women ruffled his hair. Men punched him gently on the shoulder. He had no idea that he sustained people, made them happy and drew out their improbable yearnings. He just ploughed along, oblivious.

I woke one night, when I was eleven, to a cold blast of air moving over me. I stumbled to the window but it was closed. I reached for the light and Corr was standing in the middle of the room. His cheeks were red. He smelled of cigarettes. He put a finger to his lips for hush and climbed back up the wooden ladder. 'Go to sleep,' he whispered. The smell of tobacco lingered in the room. In the morning he jumped down from the bed, wearing his anorak over his pyjamas. Shivering, he opened the window and tapped the sand from his shoes into the garden below.

'Where did you go?'

'Just along the water,' he said.

'Were you smoking?'

He looked away. 'No.'

'You're not supposed to smoke, you know.'

'I didn't smoke,' he said.

Later that morning our mother walked us to school. Down by the school gates she went on one knee, put her arms around us and kissed us one after the other. When she stood up, her gaze was caught by a dark form wrapped in a red blanket on the other side of the road by the railings of the church. The man raised a hand in salute. Corrigan waved back.

There were plenty of drunks around Dublin but my mother seemed taken by the sight, and for a moment it struck me that there might be a secret there.

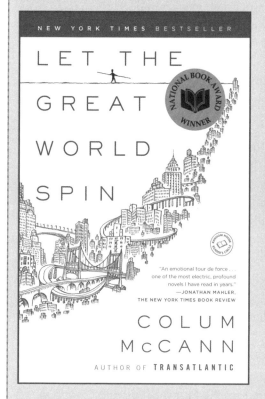

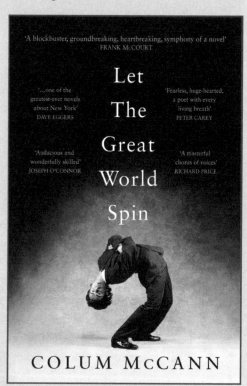

'Who's that, Mum?' I asked.

'Run along,' she said.

My brother walked beside me, silent. 'Who is it, Corr?' I thumped him. 'Who is it?'

He disappeared towards his classroom. All day I sat at my wooden desk, gnawing my pencil, wondering – visions of a forgotten uncle, or our father somehow returned, broken. In those days, nothing was beyond the realm of the possible. The clock was at the rear of the room but there was an old freckled mirror over the classroom sink and I could watch the hands crawl backwards. When the bell went I was out of the gate but Corrigan took the long road home, taking short steps through the housing estate and along the sea wall.

There was a soft brown paper package waiting for Corrigan on the top bunk. I shoved it at him. He shrugged and ran his finger along the string, pulled it tentatively. Inside was a soft blue blanket. He unfolded it, looked at our mother and nodded.

She touched his face with the back of her fingers and said, 'Never again, understand?' Nothing else was mentioned, until two years later he gave that blanket away too, to another homeless drunk, on another freezing night, up by the canal on one of his late-night walks, when he tiptoed down the stairs and went out into the dark. It was a simple equation to him – others needed the blankets more than him, and he was prepared to take the punishment if it came his way.

It was my earliest suggestion of what my brother would become.

Question A

(i)   From your reading of this extract, what impressions do you get of the narrator's mother? Refer to the text in support of your answer.   (15 marks)

(ii) Which of the two book covers (pictured on the previous page) do you find more appealing in encouraging you to read the novel, *Let the Great World Spin*? Support your answer by reference to both covers and to the written text.   (15 marks)

(iii) 'Colum McCann makes effective use of narrative and aesthetic language to engage the reader in the above extract.' To what extent do you agree with this statement? Support your answer with reference to the text.   (20 marks)

Prompt!

- Study the wording of the question closely.
- Check how many aspects there are in the question.

Ideas for answers

(i)   Impressions of the narrator's mother:
- Affectionate and loving – 'put her arms around us'.
- Fine musician who 'played with a natural touch'.
- Home-maker – 'we enjoyed each other'.
- Somewhat mysterious – 'Nothing was ever said'.

(ii) Cover A:
- Symbolic light background suggesting hope.
- Risk-taking figure on tight-rope seems heroic/vulnerable.
- Life is a balancing act.
- Imposing cityscape sketch of high-rise buildings.

- Bridges suggest adventurous journeys and possibilities.
- Bland, uninformative.

Cover B:

- Darkly symbolic background colour.
- Distorted central figure suggests human interest story.
- Life is a balancing act.
- Minimalist, vague.

(iii) Narrative and aesthetic language:

- Vivid setting – evocative sense of time and place.
- Cinematic details – 'radiator tick', 'freckled mirror'.
- Rich visual images – 'cheque which spun in the air'.
- Poignant metaphorical language – 'the museum of those afternoons'.
- Contrasting characters are engaging.
- Raises intriguing questions about Corrigan's later life.

Practising State Examination Commission Past Paper questions can be a useful revision exercise.

- Study the wording closely to identify the main elements of the question.
- Work within a realistic time frame.
- Organise key points into paragraphs.
- Use suitable textual support when appropriate.
- Write clearly and carefully at all times.

Be prepared to use your prescribed texts from Paper 2 to an answer in Paper 1, e.g. 'From the texts you have studied for your Leaving Certificate course, identify a place that gripped your imagination. Explain in detail why this place gripped your imagination.'

2 Paper 1: Comprehending B

- Learning to write for a specific, practical reason.
- Addressing all the elements of a question.
- Writing in a variety of formats.

Comprehending B at a glance

The Comprehending B section (worth 50 marks) is often referred to as 'functional writing' and asks you to write for a specific purpose.

You are likely to use a particular format, e.g. a talk, letter, email, diary, proposal, blog, opinion piece, speech, introduction, interview, report, review, etc.

For each Comprehending B task, it is essential to use the **appropriate register** (language, tone and format). Aim for at least 450 words, written over 35–40 minutes.

Marking scheme

Purpose: Are all aspects of the task being addressed? (15 marks)

Coherence: Is the response controlled, paragraphed and sustained throughout? (15 marks)

Language: Is the writing appropriate to the task (register, fluency, punctuation)? (15 marks)

Mechanics: Are spellings and grammar accurate? (5 marks)

Comprehending B tasks – Key revision points

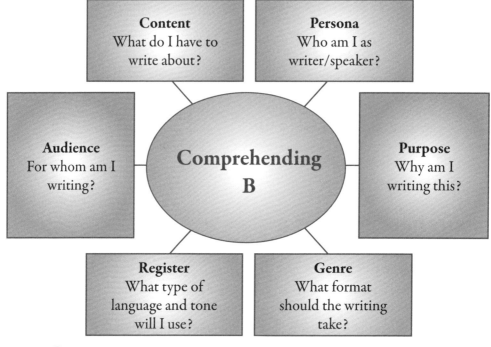

An appropriate format and layout will be expected for some functional writing tasks (e.g. reports, diaries and interviews). This may not be required for opinion pieces and blogs. The register is key. Your writing must have the 'feel' of a real news article, email, talk, etc.

The opinion piece

Opinion pieces or feature articles are written prose pieces that usually appear in the print media or on websites. They often focus on people or issues, rather than events. Opinion pieces inform, entertain and persuade. They offer another personal, sometimes humorous, perspective.

Key features of opinion pieces

- Personal engaging tone.
- Humorous touches.
- Lively anecdotes or illustrations.
- Conversational and emotive language.
- Repetition, short sentences.

Sample Comprehending B question

Question

The views people hold today are often influenced by the news and information they receive from the online world of the internet and social media. Write an opinion piece, for publication in a national newspaper, in which you give your views on the extent to which people today rely on the online world as a source of news and information, the reliability of these sources and the impact of this development on society.   (50 marks)

SEC marking scheme guidelines

Allow for a variety of approaches to the task.

Mark ex* 50 by reference to the criteria for assessment using the following breakdown of marks.

P: Understanding of genre – an opinion piece suitable for publication in a national newspaper. Address all aspects of the question – the extent to which people rely on the online world as a source of news and information; the reliability of these sources; and the impact of this development on society.
Freshness and originality, etc.

C: Sustained focus, continued control of register, management and sequencing of ideas, etc.

L: Language managed and controlled to achieve clear communication, quality of expression, style, fluency, etc.

M: Accuracy of mechanics.

Candidates should engage with all aspects of the question, although not necessarily equally.

*ex = out of

Deconstructing the task

- **On what do I have to write?** (Content)

  The extent to which people today rely on the online world as a source of news and information, the reliability of these sources and the impact of this development on society (three separate discussion points)

- **Who am I as writer/speaker?** (Persona)

  I am a writer for a national newspaper

- **Who am I addressing?** (Audience)

  The readers of a national newspaper

- **Why am I writing this?** (Purpose)

  To give my views and opinions on how the online world of the internet and social media impact news and information

- **What type of language will I use?** (Register)

  Persuasive, emotive, humorous and informative language

- **What format should the writing take?** (Genre)

  Feature article in a newspaper

Sample answer

Fake news, real news, whose news? The world of journalism has progressed into a new technological age. Today, we see more and more 'amateur footage' through tweets, snaps or posts on our internet devices. But how reliable is the information presented? What impact is this development having on society?

A fundamental change has occurred in the news business. Due to the internet, we no longer have to buy information in pre-fabricated packages like newspapers. Instead, we can just go online and individually select what we want to read. People get to choose their own adventure. There are many websites and blogs available, often pre-selecting articles and providing links to related sites.

But how reliable is all this news? Online organisations charge advertisers based on the number of hits they can get on a site. Several online news organisations could cover the same story. Which version is going to get the most hits and therefore generate most revenue? Usually the most sensational ones. Reporters are being pushed to extend the boundaries of provocation online. The 'Domino effect' then kicks in. Other online news sites pick up the 'story' that is now trending and it soon goes viral.

This impacts positively and negatively on society. In the past, news flowed from the few to the many. Old style reporting consisted of spotting the news story, checking the sources and writing it up. Nowadays, news flows from the many (the web) to the many.

The shocking events at the World Trade Center in 2001 foreshadowed how events are covered today. Feeds from social networking services such as Facebook and Twitter provide a snapshot of such events happening worldwide from the viewpoint of first-hand witnesses. Just think of the coverage from the recent tragedies on London Bridge, Nice or Hurricane Harvey! But there are dangers. First-hand witnesses cannot see the big picture.

The easiest way to broadcast content on a large scale is through the internet. It is easily updated. 'Breaking news' is available instantly. It allows people to engage by leaving comments or starting online discussions. This is quicker than writing a letter to a newspaper – especially since it may not even be published. Online news helps the public become a thinking reasoning society. However, people may confuse fact with opinion.

This blurring of the line between fact and opinion has created an environment where extreme thought flourishes while balanced judgement is in danger. Many newspapers' sales have declined sharply and they only provide online content. The cost of doing challenging, independent reporting has become cost-prohibitive worldwide.

Yet, I hope we might have the best of all worlds. Radio, television and film co-exist side by side, at times feeding off each other. Perhaps newsprint and online news could take a lesson from them? Wouldn't it be to the benefit of everyone to have the advantages of 'breaking news' coupled with carefully sourced, reflective journalism?

(480 words)

EXAMINER'S COMMENT

Successful top-grade response that addresses all the elements of the task, using a suitably discursive tone. Well-informed and illustrated article, exploring interesting aspects of the development and impact of online news. Engaging opening draws in the reader. Perceptive points throughout, although some lacked development (e.g. paragraph 4). Despite some repetition, overall expression was impressive ('extend the boundaries of provocation online', 'carefully sourced, reflective journalism').

Revision exercise

Write an opinion piece for publication in a magazine in which you consider the importance of being happy, reflect on the obstacles to achieving happiness for young people in contemporary Ireland and offer advice on how they can adopt a positive outlook on their lives.

Allow about 40 minutes and aim for at least 450 words, arranging main points in paragraphs.

Prompt!

When you are writing your response, aim to persuade the audience to your viewpoint by conveying your opinions clearly and confidently. Be careful not to overdo the emotional appeal. Make sure that your arguments are as coherent, well-informed and as convincing as possible.

Talks

A talk is an oral presentation aimed at a particular audience. In Comprehending B questions, you may be asked to write the text of a public talk which addresses a topic. It is often a mixture of argument and persuasion. Its purpose can be to inform, reflect, influence or describe. Narrative writing, in the form of anecdotes (short personal stories), can be used.

You might be asked, for example, to write a short talk (or speech) welcoming a well-known person to your school. The tone in that case will be very different to a talk to your classmates about an important issue that affects young people.

A radio talk is 'writing for the ear'. It allows the listener to 'see' what is being described. Informal radio talks are popular in chat shows, sports commentary or music programmes. Formal radio talks are used for reporting news or current affairs.

Key features of talks

- Address the audience.
- State what is to be covered and the angle to be taken (e.g. dangers of plastic packaging – negative approach to subject).
- Rhetorical questions to engage audience ('given how hard you work at school, don't you deserve time off?').
- Repetition for emphasis ('that's the truth, and nothing but the truth').
- Emotive language to establish empathy with audience ('we teenagers face a barrage of pressure').
- Personal anecdotes – memories, short stories to illustrate points.
- Humour to entertain ('at the very start, let me say we both have something in common – you don't know what I am going to say and neither do I!').
- Thank the audience for listening.

Sample Comprehending B question

Question

You have been asked to take part in a radio programme entitled 'Reflections on a Changing World'. Write the text of a talk to be broadcast in which you imagine yourself as an older person describing the changes you have noticed and reflecting on the world as you once knew it.   (50 marks)

Deconstructing the task

- **On what do I have to write?** (Content)

  The changes in my world

- **Who am I as writer/speaker?** (Persona)

  An older person

- **Who am I addressing?** (Audience)

  Radio listeners

- **Why am I writing this?** (Purpose)

  To describe and reflect on changes I have noticed

- **What type of language will I use?** (Register)

  Descriptive, nostalgic, reflective, narrative, informative, humorous

- **What format should the writing take?** (Genre)

  A radio talk

Sample answer

I would like to welcome Mrs Connolly on to our show, 'Weekend Miscellany' this morning to reflect on the changes she has noticed from when she was young.

Good morning Brian, thank you for having me. And good morning, listeners.

This morning I left my grandsons to school and set off, once more, down the familiar route of Dublin Street. On the left is 'Handy Stores'. I used to accompany my gran when she went to get blue methylated spirit in an old lemonade bottle for her Primus stove. Next door is 'Mayfair Jewellers', closed down now due to the strict No Parking rules. On its left is 'Hong Kee', a new Asian grocery shop – its pungent spices perfuming the pavement, and by its side is 'Halal Meats'. Ireland's diversity is on rich display within 500 yards. Now I've done it – 500 yards. I've forgotten they don't use imperial measurement anymore!

Turning the corner, I see 'Morgan the Fishman's' white van. I pull up to get some fresh herrings. Hopefully, the traffic wardens are not prowling yet!

'Raw day, Mrs Connolly,' he says, 'The usual, I suppose?'

'Sure, Michael,' I reply. 'Any news?'

'*Modern Fashions* is closing down.'

'No!'

'Can't compete with the big chains, parking is a nightmare on the main street. Six euros, please.'

'Thanks, Michael. See you next week, God willing.'

Climbing back into the car, I drive past the Square. I smile as I recall my grandfather's story of the day the Irish Volunteers defied the British army here. They stood on the Maid of Erin statue plinth singing Irish songs, 'God Save Ireland' soared over the British army playing in celebration of the new King.

'They couldn't arrest them, y'know,' my grandfather said.

'Why's that?' I asked.

'They were standing on the plinth … paid for by the townspeople, so they were on private property. They couldn't be arrested for singing songs on private property!'

Next is 'Modern Fashions' and splashed across the window – 70% off! Closing Down Sale. I got my First Communion dress here when I was seven. I remember the veil and flower headdress. I thought it was the most beautiful dress in the world. Next door is another new business, 'Digital Tech' – laptops, iPads, iPhones line up in the new shiny window. We must all update.

I approach the Green Church, its copper spire soaring high. St Richard FitzRalph is buried here. During the Black Death plague in the 14th century, he criticised the clergy and condemned the merchants for wasteful extravagances and under-handed practices. His tomb's exact location is unknown today – just like many of the old town businesses. Time passes. Everything changes …

(440 words)

EXAMINER'S COMMENT

Excellent top-grade response established the radio talk format from the start and sustained the reflective narrative voice and nostalgic tone throughout. Effective use of suggestion (speaker's age, interests, attitudes towards change, etc.). Colourful detailed illustrations contrasted past and present while the short conversation added some drama and variety. Overall, a well-structured and engaging talk.

Letters and blogs

Categories

Formal letter

Formal letters are required as covering letters for job applications, research questionnaires or to make a complaint, etc. These letters shape other people's perception of you. Letter writing is a necessary skill for successful progress both in your business and personal life.

Informal letter

Informal letters add a uniquely personal touch to communication, despite the popularity of digital communication such as email, WhatsApp, Snapchat, etc. Digital communication is often instantaneous, emotive and brief. Physical letter writing encourages reflection and has a lasting quality. Informal letters show that the sender has taken care and time to share thoughts, feelings and experiences. These personal letters are usually seen by only one person and are often treasured by the recipient.

Blog ('web-log')

Blogs are online diaries that share views, experiences, offer advice and connect people with an online community. They can focus in a personal interest – current affairs, music, entertainment, health, education, cooking, sport, travel, fashion, etc. Blogs need instant appeal and should be easily scanned. They include links to other web pages, visuals, video clips, etc.

Key features of letters and blogs

Formal letter	Informal letter	Blog post
Layout		
• Place address of letter writer on top right-hand corner of page and the date underneath. • Name, title and address of person/business of receiver goes on left-hand side of page, below the date. • Greetings are formal. • An unknown person is addressed as 'Dear Sir', 'Dear Madam' or 'Dear Sir or Madam'. • A known person is addressed by name, 'Dear Mr Murphy'.	• Place address of letter writer on top right-hand corner of page and the date underneath. • Do not write the name or address of the receiver. • Greetings are friendly, informal, and use the first name of the person, 'Hi Mary', 'Dear John'.	• Catchy title that pops up easily in search engine. • Address readers directly. • Focus on one central idea. • Employ headings and sub-headings. • Underline phrases to emphasise certain points. • Include links to other pages with similar themes. • Encourage comments or interactions from reader.

Formal letter	Informal letter	Blog post
• Letter concludes with 'Yours sincerely' or 'Yours faithfully', followed by writer's signature underneath.	• Letter concludes informally, 'Love', 'See you soon', 'Best wishes', followed by sender's first name.	• Use name of person who posted blog and contact details. • Date.
Tone		
• Professional, formal, polite, objective. • Use Standard English. • Avoid slang, contractions and colloquialisms.	• Friendly, informal, chatty, emotional. • Informal grammar, such as dashes, exclamation marks. • Contractions and colloquialism can also be used.	• Social, chatty, interesting, friendly, provocative, informative.

There is no exclusive style of functional writing. In Comprehending B questions, different writing tasks can overlap. Blogs, opinion, pieces, letters, talks, etc. are often similar in both content, format and language use.

Sample Comprehending B question – Informal letter

Question

Imagine that you are a successful thirty-year-old adult. Write a letter from your 'older self' to you as a teenager offering guidance, advice, reassurance and encouragement to help you progress successfully, both in your career and your personal life.   (50 marks)

Deconstructing the task

- **On what do I have to write?** (Content)
  Guidance, advice, reassurance and encouragement to younger self
- **Who am I as writer/speaker?** (Persona)
  My adult successful self
- **Who am I addressing?** (Audience)
  My younger teen self

- **Who am I as writer/speaker?** (Persona)

  To help my younger self make the transition into adult life
- **What type of language will I use?** (Register)

  Positive, persuasive, encouraging, informative, humorous
- **What format should the writing take?** (Genre)

  Informal letter

Sample answer

'Mountain View'
Longford Road
Sligo
21 April 2030

Dear James,

First, the important things. Let me assure you, the future will definitely be brighter. Not everyone gets to become a famous sports star. And who is to say that this is success anyway? Someone has to make up the crowd too. In fact, that's where most people end up – which is fine by me. There's a place for each one of us and our own unique gifts.

You are seventeen at the moment – and not exactly fighting off countless girlfriends. Despite what you think, you don't really know a lot about life yet, but you will. Being a teenager can be pretty lousy at times. I know you're not a geek, and you don't and never will like computers or chess. But you are determined and you have more than your share of good qualities. Believe me, these will stand to you in the years ahead.

Perseverance and willpower takes you far. Just stay calm and focus on the good things! Make time for those who are close to you. They will be there to help in happy and dark times. They stand in your corner, despite all the rows. It's well worth letting family and friends know that you value them. You should continue to enjoy your sports and music – you love both. And keep reading. A good book is a friend for life. It's always there and doesn't judge you.

So go for your dream, even if it doesn't work out as you planned. The journey is worth it and there is always something great there, if you keep going. Open your eyes and mind and be ready to see it. Keep talking, keep smiling and don't give up on those corny one-liners that probably belong in Christmas crackers. They'll get better too, and are useful to break the ice at a tense moment in life.

There will be regrets, but learn from mistakes. Don't agonise over them. Can I improve? Absolutely! You never remember your Mock results. As far as I'm concerned, it's a great big, beautiful life. All kinds of opportunities await you. Have the courage to try. Failure is just something which didn't work on that particular day. There is always another time, and there is always something else.

Of course, you will probably still mope around a bit and sport some weird hairstyles. But that's all fine. Believe in yourself. One final word of advice ... Don't hurt others or allow yourself to be hurt. Otherwise, enjoy yourself. Keep your friends and family close.

The older James

(415 words)

EXAMINER'S COMMENT

Successful use of the informal letter format. Tackled the key tasks in the question – particularly effective register of suitable tone of support and encouragement throughout. The advice tended to be vague and clichéd at times, however. Language use was clear and included some welcome variation in sentence length and expression. Overall, a high-grade response.

Sample Comprehending B question – Formal letter

Question

'National Treasures' is a campaign to collect objects cherished by people and families which explore the history of the island of Ireland over the past 100 years. Write a covering letter to the museum manager to explain how you first heard about the exhibition, what your chosen object is and why you think it is a 'national treasure'. (50 marks)

Deconstructing the task

- **On what do I have to write?** (Content)
  How I learned about the exhibition, what my object is and the reasons I think it adds to the Irish story

- **Who am I as writer/speaker?** (Persona)
  Teenager (myself)

- **Who am I addressing?** (Audience)
  Manager of exhibition

- **Why am I writing this?** (Purpose)
  To explain my reason for sending in object

- **What type of language will I use?** (Register)
  Polite, formal, no contractions or colloquialisms

- **What format should the writing take?** (Genre)
  The form of a formal letter

Sample answer

32 Upper Marsh Road
Shandon Park
Cork
23 February

Tony Candon
Manager Keeper
Museum of Country Life
Turlough Park
Castlebar

Dear Mr Candon,

I recently watched the programme 'National Treasures' on RTÉ after a family friend had recommended it. This travelling roadshow presented by John Creedon was telling the story of the Irish nation through ordinary people's mementoes. For some reason, I became really engaged with this personal approach to history and heritage. I found it really fascinating how a portrait of Ireland could be assembled from the keepsakes and bric-a-brac that were lying about the place, but which people couldn't bring themselves to throw away.

My great-grandfather was Denis Mulcahy Snr from Clonakilty. He owned a jeweller's shop in Peter Street, Cork. In 1920, during the War of Independence, the Black and Tans, who formed part of the British force in Ireland at that time, had been attacked in the countryside. They proceeded to carry out raids on the shops in the city. They entered our jewellery shop. There was no-one in the shop at the time except my grandfather. He put up his hands. A door in the back slammed with a cross-wind. A soldier emptied his rifle, firing wildly at the glass cabinets and then taking deliberate aim at my great grandad's heart. Although he immediately collapsed with the impact, my grandfather's life was saved by the silver cigarette box inside his waistcoat. He used to joke how 'this was a rare case where cigarettes are good for you'.

I would like to submit this small – but treasured – item for your exhibition. Apart from the natural pride within the wider Mulcahy family, I think the cigarette box is a reminder not only of the harsh struggle for independence, but also is a witness to the cheerful, optimistic attitude of ordinary Irish people, despite living in challenging times. I believe this item will be of interest to others and add another piece to the rich tapestry of our rich social history. I also include three photographs of the bullet-marked cigarette case for your online archive.

I am looking forward to hearing from you whether you consider this item a suitable object for your exhibition. I think it is a great initiative and will be very popular with everyone who has an interest in our country's history.

Yours sincerely,
Tom Mulcahy

(370 words)

Sample Comprehending B question – Blog

Question

Imagine that you are a sports dietician and you have been approached by a parents' group asking you to write for them a blog aimed at promoting and encouraging a healthy, active lifestyle for teenagers who are interested in sport. Write a suitable post for this blog.   (50 marks)

Deconstructing the task

- **On what do I have to write?** (Content)

  How to promote a healthy diet for teenagers who do sports

- **Who am I as writer/speaker?** (Persona)

  A dietician

- **Who am I addressing?** (Audience)

  Parents of teenagers interested in sport

- **Why am I writing this?** (Purpose)

  To inform parents how to care for the dietary needs of their teenagers

- **What type of language will I use?** (Register)

  Informative, encouraging, supportive

- **What format should the writing take?** (Genre)

  Blog post

Sample answer

Feeding the Sporty Teenager

'Back to school' time has come round again. Routine and order reign supreme as the days become subject to a strict schedule. Suddenly food assumes a big role. For parents with sporty teens, organising <u>food</u> on the go around training sessions and matches stretches the food routine beyond the usual three meals a day.

After school training usually means dinner later in the evening. Yet your teenagers need something quick, easy and healthy. Don't let them fall into the trap of grabbing a fizzy drink and bag of crisps. Click on my link 'Fuel your body', which guides you to feed and water your sporty teen with healthy options.

Parents are concerned about sports supplements. Protein shakes are popular with boys who are anxious to 'bulk up'. Girls favour herbal preparations.

Sports supplements are not recommended for teenagers for some very good reasons:

- lack of safe testing on the growing teenage body
- lack of tight regulations on the sports supplement industry
- extra ingredients can be included that are not listed on the packaging.

Many sports heroes take their privileged position seriously and regularly speak on the importance of healthy eating and keeping well hydrated. Our media also play their part. They come down heavy on those who attempt to cheat the system.

Remember: One in four teenagers carry excess weight. Sport is therefore a great way to keep young people active and healthy.

Healthy Additions – increasing fruit and veg intake

Breakfast
Glass of unsweetened fruit juice
Fresh fruit or dried fruit added to cereal
Chopped banana and yoghurt smoothie

Lunch
Salad veggies and fresh sandwiches
Small side salad with cooked meal
Fruit and raw veggie sticks in lunchbox

Dinner
Two vegetables instead of one
Fresh or tinned fruit in juice topped with natural yoghurt for dessert

Finally, for more healthy eating tips for teenagers, click on the following links:
Healthy eating options
Boost your brain power

(As always, we love to hear what you think!)

Posted by Deirdre Rahill
Sports dietician with the Irish Nutrition and Dietetic Institute

(340 words)

Business communications: Memos, proposals and reports

Categories

Memo

A memo is a formal business communication to bring attention to a problem and offer a solution. The receiver is usually informed of new information – policy changes, price increases, briefings, proposals. A memo persuades the receiver to take effective action – attend a follow-up meeting or introduce a new procedure.

Report

A report is a concise, factual document, written for a particular purpose and audience which communicates information compiled through research and analysis. It is often presented with a section as a bullet-pointed list. Reports recommend future action. Formal, impersonal language is used. This means avoiding the first-person pronoun 'I', opinions, slang, colloquialisms, jargon, etc.

Proposal

A proposal is an action plan for the future. It is aimed at persuading and making recommendations. Proposals are based on facts, but can use persuasive language, unlike reports. They use formal language (avoiding slang, jargon, clichés, colloquialisms, etc.) Reports should be logical and practical, using a timeline and detailing costs where appropriate.

Key features of business communications

Memo	Report	Proposal
Layout		
• **To**: names, titles • **From**: your name, job title • **Date**: • **Subject**: introductory paragraph, reason for memo • New information • Action required • Closing, offer thanks	• **Subject**: • **To**: names, titles • **Commissioned by**: • **On behalf of**: • **Date**: • Introduction gives purpose of report • Research methods employed • Main findings • Conclusions • Recommendations • Acknowledgements • Appendix	• **To**: name and title • **Date**: • **Subject**: • Introduction: identify problem, detail why it has not been addressed before • Details about problem • Proposal/solution • Timeline • Costs (if appropriate) • Conclusion: restate problem, proposed solution, offer thanks for consideration
Tone		
• Formal, concise, succinct, persuasive • No slang, jargon, clichés, colloquialisms • Call to action	• Formal, factual concise, structured • No persuasion, or personal opinion • No use of 'I' • Avoid slang, colloquialisms, clichés, jargon, etc. • Call to action	• Formal, factual, persuasive, lively • Timeline • Costs • Avoid slang, jargon, colloquialisms, clichés, etc. • Make a request for consideration

Sample Comprehending B question – Proposal

Question

Imagine that you are a reporter for your school magazine. You have been asked by the school management to write an article about your school's latest stage production to promote the cultural side of the school. Write the proposal you would send to the editor in which you suggest ideas for the article, identify whom you plan to interview and explain how you hope to engage the readers.

(50 marks)

Deconstructing the task

- **On what do I have to write?** (Content)
  School's new stage production, ideas for article, whom I will interview, how I will engage readers
- **Who am I as writer/speaker?** (Persona)
  Teenage reporter
- **Who am I addressing?** (Audience)
  Editor of school magazine
- **Why am I writing this?** (Purpose)
  Response to a school management request to promote the cultural life of the school
- **What type of language will I use?** (Register)
  Formal, concise, factual, persuasive
- **What format should the writing take?** (Genre)
  Proposal

exam Q

Sample answer

From: Patrick Dunne
To: Mary Fallon, Editor 'School Blues'
Date: 31 October
Subject: Proposal to write an article on the school's forthcoming stage production.

St Colman's College is currently preparing to stage the musical, 'Cats', over the weekend starting 30 November. The school management has requested that an article should appear in the end-of-term magazine to record this important cultural event. The magazine is not just a record of school life for current pupils, it celebrates activities for past pupils into the future. Over recent years, the Department of Education Inspectorate have taken a great interest in this publication because it recognises achievements outside of the classroom. The management is also keen that extra-curricular activities are documented.

I am proposing a 1,200-word piece on the upcoming production of this classic Lloyd Webber musical. This would be spread across four pages and include a brief background of 'Cats' plus profiles of the five stars of the school production. There would also be short interviews with those involved behind the scenes – creating sets, costumes, music, rehearsals, etc. The ticket-sellers and advertising team would also be interviewed. This would acknowledge the 'unseen' work which often goes into making a successful show. The parents' council contributed generously to fund the production and a picture of the chairperson handing the cheque to the director would certainly be of interest.

Readers of the college magazine would surely be engaged by this article because younger students could look at the celebration of the show as something to which they might aspire in the future. Current senior students would take tremendous pride in reading about 'their' production while parents and past pupils would also enjoy seeing a brief list of previous school shows.

The article would also help the school management in promoting the vibrant cultural aspect of school life since all Fifth Year students have been involved in some capacity. Hopefully, other students in the future will be encouraged to take part in the less glamorous side of staging a show if there is an acknowledgement of the importance of all aspects of staging.

In conclusion, the piece would be lively, interesting and informative, benefitting not only the young performers involved but also the crew, parents, present and past students and management. The complete article (including photographs) would be submitted no later than 20 November. Thank you for taking the time to consider this proposal.

Patrick Dunne

(400 words)

EXAMINER'S COMMENT

Well-organised top-grade response arranged in a series of succinct paragraphs. The central idea was clearly introduced and supported by a range of convincing arguments. The assured, enthusiastic tone was persuasive throughout. Expression was carefully controlled and made effective use of varied vocabulary and sentence length.

Diaries and interviews

Categories

Diary

A diary is a way of keeping track of your memories, but it has other benefits too. Diaries are also good for your creativity and mental health. Keeping a diary gives you an opportunity to express your emotions on paper, to vent anger and frustration, to voice sadness, excitement and happiness. It helps you reflect on daily life. What am I thankful for? What lessons did I learn from this experience? It is a judgement-free zone where you have a conversation with yourself about what you did, who you met, how you feel and what you hope for. A diary helps you get to know yourself better.

Interview

An interview is a one-on-one conversation in which someone is questioned about background, lifestyle and experiences, failures and successes. The person asking the questions is the interviewer and the person answering is the interviewee. The purpose of the exchange is to find out more about the interviewee, often for a magazine article or news report or for a job. The interviewer should have researched his/her subject and know what information, qualities, attitudes, etc. of the interviewee he/she wishes to explore. Imagine what your audience would wish to know about your subject.

Key features of diaries and interviews

Diary	Interview
Layout	
• **Date:** this timeline helps you to examine your progress or lack of progress over a particular period. • **Address:** 'Dear Diary', Dear (choose a name for your diary). Remember, you're talking to a friend. • **Record** your experiences, feelings, ideas, wishes, etc. • **Reflect** on personal development, so that there is a sense of sequencing. • **Conclusion:** sign off with your first name or a pen-name.	• **Set the scene:** name the interviewee, what interested you about this person, when and where the interview took place, what the interviewee is wearing and acting. • **Format:** question and answer. • **Opening and closing:** use provocative questions to open and close your written record of the interview to engage your audience. • **Conclude** with an evaluation of what you have found out about your subject.
Tone	
• Informal, informative, intimate confessional, candid, humorous, etc.	• Probing, encouraging, coaxing, persuasive, personal, humorous, etc.

Interviews

Do:

• Ask open-ended questions, e.g. 'They call you the next Johnny Sexton ... what three qualities do you share with this great player?'

Don't:

• Conduct an interview like an interrogation – it is a dialogue between people.
• Sacrifice the interviewee's privacy in order to be edgy or interesting. Respect boundaries.
• Ask boring or obvious questions. They usually lead to boring answers.

Sample Comprehending B question – Diary

Question

Write at least three diary entries which record and reflect on the details of a recent argument (real or imaginary) that you had with your best friend. Include the lead-up to the argument, the heated exchange and the outcome of this event. **(50 marks)**

Deconstructing the task

- **On what do I have to write?** (Content)

  An argument with my best friend, lead-up to argument, heated exchange, outcome of event

- **Who am I as writer/speaker?** (Persona)

  Teenager (myself)

- **Who am I addressing?** (Audience)

  Myself

- **Why am I writing this?** (Purpose)

  Personal response to an upsetting incident

- **What type of language will I use?** (Register)

  Informal, personal, factual, reflective

- **What format should the writing take?** (Genre)

  Diary entry

Sample answer

10 May

Dear Diary,

I am so mad I can barely write! To start off, I think I failed my French test. I know I should have studied more … But I just couldn't concentrate. Why? Well, you just won't believe what my so-called best friend Sheila did. She put up six pics on her Instagram profile of me eating a chicken burger (with all the trimmings) in KFC. I look like a disgusting pig. How could she? She then captioned the pics – 'Having a great time in KFC with my bestie!'

What is it with her? I know I went to 'Country Fest' with Niamh on Saturday, but really! I am apop … (Hold on – dictionary moment) apoplectic! I am not going to let this go. I am going to challenge her at hockey practice tomorrow.

Meantime, Dad's on my case about my lack of study. Honestly parents! Don't they want me to be a well-rounded person? I have other things on my mind just now, like Sheila!

Kate

11 May

Dear Diary,

Well, I met Sheila in the locker room before hockey. I told her straight how upset I was over the pics she had posted. To my surprise, instead of getting mad, she began to cry. She had put up the pics to show what good friends we were and what a great time we have together. The 'bestie' referred to me, not to the chicken burger. Well, I stood with my mouth hanging open. She said she would remove the pictures immediately. She had just wanted to show Niamh that she and I could have good times together.

Coach called and we headed off for practice. I didn't play very well. I checked Sheila's post after we had finished. They were gone.

I began to feel a bit bad. I suppose I could have invited Sheila to come with Niamh and myself to 'Country Fest'.

Kate

12 May

Dear Diary,

Didn't sleep too good last night. Realised I needed to do something. Texted Sheila to ask if she wanted to do lunch today. She said sure. I explained to her that just because I was hanging around with Niamh didn't mean I wasn't friends with her. She said sorry again for uploading the pics. I told her it was ok, I had just misunderstood what was going on. I reminded her of the time we were in primary school when I had got in to trouble for misreading the sign for 'toilet' because the 'i' had fallen off and I thought it said 'to let' and that the school were going to sell the toilets and what were we all going to do?

Meantime, on the parent front – I have agreed to stay for after school study to help improve my grades. At least it will be a tea-free zone!

'Get up, get out, start living the dream

Stand up, stand out you know what I mean

Get up, get out you're well on your way'

I can't wait …

Kate

(495 words)

EXAMINER'S COMMENT

Successful high-grade response that addresses all parts of the task, using a suitably reflective approach. Uses the diary format and maintains a good sense of sequencing when recording events. Engaging details throughout and a variety of personal tones – lively, humorous, confessional and informative.

Introductions and presentations

Categories

Introduction

An introduction presents something new to an audience, e.g. the opening section of a book, newsletter or a theatre programme. Introductions are used by publishers to pitch publications to prospective readers. An opening statement (often by a celebrity or expert) adds credibility to the text and puts a stamp of approval on the work. Introductions stimulate curiosity and interest.

Presentation

A presentation is a speech which introduces and explains a new product, idea or exhibition. It usually informs, persuades, inspires or educates.

Key features of introductions and presentations

Introduction	Presentation
Layout	
• **The hook:** 'Do you find yourself daunted by ...?' • **The benefits:** 'Discover the way in which you can ...'. • **Content:** include a brief sample or excerpt. • **Invitation:** motivate the reader or audience. • **Signature, title.**	• **Welcome audience.** • **Opening:** attention grabbing – provocative statement/humorous anecdote. • **Structure:** say what the presentation will be about, main body – two or three points, conclusion – sum up what you said. • **Memorable:** sharp, vivid, emotional descriptions; lively personal anecdotes. • **Pronouns:** use inclusive pronouns, 'we' and 'you' rather than 'I'. • **Rhetorical questions** and **repetition** engage and make it easy to remember. • **Conclusion:** summarise main points, thank audience, and end on a strong note. • **Invite questions.**
Tone	
• Informative, persuasive, confident, encouraging, etc.	• Informative, persuasive, personal, humorous, inspiring, etc.

Sample Comprehending B question – Introduction

Question

Write the introduction for a new collection of key scenes from any three Shakespearean plays (e.g. *Hamlet, Macbeth, King Lear, Romeo and Juliet, The Merchant of Venice*, etc.). In the introduction, you should discuss the relevance of the three plays to today's world, the enduring appeal of the central characters, and the productions of these plays that you have seen on stage or on screen.

(50 marks)

Deconstructing the task

- **On what do I have to write?** (Content)
  A new Shakespeare collection, relevance of three plays to today's world, enduring appeal of central characters, reference to production/s you have seen
- **Who am I as writer/speaker?** (Persona)
  Myself
- **Who am I addressing?** (Audience)
  Readers interested in Shakespeare
- **Why am I writing this?** (Purpose)
  To promote a new collection
- **What type of language will I use?** (Register)
  Factual, formal, lively, concise, persuasive
- **What format should the writing take?** (Genre)
  Written introduction

Sample answer

As a great fan of Shakespeare's best loved dramas, I was delighted to accept the invitation to write this short introduction to Gill's exciting new eBook, 'Sampling Shakespeare for Teenagers'. This attractive collection includes famous scenes from three of my favourite dramas, 'Hamlet', 'The Merchant of Venice' and 'Romeo and Juliet'. All the great themes are here – family relationships, fitting in, fighting corruption, love, hate, racism and the disastrous effects of absolute power. These issues are still the concerns of our modern world, even though the plays were mainly written in late 1500s England. Shakespeare's timeless stories have travelled through every culture and every generation since they were first performed.

The world's greatest playwright has created hugely memorable characters. The tortured, indecisive Hamlet was sensitively played in a recent modern-day version of the drama by the Irish actor, Andrew Scott. It was an unforgettable portrayal of a brilliant young prince suffering indescribably. The actor's frantic movement on stage was particularly impressive. The unhappy Hamlet convulsed with barely contained emotion, his hands fluttering like SOS signals. The prince's disgust with the corrupt Danish court was particularly evident after his father's sudden death and his mother's hasty remarriage to his uncle. For me, the most revealing moment occurred in his heart-breaking speech about this 'quintessence of dust'. It was a mesmerising performance.

We are all familiar these days with surveillance cameras watching our every move in public places. The director presents a Denmark that is totally spied on, opening the play with a patchwork of screens tracking the characters' movements. Hamlet's ghost appears stalking through deserted vaulted rooms. The haunting songs of Bob Dylan added to the tension, especially in the final duel between Hamlet and Laertes. The line, 'Feel like my soul has turned to steel', eloquently accompanied the flash of swords between the two young opponents as they fight to the death.

Similarly, in the excerpt from 'The Merchant of Venice', the veteran Hollywood actor Al Pacino puts in a moving performance as the ultimate outsider, the Jew in a predominantly Christian city. Click on the link below to see Shylock speak the tortured words of every despised outsider, 'Hath not a Jew eyes?' Venice, like most of our modern cosmopolitan cities, was a melting pot of many different nationalities, struggling to live side by side, as they conduct business. Shylock is a timeless victim who challenges us to be compassionate.

Link – Al Pacino in The Merchant of Venice: alpacinomerchantofvenice

Shakespeare's 'Romeo and Juliet' is also presented in a modern setting in Baz Lurhmann's dazzling film production about gang warfare in modern America. It really 'spoke' successfully to today's teenagers. Who could not have anything but sympathy for these two star-crossed lovers?

The new collection contains an exciting selection of excerpts from three astonishing stories by the greatest playwright who has ever lived. And all available in a modern accessible format in this new eBook. Dip in and enjoy!

Maia Dunphy

Television producer

(480 words)

EXAMINER'S COMMENT

Successful top-grade response addressing all three elements of the task, though not equally. The opening is enthusiastic and engaging. The introduction is clearly focused on *Hamlet*, but inevitably at the expense of the other two plays. Mature and perceptive discussion throughout, backed by impressive illustration and reference. Excellent register and expression.

3 Paper 1: Composing

The Composing section is the most important on the Leaving Cert English paper and is worth 100 marks (25% of the overall total). The question provides an opportunity to display a variety of writing skills and a flair for language use.

Aim for at least 900 words (written over approximately 80 minutes).

Types of Leaving Cert essay

Personal essay	Speech/talk/debate
Purpose: to share an experience and reflection. **How**: take a personal stance, use of 'I', description appealing to senses, personal anecdotes, offer reflective insights, confessional tone, humour, exaggeration, individual observations.	**Purpose**: to convince an audience to agree with your point of view. **How**: language of argument and/or persuasion, awareness of audience, use of allusions, illustrations, rhetorical questions, emotive language, personal anecdotes.
Informative article	**Feature article/opinion piece**
Purpose: to offer a factual account and to educate in an interesting way. **How**: use informative language, presenting arguments and counter-arguments, analysis, facts, statistics, sources, synthesis.	**Purpose**: to inform, entertain, reflect and persuade readers. **How**: offer a view into the human experience using emotive language, detailed description, personal anecdote, exaggeration, humour.
Dramatic dialogue	**Short story**
Purpose: to enable a reader hear a serious/humorous discussion from more than one voice on a topic. **How**: create distinct voices/characters, dramatic tension, dramatic development, variety of tones – comic, sincere, satirical, sceptical, persuasive.	**Purpose**: to write a narrative about fictional events and characters. **How**: use plot, characterisation, setting, description, atmosphere, dialogue, narrative shape, tension, suggestion, flashback, climax, resolution, aesthetic qualities.

Descriptive essay	Discursive essay
Purpose: to describe a person, place, or thing in vivid detail and involve readers in the experience. **How:** descriptive writing, imagery, setting, anecdote, atmosphere, attention to detail, appeal to senses, quality of observation, vivid vocabulary, aesthetic features.	**Purpose:** to explore both positive and negative aspects of a topic. **How:** discursive writing, allusions, arguments and counter-arguments, illustrations, analysis.

The personal essay

A personal essay explores your opinions and feelings about a subject or issue in an engaging and interesting way. It should be both **personal** and **reflective**. You are expressing your outlook or explaining your point of view.

What is personal writing?

'I have been very proud to hear how my great-grandparents helped other families less fortunate than themselves with food and fuel during those bitter winter months.'

Personal writing, using the personal pronoun 'I'.

'Previous generations helped other families less fortunate than themselves with food and fuel during those bitter winter months.'

Informative writing, non-personal, no use of personal pronoun 'I'.

What is reflective writing?

'I was bullied at school when I was ten. I realised I had a choice, I could allow myself to be bullied or I could stand up for myself. It was up to me.'

Reflective writing shows the writer thinking about an experience and sometimes drawing a lesson from it.

N.B. *'The general functions of language outlined here will continually mix and mingle within texts and genres. So, there can be an aesthetic argument, a persuasive narrative, or an informative play.'* (Department of Education English Syllabus)

Aesthetic writing refers to language that appeals to our sense of beauty. It is closely associated with an imaginative and carefully crafted poetic style. Aesthetic language is most likely found in descriptive, narrative and personal compositions.

Don't just re-tell experiences and memories – interpret and discuss them.

Purpose

To describe, share and **reflect** on an experience/relationship between **yourself** and someone/something else.

How?

- Decide on a **goal** – what do you want to show, share, understand?
- Identify your **target audience**.
- Use **descriptive, humorous, discursive** language.
- Include **autobiographical anecdotes** (experiences, either fictional or real from your life).
- **Personal feelings** should be expressed sincerely and convincingly.
- Write in a **confessional, intimate tone**.
- Use **first-person pronouns**: 'I', 'me', etc.
- **Reflective insights** (considering what the experience you have described meant to you).

> **key point**
>
> Do you have any knowledge or experience of this subject? Do you hold strong opinions on it? If not, don't choose this type of essay.

Remember!

Personal essays are usually distinguished by their lively, conversational language. The tone is often candid and confessional. You are likely to be writing about something that has really changed your view of life, such as a turning point that taught you a lesson about social inequality.

How is the Leaving Cert essay marked?

The criteria for assessment (usually referred to as the **PCLM**) are as follows:

Clarity of purpose (30%)

This refers to engagement with the task. Has the candidate engaged with the question? Relevance, focus, originality, freshness, clear aim, and understanding of genre are rewarded here.

Coherence of delivery (30%)

This refers to the ability to sustain the response over the entire answer. Continuity of argument, sequencing, management of ideas, use of examples, control of register and creative modelling are all rewarded in this section.

Efficiency of language use (30%)

This refers to control of language to achieve clear communication. Has the candidate used language suitable for the task? Vocabulary, syntax, paragraphing, punctuation, and use of lively expression are examined here.

Accuracy of mechanics (10%)

This refers to spelling and grammar.

Sample essay question

Question
Write a personal essay in which you reflect on significant moments of insight and revelation that you have experienced.

PCLM Marking Scheme guidelines:

- Always address the question. The 'P' element of PCLM requires candidates to focus on the task. Your response must be a personal essay containing reflections on significant moments of insight and revelation experienced.

- In this case, the writing can be informative, argumentative and persuasive (depending on the stance you have chosen).

- Allow about 80 minutes and aim for 900 words.

Sample answer

1 This year, above any other year, I need a moment of revelation. I need a totally reliable test which would tell me with pin-point precision – Yes, I am supposed to be a world famous scientist, No, I am not supposed to be an actor even though I was the lead in the TY school musical, 'The Sound of Music'. But I have found revelation comes when you least expect it.

> Personal response, reference to question.

2 Last July I was in New York for a week during a heatwave. At one of the gates going into Central Park, a little lady was selling 'blue' roses. I shook my head in disbelief. Sadly no rose, genetically, can be blue. The sticky summer afternoon had a line of kids ordering 100% artificially azure blue snow cones. The ice-cream van tinkled, the kids giggled. The ice-cream man presented the children with mouthfuls of frozen, sweet idealised 'sky'. I suddenly realised that not everything has to be judged scientifically. Humans dare to make impossibilities possible, even if only with syrup and food colouring.

> Personal experience, reflective insight.

3 If an experience goes so deep that a special sense of knowing emerges, then this is when insight occurs. When I went off to secondary school, my Gran bought me a new lunchbox. She used to say, 'I don't know where the years go to!' I don't think it had registered with her that I was twelve, pretending to be fourteen, not ten! In the canteen, on that first day I went in, a second year student sneered, 'Oooh, look at her, with her new shiny lunchbox!' I cringed. Is this what secondary school life was going to be like? When I went home, I went straight to my computer

and posted an urgent message on Facebook. It announced that the director of 'Frozen' was coming to our area tomorrow and was looking for a teenager who had merchandise associated with the film. A picture of this student would be taken with the director.

4   Next day I arrived in the canteen, proudly carrying my 'Frozen' lunchbox. Some of my classmates crowded around me excitedly. A hush descended. A group of the second years were coming.

'How much for that lunchbox?'

'Not for sale, my Gran bought me it.'

'Where?'

'Woodies.'

'Let's go!'

I smiled to myself. I realised that Gran sometimes knew what she was talking about when she said, 'You gotta be smart!' There would be no more problems with these older students. Must make sure to report that the director went to the neighbouring village by mistake!

Personal experience, reflective insight.

5   When I was in TY, we did a project on Seamus Heaney. I really felt that this poet could communicate moments of insight. Who can forget Heaney's home-place, Mossbawn, with its 'water honeyed in the slung bucket' on long sunny afternoons? For me, my oasis of calm against the crazy world is my quiet living room where I lie spread-eagled on the couch, trying to snatch a few precious moments of extra shut-eye before school. My living room marks the celebration of the year, Christmas. It captures the intoxicating excitement of the day. The tall Christmas tree takes pride of place, ornaments glittering, lights twinkling. An hour after our family's exchange of presents, the room looks like a bomb site with torn wrapping paper covering every part of the floor. We raise a toast to my late Gran's picture, her eyes shining as brightly as the lights on the tree. Just like Heaney, I know that in this ordinary room 'is love like a tinsmith's scoop sunk past its gleam in the meal-bin'.

Reference to Heaney's insight adds interest.

6   Of course, poetry isn't for everyone – and there's no law saying that you have to like it or learn by it. But it's interesting that most of my so-called life-changing experiences have happened with my family or at school. Back when I was in 6th Class, the most memorable moment happened during a History lesson when the teacher began discussing World War 2. Although I had heard of the war and the Holocaust, it had not really made an impact on me. Like most young children, I didn't relate to statistics. It wasn't until I read the number '6 million' on the board – and the teacher explained that this number was much greater than the entire population of Ireland, North and South, that I began to understand. In a way, it was the beginning of growing up. In the years since then, I have learnt much more about the reality of what happened to innocent Jewish victims during the 1940s. I still don't understand how such inhumanity could occur in a civilised part of Europe

less than 100 years ago, but I am still as shocked as ever by what some humans are capable of doing to one another.

> Reflective anecdote broadens discussion.

7 Luckily, life is generally not so horrific. During the holidays I always enjoy taking some quiet time to chill. Now I rise early and in the stillness of the dawn I like to be in my bedroom looking at the graceful silver birch swaying smoothly against the blue sky. I switch off my phone and close my eyes. Some days I imagine I am like the tree, my feet growing roots down through the floor into the soil, connecting with the earth. I follow the gentle pace of my breath, flowing in and out. Time drifts by. I open my eyes and stretch. The silver birch is still there, gently rocking to its own beat. It's then I realise I am part of this wonderful blue planet's creation.

8 Flashes of insight occur when our minds are quiet and our aware self is at rest. The genius inventor, Thomas Edison, would often let his mind wander, hoping to capture fleeting bits of original thought which he would jot down. Anxiety creates 'noise' in the brain, drowning out the space for revelation. Often we are told to think long and hard before making an important decision, like what should I choose to be in the future. I now realise that moments of insight and revelation pop up without warning, just as life happens while you are planning it. I think that's what I'll do with my career choice. Let's just see what pops up!

> Conclusion links ending with opening paragraph, rounding off the essay.

(1,020 words)

EXAMINER'S COMMENT

- Well-written, focused response.
- Good structure in organised paragraphs.
- Reflective approach sustained throughout.
- Effective use of a range of personal anecdotes.
- Engagingly lively and discursive tone.
- Slightly awkward expression and repetition of 'went' in paragraph 3.

GRADE H1

P = 30/30

C = 30/30

L = 28/30

M = 10/10

Total = 98/100

key point

A personal essay will be **sharply** penalised if it reads like a short story and lacks a reflective quality.

Persuasive speeches and talks

Purpose

To make an impact on the audience to **convince** them to agree with your point of view.

How?

- Decide on a clear **stance** (agree or disagree with topic).
- Identify target **audience** (e.g. adult professionals, teenage students, etc.).
- Emphatic language is **persuasive** (repetition, rhetorical, exaggeration, etc.).
- **Emotive** language (anecdotes/personal stories appeal to feelings).
- **Inclusive** language involves audience (use of 'we', 'our', etc. to influence audience attitudes).
- Anticipate **opposing** points of view.

Language of persuasion

- Appeals to audience's emotions.
- Persuades through flattery, e.g. 'This intelligent audience is well aware that I am right'.
- Manipulation through fear, e.g. 'The planet cannot survive any more pollution'.
- Use of allusions, references.
- Engaging humour.
- Rhetorical questions imply the answer, e.g. 'Who doesn't want success?'
- Emotive language, e.g. 'The ocean is under attack due to man's careless behaviour.'
- Rule of three, e.g. 'Stop, look and listen.'
- Rhythm, repetition, memorable phrases.
- Use commands, e.g. 'Come and join us!'
- Exaggeration.
- Personal pronouns – 'I', 'you', 'we'.
- Persuasive style is used in school debates, political speeches, propaganda, advertising, etc.

Sample essay

Question

Write a persuasive speech to be delivered to a youth conference, in which you give your views on how freedom and democracy can be encouraged in the world today.

PCLM Marking Scheme guidelines:

- Address the question. The 'P' element of PCLM requires candidates to focus on the task. Your response must sound like a speech, using the type of language suitable for delivery to a young audience.

- In this case, the writing can be informative, argumentative and persuasive (depending on the stance you have chosen).

- Allow about 80 minutes and aim for 900 words.

Sample answer

1 Chairperson, conference delegates, it is my privilege to have the opportunity to address you on how I believe that freedom and democracy can be supported in the world today. Democracy comes from the Greek word *demokratia*, which means the rule of the people. It is a system of government in which the citizens exercise power by casting a single vote, no matter how wealthy or well-connected they are. It is one person, one vote. Over recent years, two democratic countries had seismic eruptions because of a vote. The UK got Brexit, the USA got Donald Trump. These results were unexpected – especially by the mass media. But these results, even if they upset some people, cannot be overthrown. To support freedom and democracy in our world, we have to agree to abide by the decision of the majority, even if some do not like it.

> Reference creates interest. Addresses audience. Stance is identified.

2 Democracy is a system which is based on freedom of speech, freedom of political expression, freedom of the press and internet democracy. This ensures well-informed citizens and voters, enabling voters to cast their votes in their own interest. How are we informed? The internet has evolved into a powerful tool for spreading information. YouTube is the most popular video sharing site in the world. The videos are monetised through Google's AdSense which places small banner ads on them or short 'pre-roll' ads that play before the videos. This has changed the world. In the recent protests in Iran, one of the first actions of the government was to disable the internet. But all is not well. YouTube has admitted to manipulating the search results for certain topics to favour news reports from mainstream media over independent ones. Channels are given 'Community Strikes'. Videos are deleted because their moderators think they contain 'hate speech' or 'bullying'. But who are these moderators? What role is YouTube really playing in our democracy?

> Repetition adds emphasis. Effective rhetorical question and specific illustration.

3 Google is more than just a search machine. It is the closest thing to an all-powerful information monopoly the planet has ever seen. It has even transformed itself into a verb. When we want answers, we now 'google' everything. Its secret algorithms determine which web pages show up and in what order. 'US News and World Report' called it 'the world's biggest censor'. It has admitted censoring results for the Chinese government. It filtered any search results about Tiananmen Square where hundreds of student protestors were killed during a pro-democracy demonstration. Is democracy being served well? Wikipedia is the most popular online 'encyclopedia'. But its editors and writers are anonymous. How do we know we can trust them? A book or newspaper has been edited by a named source. The writer's name is publicly displayed. If there is bias or inaccuracies, it can be challenged. It is difficult to question anonymous sources. Is our ability to be well-informed being denied by the very sites that claim to be informing us? We need to be aware of where we get our information.

4 Being offended has become a full time job for some people. We are all different, unique, but we are all equal. Remember, one vote for one person. We have to learn to co-exist. This means accepting that others think differently than you do. They have a right to hold this opinion. You have a right to disagree with them. We have all heard of 'hate speech'. We all agree bigotry and racism is wrong. But in a true democracy, there must be room for opposing points of view. I believe class debates are a wonderful starting point to teach teens that they can argue with or attempt to persuade others to change their point of view. Each side is given the opportunity to speak and be heard. In Ireland there will be more referendums on serious issues. This will produce heated arguments, but in the end, the people of the country will decide. You may not like the outcome, but this is democracy in action. The social contract is to accept majority rule. If this is disputed, the options are an oligarchy or monarchy. Would you want that?

> Short sentences and final question add emphasis. Effective debate illustration.

5 How can we promote respect for the individual and democracy in the classroom? A teacher offers a choice of three films to her students to run on the last day of term. Each student will get a vote, having listened to a supporter of each film. A vote is taken. The film which gets the most votes will be shown. Those who don't get their choice cannot sit with their backs to the screens sulking for the duration of the film. They have had to learn to accept that the agreement has been made that majority rules. In other words, it's civilised to agree to disagree.

> Use of personal light-hearted tone.

6 Discussion, informed discussion, is the basis of our freedom. Shutting people up by dubbing their views as 'hate speech' destroys democracy. Freedom thrives on robust discussion and debate. We listen to those with whom we disagree, consider what they propose, question, challenge and decide for ourselves what our view on a topic is. We cannot close our ears. We have to become aware and informed. We

have to ask, who is speaking? What is their agenda? What are the facts? Are their opinions sound? This takes effort, time, and energy. But it is worth it to live in the dynamic and challenging system that is a true democracy. A democratic society is not a 'safe place', but an invigorating experience. Freedom does not mean screaming matches, vile insults or violence to force people to think as you do. Democracy puts forward reasoned argument, powerful persuasion and is willing to adapt to the will of the people. Thank you for listening.

> Well rounded-off.
> Strong conclusion.
> Expression of thanks.

(960 words)

EXAMINER'S COMMENT

- Generally well-written and focused response.
- Clear stance sustained throughout.
- Effective use of supportive discussion points about social media.
- Attempts to use informative details and references to history.
- Some generalisation regarding China.
- Emphatic rhetorical questions.
- Repetition in paragraph 6.
- Speech is rounded off confidently.

GRADE H1

P = 27/30
C = 27/30
L = 26/30
M = 10/10
Total = 90/100

Discursive writing

Purpose

To discuss a given topic and present an argument related to it.

How?

A discursive piece usually presents an objective examination of a subject, exploring both the positive and negative aspects, although not necessarily equally. The discursive style can be formal or informal, primarily using the language of argument.

key point

Discursive and argumentative essays aim to show a **more balanced** discussion. Nevertheless, your approach does not have to be completely neutral.

Language of argument

- Appeals to logic and reason to elicit agreement with views expressed through clarifying and explaining.
- Evidenced-based points.
- Balanced argument, presents counter-argument, e.g. 'Uniforms are criticised for depriving students of individuality, yet create a sense of belonging and pride.'
- Use of statistics and facts.

- Evidence of research.
- Interpretation of data.
- Coherent central argument.
- Well-organised structure.
- Linking phrases – so, therefore, because, in order to, etc.
- Inspirational tone.
- No slang!
- Discursive style used in articles, formal planned speeches.

Sample essay

Question

You are participating in a public speaking competition for second-level students. Write a discursive speech (serious, amusing or both) in which you give your views about government bans on the use of plastic.

PCLM Marking Scheme guidelines:

- Always address the question. The 'P' element of PCLM requires candidates to focus on the task. Your response must be a discursive speech giving your views about government bans on the use of plastic.
- In this case, various approaches can be used (personal, informative, reflective, etc.). However, the essay should contain a strong discursive/ argumentative element.
- Allow about 80 minutes and aim for 900 words.

Sample answer

1 Judges, ladies and gentlemen, fellow students. To ban, or not to ban, <u>that</u> is the question. I would like to explore the concept of government bans on the use of plastic by presenting you with some key ideas about recent bans on that controversial substance, plastic.

> Succinct, clear introduction.

2 We use one trillion plastic bags every year, according to the magazine, 'Waste Management'. The National Oceanic and Atmospheric Administration (NOAA) are issuing warnings about the Great Pacific Garbage Patch – vast shifting waves of trash which marine life are ingesting. By the Year 2050 there will be more plastic than fish in the sea. BBC's 'Blue Planet II' highlighted this problem, 71% of

> Effective use of factual references.

seabirds and 30% of turtles have plastic in their stomachs. Sky News carried the sad story of a stranded whale that died with a stomach full of plastic bags.

3 The rare Cuvier beaked whale feed far out at sea, diving to depths of 3 km. The water is completely dark. The whale uses sound beams to find squid. But this has a sonic echo which is similar to that produced by plastic bags. And plastic sinks! Three times the distressed whale swam into the shallow cove near Bergen in Norway. The first time the residents pushed it back out to sea. The next time it was the fire brigade. Returning a third time and completely exhausted, the local marksman was called to kill the tormented mammal.

4 Inside the whale there were 30 large pieces of plastic, mostly plastic bags with creepy writing – a chicken wrapper from the Ukraine, an ice-cream wrapper from Denmark, a crisp bag from the UK. Professor Lislevand, a local scientist from the University of Bergen stated that some form of human action could have stopped this plastic from getting into the marine environment. People must understand that plastics in the ocean is a problem that requires urgent action. Everyone has to play their part. Is anyone listening to this silent messenger from the deep?

> Details establish need for government controls.

5 Ireland has led the way. In 2002, it was the first country to impose a tax on plastic bags of 15 cents. We were using up to 1.2 billion plastic bags every year. Within 5 years there was a 90% reduction in single-use plastic bags. This stunning success was slowly copied by other countries.

6 But the use of plastic has increased in almost every industry. The production of plastic products in the whole of the 20th century equals that of the first ten years of the 21st century. Plastic is durable, easily moulded, sterile and inexpensive. Mobile phones, laptops, cabins cars use high quality plastic. Low quality plastic is used in utensils, bags, water bottles. The problem is that it is non-biodegradable. It cannot be recycled into new organic molecules and life. It is a man-made product – from oil. It doesn't occur naturally. Governments and people have to act. Bans have to be implemented to make us think about what we are doing.

> Paragraph 6 opening sentence is unclear. Ireland or worldwide?

7 Look at the scene from a typical morning rush hour. Workers scurry clutching plastic coffee cups. The type of coffee and where you get it says a lot about you. It's a sign of sophistication. 500 billion coffee cups each

year are used which would circle the world 1,360 times. The plastic waterproof lining cannot be recycled. Normal compost heaps cannot compost even biodegradable coffee cups. All go into a landfill.

8   The World Economic Forum advocates a circular economy. Their aim is to have disposable cups made from recyclable material. But that will take the right infrastructure to collect and reprocess the material. Once again Ireland is leading the way, Dublin City Council wants to ban the use of non-recyclable coffee cups in its buildings. But in the meantime, is there anything we can do without being forced to by government bans? Yes, we can reduce, reuse and recycle. Instead of a takeaway coffee, we can sit in the coffee shop and drink from a warmed ceramic cup and saucer. We can refuse to have a lid on our coffee. We can buy reusable containers if we must have a takeaway. 'Responsible Cafés' are springing up which will give a discount to customers with reusable takeaway cups.

> Interesting ideas, but not directly focused on issue of bans.

9   Another item of plastic which is causing havoc in the ocean is the humble plastic straw. 500 million straws are used annually, usually for one period of twenty minutes, enough to circle the earth two and a half times. They are too lightweight for any form of recycling. They take 200 years to break down into smaller pieces, but never fully disintegrate into the environment. Once more Ireland is showing its green credentials. TCD has already announced they will eliminate single-use plastics, following a year-long campaign by TCD Plastic Solutions Group.

10 Through information, education, thoughtfulness and government bans, we can act as responsible custodians to our beautiful blue planet. NASA astronaut Ron Garan described the earth as a 'fragile oasis'. We don't trash our 'pale blue dot', we take care of it! Thank you for your attention.

(835 words)

EXAMINER'S COMMENT

- Informative, thought-provoking ideas and illustrations on aspects of pollution and the use of plastic.
- General, one-sided discussion lacked focus on the issue of government bans, reducing the 'P' award.
- No counter-arguments considered (e.g. government intrusion on personal freedom; pollution/costs from further reliance on alternatives to plastic, etc.)
- Sustained use of lively, detailed references in favour of official controls.
- Excellent expression and good sense of a public speech.
- Essay was rounded off effectively.

GRADE H3

P = 23/30

C = 22/30

L = 23/30

M = 10/10

Total = 78/100

The descriptive essay

Purpose

To describe a person, place or thing in vivid detail so that a clear impression is formed in the reader's mind. Close attention is paid to details and all five senses are used (sight, sound, touch, taste and smell). A descriptive essay delivers a deeply involved experience.

How?

Imagery, setting, vivid vocabulary and aesthetic appeal are key features of effective description. Atmosphere is often created through striking visual and aural images. This type of writing uses careful observation to enable readers to reflect on the significance of what has been described.

Most forms of writing involve some description. In narrative fiction, for example, characters and places need to feel authentic. Evocative description of people, events, feelings and atmosphere helps to achieve this.

Variety makes writing interesting. Careful choice of adjectives and verbs can help to improve descriptions.

Sample essay

Question

Write a descriptive essay entitled 'Night Scene'.

PCLM Marking Scheme guidelines:

- Always address the question. The 'P' element of PCLM requires candidates to focus on the task. Your response must be a descriptive essay about a night scene.

- In this case, various approaches can be used (personal, narrative, reflective, discursive, etc.). However, the essay should contain a strong descriptive element.

- Allow about 80 minutes and aim for 900 words.

Sample answer

1   I just can't do anymore! My head is bursting. I fling the textbooks to the floor and stomp out into the balmy June night. I plug in my earphones, a softly strummed guitar is followed by Ellie Goulding's gentle, 'Starry, starry night … Paint your palette blue and grey'. I hum along half-heartedly. 'With eyes that know the darkness in my soul …' My breathing is slowing now. I smell the lilac bush, Mum's favourite, 'Swirling clouds in a violet haze'. I smile too as I pop out my earphones and breathe in the sweet scent perfuming the evening air. I lean against the cool stone wall and close my eyes, 'I cannot see what flowers are at my feet, Nor what soft incenses hangs upon the boughs'.

> Lively, engaging opening establishes the night-time setting.

2   Further up the street, a gate creaks. A small girl, blonde curls bobbing, runs and fires herself into her waiting Daddy's arms. She curves her head gracefully, like a little bird, into his broad shoulder. Safe and secure now, protected against the night. Father and daughter walk back into their house. As I watch them, I think of childhood memories – of not fearing the dark.

3   A pair of heavy steps ring out on the cobbled pavement and a young lad struts into view – Docs, black jeans and the ubiquitous leather jacket. Hands stuck in pockets, shoulders hunched, he weaves his way home like a dark bird of prey, 'Makes wing to the rooky wood'. I shiver slightly. Walking across the grass verge, I hear a party in full swing. Laughter rises, bottles clink. Boys laugh

> Atmospheric images add interest throughout paragraphs 2 and 3.

loudly. Some of the young college students are having one last blow-out before their finals. I remember Gatsby's 'blue gardens'. All that glitter and anticipation where men and girls 'came and went like moths among the whisperings'. The heavy dance music thrums out its insistent beat. A young girl breaks from the crowd, arms moving sinuously to the hypnotic beat … The crowd hushes. I stand transfixed. She is caught in the moment, her hands floating gracefully through the soft air, her body swaying to the pounding rhythm. Friends join her and they dance together, unaware of everything and everyone else.

4   Strangely, in the dead of night, in spite of the electric lights, this seems an alien place, especially if you are walking through it alone. There are alleys and street corners and shop entrances where the darkness seems to collect in a dense mass. I walk on. An empty plastic bag hangs limply on a hedge. The bag shape rustles in the ghostly light. Had it once held a book of nursery rhymes for a favoured grandchild, or some dream-filled magazines for a weary commuter? Or perhaps something more sinister? Who can be sure about the secrets hidden in these dark places?

5   Once the pubs are closed, there is only the 24-hour convenience store and the flickering striplight from a sleepy taxi. I pass the 'Polski Sklep', still open for business to catch the shift workers as they make their weary way home in the gleam of the street lamps. Large pink rings of salami, pale cheeses and boxes of smoked fish are piled high in the shop window. I wonder if the shopkeeper looks out at the moon and thinks of loved ones

far away. Are they also are looking at the moon, a slender channel of communication, linking one who went and one who stayed.

6   From time to time, there are the ominous silhouettes of other solitary individuals. They seem as threatened by your presence, no doubt, as you are by theirs. Despite the artificial light, it never fully removes the suspicion that night people are up to no good. To be alone in the streets, even when walking determinedly, nearly always gives the impression of being on the run, either from oneself or from someone else.

> Focus on people makes the essay more thought-provoking.

7   I wonder about all those who walk alone in the streets at night? The lost, the lonely. The sleepless, the homeless. All the city's internal outcasts. The night has always been the time for such dispossessed people – the different. Am I one of those? Popping in my headphones, I turn on Goulding again, 'And now I think I understand what you tried to say to me'. I head for home. Time to have another look at all those writers.

> Well-controlled ending echoes the introduction.

(715 words)

EXAMINER'S COMMENT

- Although short, this is a succinct top-grade descriptive essay – with a sustained focus on the night-time experience.
- Vivid cinematic details add drama and a strong sense of immediacy.
- Paragraph 2 is slight and could have been more developed.
- References to songs and poems enrich the description and add an aesthetic quality.
- Reflective conclusion further involves the reader.
- Expression is in keeping with the overall register and the underlying sense of unease.

GRADE H1

P = 28/30

C = 27/30

L = 28/30

M = 10/10

Total = 93/100

Informative writing

Purpose

To offer a clear, factual account and to educate in an interesting way.

How?

Information should be conveyed efficiently and effectively. Always keep your audience in mind. Readers should know more about a subject after they have read an informative piece of writing.

Language of Information

Structure

- Clear opening.
- General information about topic.
- Specific information about topic.
- Succinct, logical conclusion.

Layout

- Straightforward, clear.
- Well-organised, accessible.
- Present tense.
- First or third person.
- Facts, statistics, sources.
- Good linkages between paragraphs.
- Use of connectives – therefore, because, resulting in, etc.
- Avoid opinion/bias/repetition.
- Questions engage reader.
- Specific examples.
- Bullet point summaries.
- Used in newspaper/magazine articles, web pages, instructions, travel guides, reference books, etc.

Sample essay

Question

You have been asked by the editor of your online school magazine to write an informative article, aimed at both students and parents, about the digital age of consent online.

PCLM Marking Scheme guidelines:

- Always address the question. The 'P' element of PCLM requires candidates to focus on the task. Your response must be a descriptive essay about a night scene.
- In this case, various approaches can be used (personal, narrative, reflective, discursive, etc.). However, the essay should contain a strong descriptive element.
- Allow about 80 minutes and aim for 900 words.

Sample answer

TEENAGE CLICKS

1 The 'digital age of consent'

The digital age of consent refers to the time from which it is legal for data controllers to hold data gathered from children and teenagers. It determines the age when these young people can have a contractual-type arrangement with an online provider. Every country has to choose a number between 13 and 16 and make it the legally binding age for their children to join social media.

> Clear opening includes precise definition.

2 The case for consent at 13

The Irish government, the ISPCC, the Children's Rights Alliance, the Ombudsman for Children and Barnardo's had all argued for the age to be set at 13. They pointed to the internet as a critical source of information for children who cannot turn to an adult for help. The government did not want to restrict free speech and does not wish to be seen to 'regulate the internet'. The Digital Youth Council also felt that raising the digital age of consent to 16 only sweeps the problem under the carpet and leaves young people at greater risk online. They preferred developing digital education and literacy for parents and children, arguing that many young people don't understand what happens when you put a personal photo or information online. Barnardo's also felt that raising the age fails to address the uncomfortable realities about children's online usage.

> Well-supported references.

3 The case for consent at 16

Gardaí, teachers and doctors advocate the age of consent to be fixed at 16. They believe that parents are unaware of what is happening and argue that if the medical age of consent is 16, then the digital age of consent should match it. Details posted by a 13-year-old stay online forever. Human resource companies can access this data years later, when the young person is applying for a job – which they believe is unfair to the thirteen-year-old. The Gardaí, who deal with the explosion of online grooming, support the age 16 level. Teachers, who deal with the daily fallout of online bullying, oppose the lower age of 13. Doctors, who deal with patient problems of sleeplessness, obesity, anxiety and depression, also want the age set at 16.

The Irish Daily Mail recently ran a campaign, 'Protect Our Kids Online', to alert the public that children who are not old enough to leave school, drive a car or vote should not be able to sign a contract which will result in such far-reaching consequences for

> Strong point, well-developed through illustration.

them. The Irish Heart Foundation also support the age 16 limit because the micro-targeting of children by junk food marketers, using data harvested by social media platforms, is now a criminal offence. Ireland would join the Germans, French and Netherlands who have all set their age of consent at the upper limit. WhatsApp has set its age of consent to 16 for all of Europe. So children under the age of 16 could not be targeted by big tech companies to collect, store and process their data. So young people will not have access to a large number of websites because they won't be able to legally consent to these sites' terms and conditions. Such groups argue that the protection this amendment offers is limited. Children can lie about their age to set up a social media account. Policing of age verification can be difficult, but there are technological solutions to this problem. Some research has shown that adolescents experience greater unhappiness through their teenage years if they go online when too young.

4 What do you think?

Is the setting of the age of online consent at the age of 16 a 'victory for common sense'? French privacy laws have put a fine for €45,000 euros on parents who post images of their kids online, because they are breaching their children's privacy. Yet Cruz Beckham, age 11, has over 300,000 followers on Instagram. For decades, the big tech companies have used a thirteen-year-old's personal information in the same way as an adult's information. In the US, big toy companies were fined $800,000 dollars collectively for ad-related monitoring of kids' online behaviour. Several leading Children's Charities have called for a number of measures to be implemented immediately, including:

- A National Action Plan on Online Safety
- Creation of the Office of Digital Safety Commissioner
- Increased Gardaí powers to detect online crime
- Enhanced digital awareness education for children, parents and teachers

5 So what's your view? Was it right to raise the digital age of consent to 16 to safeguard children's safety online? Please click on the link below to add your comments on this issue.

Effective conclusion inviting a response from readers.

Online consent in Ireland

(745 words)

EXAMINER'S COMMENT

- Informative article rooted in a clear factual context.
- Opposing arguments presented without obvious bias.
- Some direct focus on attitudes/behaviour of students and parents expected.
- Headings and layout aids accessibility.
- Generally well-controlled expression, apart from some repetition.

GRADE H2

P = 26/30

C = 26/30

L = 25/30

M = 10/10

Total = 87/100

The short story

Purpose

To entertain and enlighten with a narrative that illustrates a moral lesson and/or insight into life, revealing a fresh perspective on the human condition.

How?

By using some of the key elements of narrative writing:
- Plot, setting, characterisation, conflict.
- Narrative shape, dialogue, narrative voice.
- Foreshadowing, atmosphere, suspense.
- Suggestion, flashback, resolution.

Plot

This is the storyline (what happens in the narrative).
- The **beginning** sets up the world of the story (where and when the action takes place), the atmosphere, the main characters and the conflict.
- The **climax** is the turning point. This is where the tension is at its height and the main character has to make a decision to act or not to act in trying to achieve his/her wish.
- The **ending** resolves the conflict happily, unhappily. The resolution can be open (a cliff hanger – the reader decides what might happen) or closed (the writer decides what happens). It can be an unexpected surprise (a twist in the tale). The ending must make sense within the world of the story.

Narrative shape

The shape of a story is usually **not** a straight line, but an arc.

Middle
- Climax/turning point
- Tension at its height
- Main character decides to act or not

Beginning
- 'World' of story – where and when the story is set
- Character – personality, aim or wish
- Conflict – what stands in the character's way

Ending
- Conflict resolved credibly within the world of story
- Character changes
- Life lesson learned, etc.

Some narrative writing guidelines

Do	Don't
• Have a small number of characters and settings. • Keep the plot (storyline) simple. • Include conflict. • Suggest mood and atmosphere, rather than explaining everything. • Create obstacles to challenge the central character. • Use dialogue to engage readers. • Establish narrative voice, i.e. first person ('I am involved in the action, telling the story') or third person ('he/she is looking in, telling the story'). • Use flashback if appropriate to explain what led up to the present situation. • Show or suggest consequences of character's choices and decisions. • Know the ending before you write.	• Tell the story – *show* it. • Have too many characters or settings. • Have a complicated plot. • Have an over-extended time scale. • Start writing without planning. • Learn off a story and hope to write it in the exam. • Have a clichéd ending ('it was all dream', everyone dies at the end, etc.). • Have an incredible ending. It has to be believable within the context of the story.

Sample story 1

Question

Write a short story in which the central character makes a decision to be true to him/herself.

Prompt!

- Identify the main elements of the question, so that your answer is focused.
- The plot is already given (a character makes an important decision or acts in a way that is true to who he/she is).
- Decide on the conflict.
- Where and when is the story set?
- Who is in the story? What is the main character's aim or wish?
- Who/what is preventing this?
- How will the story end?
- Will I begin mid-way through the narrative or at the beginning? Will I use flashback?
- Where will dialogue, suggestion, tension, etc. be useful in engaging readers?

PCLM Marking Scheme guidelines:

- Always address the question. The 'P' element of PCLM requires candidates to focus on the task. Your response must be a short story in which the central character makes a decision to be true to him/herself.
- In this case, various approaches can be used (personal, descriptive, reflective, etc.). However, the essay should contain a strong narrative element.
- Allow about 80 minutes and aim for 900 words.

Sample answer

Robbie shook his head at his old Grandad. Half-dozing in his favourite red armchair, he was watching yet another Western.

'A man's gotta do what a man's gotta do,' he echoed John Wayne striding across the wide open spaces of Texas beneath the technicolour blue skies. Robbie flung his bag at the cat and thumped up the stairs two at a time. Goth nirvana awaited. Slipknot or Rammstein? Robbie tapped his MP3 player and the raw guitar of 'Psychosocial' shook the room. The thunder beats of the drums and Corey Taylor's guttural lyrics thrummed through his brain. Bliss! Robbie grinned – good job Grandad was half deaf. But now, to business! Every death metal, long-haired Viking Goth had to have a tattoo.

Scrolling quickly through BuzzFeed on his laptop, Robbie checked out how the skin takes ink, how the body heals, noting the areas to avoid – back of knees, elbows. The feed stated 'beach bums in particular will need to avoid getting a tat in the summer because sun exposure and water submersion can damage the new tattoo'. Robbie laughed wryly to himself as he gazed out at the grey drizzling Irish rain misting down the window. Same colour as Carly's eyes – biggest Justin Bieber fan in the world – but a cool babe.

> Narrative voice ('he') of main character introduced. Foreshadowing – wish to have tattoo.

This was it. He thundered down the stairs.

'Just goin' out, Gramps,' he roared.

'Aye lad, mind yerself.'

Dressed now in a faded denim jacket adorned with icons of his favourite rock gods, sleeveless black vest, bullet casing belt, black jeans and Docs, Robbie strode through the damp streets of Monaghan with the libido of a Nordic god, Slipknot pulsing through his earphones. He was going to get this tattoo. He was going to show Carly this wasn't just a phase. Heavy metal was in his blood, in his DNA. He wasn't changing. His eye lit on the 'Afters' Club. Great nights there, an image of the all-male line in front of the altar of heavy metal popped up, heads swaying to the deep beat, long hair pulsing in waves ...

> Good use of flashback.

'And the rain will kill us all,

Throw ourselves against the wall

But no one else can see,

The preservation of the martyr in me ...'

'Marking your body for life is a big decision,' Carly had said. 'What if somebody at an interview asks you what it means?'

Robbie bit his lip. He was standing outside Crazy Joe's tattoo parlour. Robbie sighed. He peered in. The heavy smell of incense seemed to seep through the dingy window. He spotted a vague shadow crossing behind the blind. He hit the door three deafening thuds. A bolt slid back. The door opened a crack.

'Yeh?'

'Are you open?' Robbie asked.

'Can ye no read?'

> Conflict – obstacle presented. Realistic dialogue and atmosphere.

'I wanted a tattoo, I have a hundred euros,' Robbie stammered.

The door opened an inch wider.

'Show me!'

Robbie pulled out the rolled-up wad from his jacket pocket.

'C'min.'

Robbie followed the bald, heavyset man into the gloom. The black walls were covered with photographs of previous clients, exhibiting legs, arms, backs heavily inked with every type of tattoo imaginable. The heavy smell of weed hung in the air. A bright spotlight was snapped on.

'D'ya wanna see the portfolio?'

'No I know what I want – the Slipknot logo.'

'A metaller!'

'Yeah, on my left arm here.'

'Remember, if ya want it removed, I have to get the saw!'

'I won't want it removed.'

'Right, let me get ya shaved.'

*** *** ***

The constant piercing of the needle made Robbie wince.

'Take a deep breath. I've had a lotta girls cry and hyperventilate even before the needle went in. Panicking will only ruin the experience, it should be a good memory ... Maybe.'

Robbie didn't feel good. A cold sweat broke out on his forehead. He started to feel nauseous. He tried to concentrate on the photos on the walls, the grinning faces began to swirl. A deep blackness descended.

A sharp slap woke him.

'Real lightweight, aren't we?' grinned Crazy Joe. '100 euros.'

Snatching the wad, he shoved a jar of Bepanthen at him.

'On the house. Apply twice a day for four weeks. Wrap yer arm in cling film before ya shower, dude.'

Robbie gazed at the undulating loops in the design of the slip knot on his forearm and muttered his thanks. Pulling on his jacket, he stumbled unsteadily into the gloomy Monaghan evening.

He began to cross the road, but stopped abruptly. Across the street were Carly and her mom.

'Ah no!' he groaned.

He scrunched himself smaller into his jacket, veering off to the left.

'Robbie, Robbie!'

Caught. Nothing for it but to face the music.

'Hi Carly, hello Mrs Armitage.'

'Good evening Robbie,' Mrs Armitage sniffed. 'Carly, I'm going into Snaubs. Don't be long. She disappeared into the clothes shop.

'Did you get it done? Can I see it?'

Robbie shook his head. Two enormous grey eyes looked into his.

'You did. I saw you coming out of Crazy Joe's.'

Carly's phone went off.

'Let me see it', Carly pleaded.

Robbie pulled his arm out of his jacket.

'What is it?' quizzed Carly.

'The Slipknot logo.'

'What does it mean?'

'The band, the band!'

'It's very big. I don't think I like it.'

'Carly, Carly dear, I was ringing you, I need your advice,' shrilled Mrs Armitage from the shop door.

'Coming, Mummy. Can you get it made smaller?'

'No, but I can have my arm sawed off!'

'There's no need to be so rude!'

'Carly, Carly …'

'Coming, Mummy!'

And it was as easy as that. The slipknot was loosed, undone by a pull. Carly disappeared into the clothes shop. Robbie pulled his arm back into his jacket, plugged in his earphones and slouched off into the misty evening. Corey Taylor's lyrics enveloped him.

> *'We could start over*
> *Just look me in the eyes and say I'm wrong*
> *Now there's only emptiness*
> *Venomous, insipid*
> *I think we're done.'*

(1,000 words)

> Another obstacle – increase of tension.

> Tension at its height. Character reaches decision.

> Credible ending. Character true to himself despite obstacles.

EXAMINER'S COMMENT

- Lively narrative response sustained throughout.
- Effective characterisation and plot development.
- Engaging use of place-names and settings.
- Detailed music and tattoo references create atmosphere.
- Excellent use of dialogue adds realism.
- Some over-writing ('Robbie didn't feel good ... nauseous').
- Well-organised paragraphs; controlled syntax, grammar and punctuation.

GRADE H1

P = 30/30

C = 28/30

L = 26/30

M = 10/10

Total = 94/100

Sample story 2

Question

Write a short story in which a character faces a moment of uncertainty.

Sample answer

1   Dave was such a good athlete. Top notch as they say in the beautiful game. We knew absolutely nothing about him before he came up. He was playing junior football, but we were League players. We never bothered looking at junior football. To us, it was not so good, just a different scene completly, a different scene altogether. But let me tell you, I don't think I've ever met a young lad who was more in love with the beautiful game as it was often called by true fans.

> Some attempt at establishing a character in a dramatic situation.

2   Our manager who was called Roy decided to try him as a strikker but he just couldn't hack it. Roy scored a couple of goals early on and I remember him saying, this is just great. I'm playing with a really good team. The rest of us were delighted. On the field during big matches against our rivals, we made sure that he was getting a good service. There'll be plenty more goals where they came from. That's what we all beleived.

3   Roy moved quickly, signing him up a semi-pro. Dave was on course, chasing the beautiful dream. The hairstyle changed. Some of the lads used to joke about him. The smart lads said he adopted the looked so well groomed that he was like one of them Afghan hounds. But only joking. Most of us lads really admired Dave. Some of the senior lads were sort of shocked by his confidence, others made faces. They seen it all before, the looking down at the rest of us and the fancy haircut. I still liked Dave because he was just a young kid who just wanted to play the beautiful game of football. But the goals dried up and Dave's confidence really began to be shattered. When you join up with us in the top Ireland team, you can really be overcome.

4   That's what happened to Dave. There was just really too much quality players around the young lad. The pace of the football, the skill of the lads the shear quality of the players really took him by surprise. He was hardly getting a touch in games now Roy switched him to midfield. It made no difference. In the defence he was just really struggling. what happened was he was out of his depth. He called me late one night a cry for help.

> Evidence of narrative shaping.

5   Jamie, he said. I don't belong anymore in the squad I really hate every minute of it. I have no touch, no timing in the box. I'm going to be out of the team Jamie. I had to save my best freind. so I made reassuring noises. what more can a best freind do! But we had all heard the grumbles from the back on the left side of the ground where Dave's real hard core fan base were.

6   Then it all came to a head one Sunday afternoon. Roy was feeling the heat of the sneery comments from the papers – another bad manager. Let me tell you fans do not like a loser. He called Dave over for a chat about an hour before kick-off. Look, Dave, the directors aren't happy with you. You've failed up front and in midfield. Your going back to centre-half possition and if that doesn't work, the next move you'll make is off the team.

7   At half-time we were 2–nil down, the Cup Dream was just that a dream. Suddenly the dressing room door burst open. Roy entered in a fierce mood and with a look in his eye. Is this what you want? Second best. Who remembers number two? But it wasn't over yet. Roy went for Dave, your supposed to be the streetwise kid? Yeah, plastered on the headlines in every street! Your hung over again. You really disgust me. Dave felt really sick because this was his moment of uncertainty.

> Build-up to story's high point.

8   During the second half, things changed. Dave hit the spot with his first touch and sent over a really wicked cross. 2–1 was now the score the fan base roared. Then Davie got the ball again, a quick chip and we were 2 all. Dave was really back to his old form. In the last minute of the match he past to me and I tucked the ball into the corner. Goal! Dave and me had won the big match.

(720 words)

Setting

- The setting is where and when the story takes place.
- A writer builds 'a new reality' into which the reader enters. Everything has to make sense, not in the real world, but in this 'new world' that the writer has created.
- The story changes if it is moved to a different place and time.
- Setting also shows the passage of time through descriptions of the weather, lighting, season and the day.
- Setting often shapes the opening atmosphere of the story.

Sample story 3

Question

Write a short crime story that centres on three characters and a car journey.

Sample answer

1 The car sneaked along the deserted streets, a gleaming dark predator in this black rain-soaked winter evening. Most people were safely settled at their glowing firesides, but not the three grim faced men in the car. They had business to attend to.

2 On to the road before Broad Street, the car made a quick turn to the right into the warm pools of yellow light, flooding from pubs and chippies. Groups of young people were pouring onto the street. Young men, greased back hair and drain pipe trousers the dominant uniform, strutted the pavements, whistling at the giggling young women with towering beehives and too much makeup. All were heading for the mecca of dreams, 'The Blue Moon Ballroom'. But there were no dreams for the steel-faced occupants of the car. It turned left into the empty market, stall covers flapping forlornly, sodden litter shifting in the wind.

'Pull in here,' came the abrupt command.

'Want us to come wi' ye?' the driver asked.

'Just keep the motor running,' ordered the front seat passenger as he slid swiftly onto the pavement.

3   Adjusting his collar, he looked quickly left and right. He felt the comforting small hard weight in his right hand pocket. It was a routine he carried out as regularly as people check their wallets and car keys. Satisfied, he strode confidently through the doors of 'The Cobblestones Pub'.

'He's a careful one,' said the rear seat passenger.

'He is that,' agreed the driver, pulling out a ten pack of Silk Cut and offering one to his colleague.

'He's no' expectin' trouble, is he?' asked the passenger, taking a deep pull.

'Nah, it's just his way. The man doesn't miss a beat!'

4   The two men nodded in agreement. The driver blew a large hazy smoke ring. The passenger stared blankly through the rain speckled car windows. They both grinned at the sight of an old man, booze wobbly legs slowly advancing from the pub – one step forward, two to the side. The car door clicked open abruptly. The two men snapped to attention.

'Any luck?' asked the driver.

'No show,' replied the front seat passenger as he settled himself into the car.

'The stupid get.'

'His place?'

'Yep, Duke Street.'

The car rumbled down the street, carefully avoiding the potholes.

'Pull up a couple of houses away.'

'Don't want them seeing us comin'?' commented the driver.

'Shut up and keep yer mind on business.'

The banter was at an end.

5   The stale stench of beer hung heavily in the air as the front seat man pushed the half open front door. His two associates hung back in the shadows.

'He's not in, lovie,' a thin woman's voice announced. 'Please don't break anything.'

Last night's powder and a faint red lipstick smear clung grimly to her prematurely old face. A lopsided grin slid quickly from her cheek as he pushed her roughly to one side. He entered the ground floor flat, followed silently and swiftly by the others.

6   An hour later they emerged, the sound of strident guitar screaming behind them from the wireless in the flat.

'He's got hopeless taste in music, eh?' said the driver, desperate to talk – anything to break the tension.

'Don't know,' said the back seat man. 'But he'll be not be dancin' in there tonight.'

The passenger laughed coldly. It had been a good night's work.

7   It hadn't been a huge debt – just two hundred borrowed and fifty paid off. A fair bit of dough, but not the biggest he'd lent, not by a long shot. He'd had his doubts from the beginning though. Never can trust these junkies – good lesson for the rest of his debtors. Doesn't harm to let them know who is in the driving seat, he thought. The car picked up speed. Behind in Duke Street, a woman cried tears of fear and hurt. Her man was lying at her feet writhing in agony.

8   The car headed north to Mill Street and pulled in. The front seat man opened the door.

'Ye don't think ye were a bit hard on him?' asked the driver.

'Nothing was broken!'

'Just his kneecaps …'

'Never trust a person who's let you down. No warning, just give the lesson. People create their own storms, then get mad when it rains.'

Quickly looking left and right, he melted into the night.

(740 words)

EXAMINER'S COMMENT

- Successful and well-crafted hard-boiled, violent 'tartan noir' story.
- Effective use of sharp dialogue builds world-weary character and advances the plot.
- Suggestion adds to the narrative tension and conflict.
- Details provide authenticity throughout.
- Impressive use of vivid verbs (e.g. 'sneaked', 'clicked', 'rumbled', 'hung back', 'melted').
- Organised structure, good build-up and engaging conclusion.

GRADE H1

P = 30/30
C = 28/30
L = 28/30
M = 10/10
Total = 96/100

The short story genre

Different genres set up different expectations in the reader. In paranormal books, world building is the key. In romantic stories, plot twists intrigue readers. Some stories contain elements from several genres.

Fantasy/fairy story

Contains elements that are not realistic, e.g. talking animals, magical powers, mythical beings, etc. happy ever after ending.

Mystery

Strangeness, solving a puzzle or crime; centred around a person who investigates wrong-doing.

Crime fiction

Elements of this genre can include the seemingly perfect crime, the wrongly accused suspect, bungling police, sharp-witted detectives, unexpected conclusion, reader accompanies detective's pursuit of clues.

Science fiction

Plot involves science and technology of the future; new worlds such as space, a different universe or dimension, set in the future.

Realistic fiction

Stories take place in modern times with ordinary characters; believable plots, these events could really happen to anybody.

Writers today often bend genres, changing what the reader expected to happen, e.g. a fairy story could have an unhappy ending.

Sample story 4

Question

Write a short story in which a closely guarded secret is gradually revealed.

Sample answer

1   'Did you see that?' Robyn dumped a fresh pot of coffee in the sink.

'Yeah,' I confirmed, pointing to the steam.

'Lady on table 51 thinks the coffee's too cold,' Robyn grimaced, stomping her foot.

Feeling her frustration, I offered my advice.

'Maybe you should spill it on her so she'll know how hot it is.'

2   We giggled, secretly wishing it was an option. I watched Robyn take the rest of the lady's order as I coiled myself in the corner of table 11, across from 4, my styrofoam cup of coffee blowing fragrant steam at my face.

> Setting and characters established.

3   'Oops!' cried Robyn as the hot brown liquid trickled onto the lady's arm. Robyn glanced over and winked. I couldn't believe she'd done it. I never would have had the nerve. Robyn dabbed energetically with her napkin as the lady curled her thin lips.

4   I liked Robyn. Her bouncy blonde hair blossomed like a daffodil from her scrunchie. She was round and fluffy. We would never be friends. We had nothing in common. We only held onto one another to stay afloat. But right now in the smoking section we were sisters.

5   'Whooh,' she pushed a whirlpool of air from her mouth. Her pale hand covered her lips as if to lock in extra giggles.

'I can't wait to make my next appointment.' She stared off into space.

'What appointment?' I snapped her out of her daydream.

'My tanning appointment,' she explained, rubbing her fingers over my hand, admiring my brown complexion.

'Isn't that bad for your skin?' I felt sorry for her. One day she'd be a prune.

'Yeah,' she admitted. 'But it feels so good. It's like you're in a tub of sun, heat soaking into every inch of your body. I love it. I go every week.'

She didn't have to explain herself anymore. I understood. Sometimes people do extreme things to feel warm.

Effective characterisation.

6   Table 4 had now been cleared and a middle-aged black lady sat waiting for her order to be taken. Robyn leaped from her seat to take the lady's order. She stood, weight on her right hip, flipping page after page scribbling furiously. When the meal was delivered it covered the entire table. Before sticking her fork into the meat, she barked,

7   'It ain't done.'

'I beg your pardon,' Robyn raised her arched eyebrows.

'I said it's got blood on it.' She shoved the plate at Robyn.

'Okay.' She smiled. 'I'll have him cook some more.'

Robyn returned with the burnt T-Bone. The lady took a deep breath.

'These eggs don't got enough cheese in 'em.'

She kept her head straight and stuck the plate in Robyn's face. Robyn's eyes met mine.

We both grinned. Robyn satisfied the annoying customer and returned to table 11.

8   'Okay,' she whined. 'Your smoking break is over. I'm sick of table 51. Next time you take it.'

'Okay.' I knew her feet were tired. My butt was numb from sitting so long.

The lady left a dollar tip. An old white man filled her place. Once seated, he opened his newspaper and started to read. I tapped my pad on the back of his seat waiting for him to finish his article and place his order. Eventually he gazed up at me. His bottom lip dropped.

9   'Coffee,' spilled from his mouth. He looked at me crossly as I left to fetch his pot of coffee. When I returned he was gone.

'What happened?' I wondered placing the coffee pot on the table.

Robyn didn't look at me. 'He forgot he had to go somewhere.'

'What really happened, Robyn?' I lowered my eyes to hers.

10   Sadly looking into my face, Robyn revealed the closely guarded secret.

'He asked me to be his waitress ... 'She swallowed hard. 'He said he didn't want a black person handling his food.'

Her words came like a flood. It drenched me in an icy cold sweat.

> Narrative climax is well managed.

'So I told him to leave.'

11   She could have got fired.

My eyes surveyed the restaurant. Everyone was a million shades lighter than me. I began to shiver.

'I really should have smacked him.'

This time I didn't giggle. My lips quivered. She would never feel this cold.

'Don't.'

12   Her arm touched my shoulder spreading a little warmth. A tear stood in her eye. She knew that this would not be the last for me. She could see a secret world she had barely known existed. We sat floating in the warmth of table 11, in the smoking section in the tranquil glow of each other's warmth.

> Ending is convincing and unsentimental.

(760 words)

EXAMINER'S COMMENT

- Authentic setting and characters engage readers.
- Plot and characterisation development through lively dialogue.
- Subtle introduction of conflict.
- Details provide an authentic atmosphere.
- Some effective suggestion.
- Organised structure, controlled syntax and punctuation.

GRADE H1

P = 30/30

C = 28/30

L = 28/30

M = 10/10

Total = 96/100

Short story endings

The conclusion or resolution is the answer to the central conflict. A closed ending means nothing more can happen, e.g. the clichéd conclusion, 'They lived happily ever after'. An open ending leaves questions about what will happen next. In the final section of your writing, you must begin to tie up the loose ends. The ending lends meaning to the story. It shows something about human nature or the human condition.

You have three main choices for your ending:

- Cliff hanger
- Twist in the tale
- Resolution.

Cliff hanger

This leaves the story without a definite conclusion or resolution. But the reader needs to be left with some clues as to what will happen next. Don't leave the ending unfinished as if you ran out of time. Plan that your story will end unresolved. You should have some idea of what will happen next, even though you are only giving clues to your reader to guess the ending.

Twist in the tale

A completely unexpected turn of events. Again you should have decided that you are going to end this way when you are planning your story. You can then drop a hint earlier in the plot to which you can refer back later.

Resolution

All the loose ends are tied up and the ending is complete and definite. Often this would be a happy ending. But, of course, it doesn't have to be happy ...

English (Higher Level) Paper 2 Overview

Paper 2 accounts for 200 marks (half the overall examination total).
You are required to answer:

- one question on **The Single Text** (60 marks – 60 minutes)
- one question on **The Comparative Study** (70 marks – 70 minutes)
- one question on **The Unseen Poem** (20 marks – 20 minutes)
- one question on **Prescribed Poetry** (50 marks – 50 minutes)

> The time limit for Paper 2 is
> **3 hours and 20 minutes**.

exam focus

- Always aim to find your own voice when discussing texts.
- Exam questions are there to be challenged.
- Exemplars of paragraphs and essays illustrate different standards of answering.
- Sample essays should not be learned off or recycled in the exam.

aims
- Revision of keys aspects of selected Single Texts.
- Developing successful responses to Single Text examination questions.

key point

For Leaving Cert English Higher Level, a play by Shakespeare must be one of the texts chosen. This can be studied on its own for the 60-mark Single Text section **OR** as one of the three texts for the 70-mark Comparative Study section.

King Lear by William Shakespeare

Prescribed Single Text for 2021

Prescribed Comparative Study Text for 2021

Storyline

King Lear, the legendary ruler of ancient Britain, **decides to divide his kingdom** between his three daughters and asks each of them to declare their love for him.

Goneril and Regan flatter their father, but his youngest daughter, Cordelia, refuses to do so. Lear disowns Cordelia and she is banished to France. The elderly king soon quarrels with Goneril and Regan. Feeling mistreated and humiliated, he rushes out into a raging storm on the windswept heath where he is **driven mad by grief** and indignation.

When Cordelia learns of her father's condition, she returns to Britain with an army to fight her sisters' forces. However, her soldiers are defeated, and she is imprisoned and hanged. **Heartbroken over Cordelia's death**, Lear himself dies soon afterwards.

Using a key scene to answer exam questions

With just 60 minutes to answer the Leaving Cert Single Text section, it's essential to **make use of relevant key scenes** or significant moments to support your discussion points.

Five key scenes

Act 1 Scene 1: King Lear's palace

Lear's public 'love test'. Acting on impulse, he disinherits Cordelia and hands over power to Goneril and Regan. These decisions will determine the play's tragic outcome.

Act 2 Scene 4: Gloucester's palace

Lear's anguish reaches its height when Regan and Goneril disrespect him. He begins to lose his mind. Lear meets the Earl of Gloucester, an old friend, who is concerned for the king's wellbeing.

Act 3 Scene 2: The heath during a storm

Lear wanders the countryside during a violent storm, accompanied by the Fool and his loyal servant, Kent. In his madness, the king rages against the weather and his daughters' ingratitude.

Act 4 Scene 7: A tent in the French camp near Dover

The exhausted king wakes from sleep and recovers his senses. He is reunited with Cordelia who has returned with an army from France. Father and daughter ask each other for forgiveness.

Act 5 Scene 3: The British camp near Dover

Cordelia is imprisoned and executed. Lear is unable to accept that she is dead and he himself soon dies of overwhelming grief. Gloucester's son, Edgar, is left to restore order and rule Britain.

Preparing for the Single Text *King Lear* question

It is essential to have a **close knowledge of *King Lear*** (particularly the storyline, characters, themes and the main features of Shakespeare's dramatic style). Your written work should show evidence of **effective analysis** of the play. **Support relevant discussion points** with suitable reference to key moments.

key point

There is no single 'correct way' to interpret *King Lear*. Answers should be based on close reading and supporting evidence.

exam focus

- Identify the main elements of the question, so that your answer is on target.
- Avoid general narrative or summary.
- Use accurate quotations when appropriate.
- Always express yourself clearly.

Key characters

King Lear

One of Shakespeare's most complex characters, Lear initially appears to be a cruel monarch who decides to hand over the responsibilities of being king after a long reign of undisputed power. A victim of his own excessive pride, he banishes his youngest daughter, Cordelia, and is then rejected by her two sisters, Goneril and Regan. He pays dearly for his misjudgement and ends up wandering the stormy heath in a deranged state. Through his suffering, Lear gains self-knowledge and is eventually reunited with Cordelia. His mind is restored and he is happy to spend time with his youngest daughter whom he now realises he has wronged.

Lear's qualities

- Lear inspires loyalty (from Kent, Cordelia, the Fool).
- Strong-willed, resilient and sympathetic.
- Recognises his mistakes, asks forgiveness.
- Becomes more human and tolerant.
- Through his suffering, he gains wisdom.

Lear's faults

- Rash, egocentric, irrational.
- Unstable, naïve, foolish.
- Vain (wants glory without responsibility).

Cordelia

The king's youngest daughter is often described as being too honest for her own good. Cordelia is principled and refuses to flatter her father. She does not trust her sisters, as it turns out, for good reason. Cordelia remains loyal to Lear despite being banished by him. Throughout the play, she is contrasted with Goneril and Regan, who manipulate their father for their own ends. Becoming Queen of France, Cordelia hears about how Lear is being mistreated and returns to England with an army to help him. The Cordelia we see at the end is gentler and more understanding than the obstinate daughter of the opening scene.

Cordelia's qualities

- Honest, selfless, honourable and insightful.
- Compassionate, forgiving and loving.

Cordelia's faults

- Headstrong and stubborn.

Gloucester

Like the old king, Gloucester is a poor judge of character and does not really know his own sons. He pays for his foolish judgement with the violent loss of his sight. He is also metaphorically blind to the truth of Edmund's wickedness and Edgar's love. His tragic fate is in many ways similar to Lear's, although he accepts what happens to him. Initially weak, Gloucester is a tormented character who eventually achieves self-knowledge and greater humanity through his suffering. His death also parallels Lear's. When he is finally reconciled with Edgar, Gloucester can die happily: 'his flawed heart ... Burst smilingly'.

Gloucester's qualities

- Loyal, brave, compassionate towards Lear.
- Recognises his mistakes and asks forgiveness.
- His moral integrity grows.

Gloucester's faults

- Initially weak and self-interested.
- Morally blind and pessimistic.

Edmund

Gloucester's illegitimate son is the 'villain' of this play. Completely amoral, Edmund lies, charms and betrays his father and brother for his own gain. He seizes every opportunity to gain his father's wealth and power. Yet he feels insecure and wants others to respect him. Edmund rejects society's hypocritical attitudes, but resorts to heartless behaviour. He is fully aware of his own unscrupulous nature and often delights in his treachery. When Goneril and Regan's dead bodies are brought in at the end, Edmund realises that even he was loved. He then tries to save Cordelia's life, but his good deed comes too late.

Edmund's qualities

- Gloucester's illegitimate son is charismatic and ingenious.
- He tries to do 'some good' before he dies.
- He accepts his fate bravely in the end.

Edmund's faults

- Hypocritical, villainous and opportunistic.
- Callous, scheming and egocentric.

Key themes

Themes refer to issues or ideas that are central to the drama. Shakespeare explores fascinating subjects in *King Lear*, including justice, madness, love, revenge and deception. All of these themes – and many others – are closely interlinked.

key point

When writing about central characters, consider their development. What is your initial impression? How do they change over the course of the story? What is your final view of each character?

Love

Love is a central theme in Shakespeare's great tragedy. The crucial question that drives the entire story is 'Which of you shall we say doth love us most?' Lear's short-sighted exercise in egotism leads to the tearing apart of his family by the conclusion of Act 1. The play explores child/parent love, the dutiful love of Kent for Lear, romantic love between men and women, and the universal love of humanity that Lear eventually experiences.

Family love

In the 'love test', the seeds of tragedy are sown. The 'glib and oily' protestations of affection from Goneril and Regan hide their true purpose – a desire for power. Goneril hypocritically declares: 'Sir, I love you more than word can wield the matter.' Lear allows himself to be deceived by her sycophancy. The king rewards both his older daughters handsomely.

In contrast, Cordelia can only 'love and be silent' on the subject of how she feels about her father. Her **restrained love** reflects the natural filial link between child and parent. Lear is devastated at what he regards as her 'untender' admission and seems incapable of differentiating between hypocrisy and sincerity. The old patriarchal king is so out of touch with his children that he allows his pride to shatter family relationships.

Over the course of the play, however, **Cordelia represents true love**. When she eventually learns of her sisters' harsh treatment of their father (Lear is turned out of doors and into a raging storm), she is outraged. Her capacity for forgiveness is total. She refuses to apportion blame – unlike the king who quantified love by the amount of land or number of knights he would retain. During the tender reunion between Lear and his youngest child, the French camp at Dover becomes a haven where father and daughter can express their real feelings.

Shakespeare emphasises the point that love cannot be measured by words alone. Like the reckless king, Gloucester is also deceived by a disingenuous child. He allows Edmund to fool him into banishing his loyal son, Edgar. The hasty decision to place his trust in Edmund has devastating results. However, **genuine emotion is seen in Edgar's unconditional care for his father**. This is particularly evident when Edgar (in disguise as Poor Tom) saves the blind Gloucester from committing suicide. We learn that when father and son are finally reunited (off-stage), Gloucester's damaged heart 'Burst smilingly'. Once again, the playwright highlights the value of expressing true feeling.

key point

When writing about themes, consider the playwright's viewpoint. How does Shakespeare introduce the theme? How does he treat and develop it over the course of the story? What is his attitude to love, deception, justice, power, etc.?

Shakespeare's dramatic style

Imagery

Shakespeare's use of imagery is a key aspect of his dramatic style in *King Lear*. The main function of imagery (pictures created by the playwright's use of words) is to aid characterisation. Patterns of imagery also help to create distinctive atmospheres and heighten evocative moods. Lear himself is defined through images and symbols, often associated with animals, clothing, sight and nature.

Animal imagery

Initially, Lear sees himself as an enraged dragon. Powerful animal images play an important part in the story – especially in depicting the characters **Goneril and Regan, who are often likened to savage creatures**. During angry exchanges with his eldest daughter, Lear compares Goneril to a 'sea-monster' with a 'wolfish visage'. He tells Regan of her sister's 'Sharp-toothed unkindness, like a vulture'. Such references emphasise the old king's sense of his 'pelican daughters' and their unnatural behaviour.

Other characters describe Goneril and Regan in animalistic terms. Appalled by their cruelty, Gloucester refers to their 'boarish fangs' while Albany eventually recognises that they are 'Tigers, not daughters'. Recurring bestial imagery suggests their **vicious, predatory nature.** Audiences tend to understand the appropriateness of linking the animal instincts of Lear's older daughters to their eventual downfall.

Shakespeare sometimes uses animal images in a more positive way. The tenderness of the reunion with Cordelia shows their close natural bond: 'We two alone will sing like birds i' the cage'. For the most part, however, animal imagery paints an intense picture of the disintegrating social order in a world where unimaginable cruelty is inflicted on parents by their children. Numerous images of beasts of prey savaging their victims create **a disturbing context** of torture and suffering. As always, Shakespeare's compelling language presents audiences with countless moments of breathless dramatisation.

Sight imagery

Although Lear can physically see, **he is blind to reality** in the sense that he lacks insight and understanding. Ironically, it is only when Gloucester has lost his eyes that he is able to 'see' the truth. When the king is first infuriated by Cordelia, he orders her to 'avoid my sight!' Kent's attempts to intervene are also dismissed – 'Out of my sight!' – to which he responds: 'See better, Lear.'

As his anger increases, the king becomes increasingly reckless. Unlike Cordelia and Kent, he is unable to see through the 'glib and oily' hypocrisy of his older daughters. His **judgement diminishes** and he loses all sense of the consequences of his actions.

Gloucester's loss of physical sight also symbolises his **metaphorical blindness**. Like Lear, he completely fails to recognise the truth about his family, and it is only through the most horrific agony that he becomes painfully aware of his past mistakes: 'I have no way, and therefore want no eyes; I stumbled when I saw.' When the two men meet after the storm, it is obvious that they have both learned valuable lessons about the world. Lear's observation that a 'man may see how this world goes with no eyes' is a timely reminder that appearances do not always reflect reality.

King Lear: Revision of a key scene, Act 1 Scene 1

Summary

Lear has chosen to step down from his role as king and hands over power to his daughters. He persists in a public 'love test' as a way of rewarding the daughter who says she loves him best. Goneril and Regan tell their father exactly what he wants to hear, but Cordelia refuses to flatter him. The king is enraged by this and disowns Cordelia. He divides her share of the kingdom between her sisters.

As she leaves for France, Cordelia warns her sisters that their hypocrisy will eventually be revealed, 'Time shall unfold what plighted cunning hides'. Once Goneril and Regan are alone, they talk about how Lear is becoming more difficult with age and how they will need to act to address the situation.

Using Act 1 Scene 1 to answer questions

Act 1 Scene 1 can be used successfully in response to a range of examination questions about the play's central themes, characters, relationships and the playwright's dramatic style.

This key scene has significant dramatic functions:

- **Establishes the main plot** concerning Lear's relationships with his three daughters.
- **Presents initial impressions of characters**. Lear is egotistical, rash and vindictive. Goneril and Regan are hypocritical and ambitious. Cordelia is honest, stubborn and sincere.
- **Introduces key themes**, such as family relations, judgement, deception and power.
- The opening scene marks **a turning point**. Lear cannot distinguish between pretence and reality, so he gives away his power both as a king and as a father.
- **Foreshadows disaster** and tragedy ahead. Act 1 Scene 1 reveals Lear's disastrous lack of judgement – something which will lead to tragic consequences.
- Power struggles increases the **dramatic tension** and engages the audience.

Successful essay writing

How do I approach the question?

> 'In the play *King Lear*, Shakespeare presents us with a powerful vision of human endurance in which the destructive forces of evil are overcome by the redemptive forces of love.'
> Discuss this view, developing your answer with reference to the text.

In this question, you need to:

- Focus on all aspects of the task (vision of human endurance, evil overcome by good).
- Identify and comment on key moments/ scenes that support discussion points.
- Adopt a viewpoint or stance by agreeing/ disagreeing wholly or in part with the question.

Marking scheme guidelines

Candidates are free to agree and/or disagree, but they should engage with **all aspects** of the statement, though not necessarily equally.

Possible approaches to answering this question

Approach 1: Viewpoint is in full agreement with the given statement.

Several central characters (particularly Lear and Gloucester) experience rejection. Dramatic scenes of severe mental and physical suffering throughout the play. Peace and reconciliation triumph at the end.

Approach 2: Viewpoint is in partial agreement with the given statement.

Horrific vision of cruelty and madness dominates the tragedy. Characters (good and evil) suffer. Forces of evil more powerful for most of the story. Lear's redemption is short-lived.

exam focus

- Identify the main elements of the question, so that your answer is on target.
- Make sure to avoid unfocused narrative. Use accurate quotations when appropriate.
- Always express yourself clearly.

The Single Text (Higher Level) question is allocated 60-minutes in the exam and worth **60 marks** in total. These are awarded by reference to the **PCLM** criteria for assessment (i.e. 3 x 18 marks for each of P, C and L plus 6 marks for M):

- **P = Purpose:** 18 (30%); Is the answer focused? Does it address the question?
- **C = Coherence:** 18 (30%); Are the ideas and discussion points well sustained?
- **L = Language use:** 18 (30%); Is the candidate's writing style effective?
- **M = Mechanics:** 6 (10%); Are there spelling or grammar errors?

Prompt!

- Opening scenes introduce an evil world of ruthless ambition, resentment and hypocrisy.
- Lear and Gloucester both endure horrific suffering – dramatic scenes in court/heath.
- Edmund's viciousness evident and in his triumphant soliloquies.
- Goneril and Regan's association with animal imagery intensifies evil vision.
- Tender moments/reconciliation provide some relief from the graphic violence.
- After all the human pain and perseverance, love wins out/is defeated in the end.

Question

'In the play *King Lear*, Shakespeare presents us with a powerful vision of human endurance in which the destructive forces of evil are overcome by the redemptive forces of love.'

Discuss this view, developing your answer with reference to the text.

Sample essay

1 In *King Lear*, Shakespeare creates a world where love, honour and loyalty ultimately overcome the powerful forces of evil. Goneril, Regan, Cornwall and Edmund are all eventually defeated by Edgar, Cordelia and a brave servant. There are many horrific scenes, but good wins over evil in the end.

> Succinct and clear engagement with the main elements of the question.

2 Shakespeare quickly establishes a mood of suspense and tension by showing the audience how evil operates. Goneril and Regan successfully flatter their arrogant father with false declarations of love. Cordelia is too honest for her own good and is punished because she 'cannot heave my heart into my mouth'. She is disowned and powerless to help her impetuous father: 'I would prefer him to a better place'. Cordelia's fears prove true. The playwright shows the hypocritical sisters immediately plot against Lear, 'we must do something and in the heat'. This tense opening scene protrays the start of a terrible tragedy.

3 The sisters' evil powers are dramatically presented through the use of animal imagery. Their brutality is matched by the savagery of the language. They humiliate their father, reducing his number of followers, 'What need one?' Gloucester is cruelly blinded on Regan's instruction, 'One side will mock another'. During angry rows with his eldest daughter, Lear compares Goneril to a 'sea-monster' with her 'wolfish visage'. The two sisters are

> Effective reference to animal imagery illustrates the immoral atmosphere.

described as 'pelican daughters' and 'tigers'. For the audience, it seems impossible that the mild-mannered Cordelia can ever overcome such a cruel atmosphere.

4   Similarly, Edmund's evil cunning adds to the nightmare vision in the play. Shakespeare uses soliloquies to show Edmund planning revenge against his naïve brother Edgar, 'Edmund the base shall top the legitimate'. Edmund shows Gloucester a letter supposedly from Edgar suggesting that they kill their father to release them from 'aged tyranny'. He totally deludes the gullible Gloucester, pretending to hide the letter, falsely defending Edgar, 'suspend your indignation against my brother'. The power of evil is very evident at this stage.

> The introduction of Edmund's evil scheming broadens the discussion.

5   The conflict between the good and evil characters takes up most of the play. At first, evil dominates. Cordelia, the faithful courtier Kent and Gloucester's heir Edgar are all banished. It seems impossible that they can ever defeat the vicious Goneril, Regan and Edmund. But at times, the forces of good fight back. A loyal servant attempts to stop Cornwall's savage attack on Gloucester, 'I have served you even since I was a child'. But the servant, although killed by Regan, succeeds in wounding Cornwall.

6   One of the most dramatic and disturbing scenes in the play takes place on the heath during a fierce thunderstorm. Lear suffers terribly on the wild heath and is almost driven beyond endurance. His rejection by Goneril and Regan along with his guilt about Cordelia, 'I did her wrong' torments him. His old heart breaks and he loses his mind. Lear has been driven mad and he takes shelter in a peasant's hovel.

7   The king is accompanied by the Fool who keeps reminding him of his stupidity in banishing Cordelia. Lear's mind is in a highly confused state and he is caught between various emotions, particularly anger and regret. But something positive comes out of this chaos when Lear meets Edgar in disguise as Poor Tom, the mad beggar. For the first time, Lear has genuine pity for the 'poor naked wretches'. The good side of the king's character overcomes the evil dictatorial side. He becomes a better man who recognises the injustice of poverty. It is an ironic moment where a vision of a just society occurs during a nightmarish scene.

> Perceptive point about how Lear endures madness and becomes compassionate.

8   Like Gloucester, the frail old king is overwhellmed by suffering. But both men are learnt important lessons in the merciless storm. Gloucester dies of a broken heart after being blinded and he is heartbroken by Edmund's treachery. He is also filled with the remorse of having misjudged his legitimate son Edgar.

> Slight paragraph, repetitive, but could be developed.

9   Cordelia, like Edgar, has to resort to desperate measures. She has had to arrive with an army from France like an invading force. But, in contrast to the evil characters, she is motivated by 'love, dear love'. In a tender scene

of reconciliation, the wronged daughter gently prays, 'let this kiss repair those violent harms that my two sisters have in thy reverence made'. Lear enquires to her, 'Be your tears wet?' Cordelia has at last found a way to express herself. There is a sense of justice as both loyal children, Cordelia and Edgar, are reunited with their elderly parents.

10 But the shadow of evil endures as the play concludes with the intense image of Lear appearing with his dead daughter cradled in his arms, demanding, 'Why should a dog, a horse, a rat, have life, and thou no breath at all?' The forces of evil, which throughout the play, have released such destruction that not only they, but also the innocent, must suffer before order can be restored. Shakespeare dramatically presents us with a world in which the powerful forces of evil are eventually overcome by the redemptive forces of love, but at a terrible price.

> Targeted conclusion makes an effective point to round off the essay successfully.

(835 words)

EXAMINER'S COMMENT

GRADE H2

P = 16/18

C = 15/18

L = 14/18

M = 5/6

Total = 50/60

- Focused essay generally addresses the key elements of the question.
- Some very good detailed analysis, e.g. in paragraphs 3 and 7.
- More developed discussion on 'endurance' needed at times.
- Uses a wide range of references and some apt quotations.
- Well-controlled functional expression overall.
- Mechanical errors ('impetous', 'protrays', 'overwhellmed', 'are learnt', 'enquires to').

exam focus

- Always aim to find your own voice when discussing the play.
- Exam questions are there to be challenged.
- There is no single 'correct' answer.
- Exemplars of paragraphs and essays illustrate different standards of answering.
- Sample essays should not be learned off or recycled in the exam.

Revision essay question

'*King Lear* is not only a tragedy about failed family relationships, it is equally a tragedy about the failure of kingship.'

To what extent do you agree or disagree with this view of the play? Support your answer with reference to the text.

Marking scheme guidelines

Candidates are free to agree and/or disagree but they must engage with **all elements** of the statement, though not necessarily equally.

Prompt!

- As a father and a king, Lear abuses power and makes catastrophic errors of judgement.
- The tragedy is due to his failure to understand the separate kingship/parental roles.
- His three daughters are/are not flawed characters who act with tragic consequences.
- Various power struggles lead to disastrous sibling rivalry.
- Through pain and madness, Lear becomes a better father and a wiser king.
- Lear and Cordelia's reunion counterbalances the tragedy in the end.
- Sense of tragedy is/is not eased when Gloucester and Edgar are also reconciled.

exam focus

Allow about 55 minutes and aim for focused and developed points organised in paragraphs.

The Handmaid's Tale by Margaret Atwood

Prescribed Single Text for 2021

Prescribed Comparative Study Text for 2021 and 2022

Overview

Genre

In dystopian fiction, society oppresses the aims and desires of the central character. The oppression is usually carried out by a totalitarian (authoritarian) government, resulting in great loss of freedom and dehumanisation.

Setting

The Handmaid's Tale is set in the Republic of Gilead somewhere within the former borders of America in the not too distant future. The country is run by a military dictatorship. Human rights are extremely limited and women are assigned specific 'uses' in this patriarchal society.

Handmaids are kept solely for the purpose of reproduction. Aunts are older women who oversee the training of the Handmaids while Marthas are women with domestic skills who work as servants. Wives are regarded as high-ranking in Gilead, but they are merely trophies and are forbidden from interacting with other men.

MARGARET ATWOOD
The Handmaid's Tale

Shortlisted for the Booker Prize

Storyline

The novel's narrator and central character is Offred, the Handmaid of the title. She is thirty-three years old and lives in the Republic of **Gilead, a male-dominated society** with a totalitarian government. The population is falling and therefore women who are capable of having children are used for that purpose.

As Offred tells her story, we gradually discover how she went from being an ordinary woman, with a job and a family, to being a Handmaid. In her own words, **a Gilead Handmaid is 'a womb on two legs'**.

Offred is not this woman's real name. She was renamed when she became a Handmaid, and her name is composed of the preposition 'of' and the name of the man to whom she 'belongs', a Commander named Fred. All Handmaids are similarly labelled – for example, Ofwarren, Ofwayne. **They are treated as belongings or objects.**

If Offred does not have a child soon, she will become an 'Unwoman', exiled to clean up toxic waste in one of the Colonies until she dies in two or three years. Unwomen, like Jews, African-Americans and Catholics are **considered undesirable** by the Gilead regime.

Much of Offred's time is spent alone in her bare room remembering her previous life and **desperately seeking some means of escape**. Eventually, she establishes a bond with another Handmaid, Ofglen, who introduces her to 'Mayday', an underground resistance group. Offred also becomes involved with her master's chauffeur, Nick, and has a secret affair with him.

Nick arranges Offred's escape, which supposedly can help her find freedom in Canada. In the final chapter, two men come for her and take her from her master's house. However, **neither Offred nor the reader is certain about whether or not she is actually being rescued**. She may possibly be under arrest as an enemy of the state, and doomed to death.

The novel ends with 'Historical Notes' from a future academic conference about Gilead held in the year 2195. Professor Pieixoto describes the discovery of old cassette tapes that might provide more information about Offred's life. There is a **suggestion that the people who helped her escape were part of the Resistance**.

Characters

Offred

The novel's protagonist is an intelligent, reflective, sometimes submissive woman who is not given to impulsive behaviour. Throughout the story, Offred struggles to survive and hold on to a sense of self. She reveals her deep unhappiness and tragic loss through a series of flashbacks and dreams.

Offred does not accept the propaganda of the new regime and stubbornly retains her right to think for herself despite being forced to endure a restricted and tormented life. She sometimes blames herself because she does not have the same courage as her close friend, Moira. Too often, she thinks, she just goes along with what is expected of her because she is simply trying to survive.

Occasionally, Offred is rebellious, even violent, in her thoughts. She does not want to end up hanging at the public Wall where the corpses of those who have been executed are left on display. However, Offred does become reckless when she gets involved with Nick.

Readers may be quick to condemn Offred for her passivity, yet her sharp observations and honest emotions, even after the terror and brainwashing she has encountered, demonstrate the limitations of Gilead's power over its subjects.

The Commander

Commander Fred (also known as 'the Commander') is the head of the household where Offred is enslaved as a Handmaid. He is the husband of Serena Joy. He often seems a reasonable, well-meaning man, and Offred sometimes finds that she likes him in spite of herself.

The Commander is powerful and wealthy. He epitomises the oppressive system that has consigned Offred to a life of sexual slavery. He seems to have some regret that Gilead's rules cause Offred and other women such suffering, but he believes in the necessity of these rules to create a better future.

Though he is a high-ranking official of Gilead who may have played a large role in its construction, Fred breaks many laws, including going to the sex club Jezebel's and spending private time with Offred. At times, his need for companionship make him seem as much a prisoner of Gilead's restrictions as anyone else.

The Commander's character is ambiguous; he seems decent at times, but he participates willingly in Gilead's oppressive patriarchal system. He believes that the regime can make things better, but, as he also tells Offred, 'better never means better for everyone'.

Serena Joy

Also known as the Commander's Wife, Serena Joy is unable to have children and has to tolerate Offred. Before Gilead, she was a singer who became famous on TV for her over-emotional Christian music. She also promoted an anti-feminist view about the sanctity of the family home and the housewife's important role. During the novel, she occupies her time gardening with Nick's help, and knitting decorative scarves for soldiers, despite her arthritis.

In Gilead Serena Joy is no longer famous and she is forced into the subdued role of housewife. She resents Offred because the Handmaid's presence highlights her failure to produce children. She is also jealous of the sexual relationship Offred has with the Commander. For much of the novel, Serena Joy resentfully ignores Offred, but towards the end she becomes more manipulative and encourages her to try to get pregnant by having sex with Nick.

Moira

Offred's best friend from her college days is a courageous woman and a staunch feminist. Moira's defiant nature contrasts starkly with the behaviour of many other characters. Rather than passively accept her fate as a Handmaid, she makes several escape attempts and finally manages to get away from the Red Centre. However, she is caught before she can get out of Gilead.

Later on, when Offred sees Moira working as a sex worker in a club for the Commanders, it seems that the authorities have managed to break her friend's spirit. After symbolising resistance for most of the story, Moira illustrates the way a totalitarian state can crush even the most independent person.

Key themes

Power

The novel is primarily an exploration of power politics. The Republic of Gilead is a dictatorship and a strictly hierarchical society, with a huge difference between the genders. Women no longer have jobs or money, leaving them desperate and dependent. Women do not have access to education. They also lack the rights to their own body as they are forced to be surrogate mothers.

The government maintains power through military control and intimidation. In Gilead, religion is also used as a basis of power and routinely abused through public hangings, murder and imprisonment. Women are used to disempower other women. The Aunts indoctrinate the Handmaids through fear. In this patriarchal society, the Commanders hold immense power over all the citizens, while the Commanders' Wives hold limited power within the household. Generally, the Handmaids have very little power because they are of a lower social class.

Despite the widespread oppression, however, some characters find ways to maintain control over themselves and others. Offred manipulates her sexuality in the subtlest ways, aware of how much influence she has simply because she is a good-looking woman. Through her relationship with the Commander, Offred gains some power, but she is afraid to test its limits.

Feminism

Atwood is very well known for her feminist views and *The Handmaid's Tale* raises many questions about the role, status and treatment of women in the modern world. Gilead is depicted as a harsh patriarchal regime where women are subservient to men in every way. While the dystopian setting illustrates the oppression of women, the author also allows readers to see how some women passively oppress themselves.

Unlike Moira who is naturally rebellious, Offred is desperate to conceive the Commander's child in order to survive. Both characters offer parallels to many women in today's world. On one hand, there are feminists who rebel against society no matter what it costs. Some of the women resist oppression as much as they possibly can while others uphold the patriarchal system.

In any discussion about the themes in a text, there is always some overlap; power and identity are obvious examples in *The Handmaid's Tale*.

The characters in the novel represent conflicting ideas about sexuality. Offred and Moira represent very different kinds of feminism. But, like most of the women, they simply make the best of second-class citizenship. However, it could be argued that the open-ended conclusion of *The Handmaid's Tale* illustrates the lack of female solidarity as contributing to the failed feminist revolution.

Preparing for *The Handmaid's Tale* Single Text question

- It is essential to have a **close knowledge** of the novel.
- **Check the plot summary** to revise how the story develops.
- Your written work should show evidence of **effective analysis**.

Using a key scene to answer exam questions

With just 60 minutes to answer the Leaving Cert Single Text section, it's essential to make use of key scenes or significant moments to support your discussion points.

Reference to **relevant key scenes** can be useful in responding to questions on:

- characters and relationships
- themes
- narrative techniques.

Extract, Chapter 2

A chair, a table, a lamp. Above, on the white ceiling, a relief ornament in the shape of a wreath, and in the centre of it a blank space, plastered over, like the place in a face where the eye has been taken out. There must have been a chandelier, once. They've removed anything you could tie a rope to.

A window, two white curtains. Under the window, a window seat with a little cushion. When the window is partly open – it only opens partly – the air can come in and make the curtains move. I can sit in the chair, or on the window seat, hands folded, and watch this. Sunlight comes in through the window too, and falls on the floor, which is made of wood, in narrow strips, highly polished. I can smell the polish. There's a rug on the floor, oval, of braided rags. This is the kind of touch they like: folk art, archaic, made by women, in their spare time, from things that have no further use. A return to traditional values. Waste not want not. I am not being wasted. Why do I want?

On the wall above the chair, a picture, framed but with no glass: a print of flowers, blue irises, watercolour. Flowers are still allowed. Does each of us have the same print, the same chair, the same white curtains, I wonder? Government issue?

Commentary

The extract in which Offred is introduced to the reader sets the scene for the novel. Her confined bedroom provides a powerful insight into her bleak existence without the normal supports of family, home and security. The description of several functional objects emphasises the lack of character of the room. This emptiness reflects Offred's meaningless and unfulfilling life in Gilead.

The narrative style is stilted, making her sound as though she has regressed to a childlike state. Offred seems obsessed by the window with its 'two white curtains'. For someone in her entrapped position, the window is likely to symbolise the freedom she desires. There is an obvious sense that she is imprisoned and under strict rules. Offred wonders whether her 'white curtains' are government issue, specially designed for Handmaids. The colour white represents hope and purity.

Some key quotes	
'It isn't running away they're afraid of. We wouldn't get far. It's those other escapes, the ones you can open in yourself, given a cutting edge.' (Chapter 2)	This quotation symbolises the lack of freedom in Gilead. The oppressive authorities are mainly concerned with preventing the possibility of suicide.
'The Republic of Gilead, said Aunt Lydia, knows no bounds. Gilead is within you.' (Chapter 5)	In Gilead, everything is controlled. The authorities make all the choices.
'There is more than one kind of freedom ... Freedom to and freedom from.' (Chapter 5)	Aunt Lydia defends the new thinking in Gilead. She argues that women should be grateful for their new lives rather than mourning the other freedoms they have lost.
'There are only women who are fruitful and women who are barren, that's the law.' (Chapter 11)	Offred's doctor reminds her that the woman's role in Gilead is primarily to produce children.

Some key quotes	
'My name isn't Offred, I have another name, which nobody uses now because it's forbidden.' *(Chapter 14)*	Identity is important to Offred. She resists being oppressed by thinking about her real name.
'It has nothing to do with passion or love or romance or any of those other notions we used to titillate ourselves with.' *(Chapter 16)*	Offred describing her purpose as a handmaid. Sex has completely lost its value. In Gilead, it is simply used for reproduction.
'Better never means better for everyone ... It always means worse, for some.' *(Chapter 32)*	Offred is taught an important lesson by her master, Commander Fred.

exam focus

- Identify the main elements of the question, so that your answer is on target.
- Make sure to avoid unfocused narrative.
- Use reference to key scenes in your discussion.
- Always express yourself clearly.

Sample essay on *The Handmaid's Tale*

exam Q

Question

'Atwood presents readers with a deeply disturbing story that explores significant aspects of power and powerlessness.'

To what extent do you agree or disagree with this statement? Support your answer with reference to the novel *The Handmaid's Tale.*

Sample answer

1 I thought *The Handmaid's Tale* was mainly an exploration of power and the misuse of power. Gilead is an oppressive country based on a mix of old-style religion and military dictatorship. This is a horrifying world where women's rights have been almost totally destroyed. Most citizens are helpless in the face of threats to their freedom. Very often they do not fully realise what is happening to them until too late. However, a few characters, including Offred, the narrator, do what they can to resist the oppressive society that enslaves them.

Focused introduction, addressing the main aspects of the question.

2 Throughout the story, there are numerous examples of how power is totally abused. The authorities use violence to keep control. We see women tortured at the Red Centre. After public hangings, the bodies of victims are displayed on the Wall as a warning to everyone else. But the government also uses fear and threats to totally control the people. Spying is widespread, carried out by the Eyes. Offred and the other Handmaids live in terror, unsure of who can be trusted. Handmaid have only one purpose – to have children. The powerful authorities have broken up Offred's family and taken away her child, so she is left totally alone and defenceless. This is one of the most effective ways by which Gilead exerts control.

> Illustrations of abuse of power provide useful background information.

3 Offred allows us to experience her own thoughts and feelings as she struggles to maintain her own individuality. When she begins her story with a memory of her time at the Red Centre, she illustrates different kinds of power that exist. For example, the Aunts who guarded the Handmaids beat them with electric prods and leather belts. Although the Handmaids had to accept such treatment, they break the rules by meeting secretly after dark and communicating quietly.

4 The Handmaids aren't the only women who are totally downtrodden. When Offred is first taken to Commander Fred's house, she is treated as being inferior by Serena Joy, the Commander's Wife who is dressed in pale blue to distinguish her higher position, saying 'I want to see as little of you as possible'. Offred is dressed in red, the symbol of her being only a surrogate or substitute style mother. Serena reminds her of the rules in which the wife is the most important woman. But Offred doesn't feel very much more inferior to the Serena. They are almost equally controlled – but just at different levels – which is totally patriarchal.

> Interesting discussion points. Some awkward expression.

5 Offred seem passive, but she does what she can to resist the authoritarian regime. She is not as brave as her friend Moira and her shopping companion Ofglen, but she never accepts the oppressive society totally. Throughout the story, she is quietly independent and involved in a whole series of disobedient acts. For example, she steals butter and uses it as beauty cream. She also stares at a man in public, which is strictly forbidden.

> Point deserves more developed consideration.

6 As Offred begins to understand more how the whole system works, she becomes more slightly powerful. The Commander wants to have a secret affair with her – treating her as a lover more than as a Handmaid. Offred uses this to her advantage, getting him to give her illegal gifts, such as magazines. In a way, the balance of power between them changes totally and he sort of becomes dependent on her. Serena also has less power over Offred. She is so keen for Offred to become pregnant that she encourages

> Effective discussion of a perceptive point. Expression awkward in places.

her to have an affair with Nick, the chauffeur. As a bribe, Serena gives Offred a photo of her daughter, who was once taken away from her by the authorities.

7   Although women are generally powerless, they are not all simply victims. I think it is ironic that women are both powerful and powerless at the same time. Their ability to have children is both their strength and their weakness because that is the only influence they have. Offred knows the odds are almost totally stacked against her, but tries everything she can to cope. Very often she lies alone in bed and escapes through memories and dreams. Near the end, however, she is despairing after the suicide of her friend Ofglen. Shortly afterwards, when Nick arranges for her to leave the Commander's house, she is still unsure whether she is about to escape to freedom or be brought to prison. We are left wondering if Offred is stepping 'into the darkness within or else the light'.

> Insightful view seamlessly interwoven with textual reference.

8   *The Handmaid's Tale* is thought-provoking on the theme of power. The story is highly disturbing when dealing with the abuse of power. Offred wants to be reunited with her family, her husband Luke and their daughter. Even though she is suppressed, she is still her own person, and dreams of women being treated equally with men. Atwood is suggesting that people will do anything to maintain their independence and power, no matter how bad circumstances are.

> Essay is rounded off well.

(810 words)

EXAMINER'S COMMENT

Thoughtful response that addresses significant aspects of power. Some well-informed and interesting discussion supported by wide-ranging textual reference, both general and detailed – including an insightful point about victims in Paragraph 7. More focus on the 'deeply disturbing' story would have improved the grade. Reasonably clear expression, if occasionally awkward (e.g. paragraphs 4 and 6). Overuse of the adverb 'totally'.

GRADE H2

P = 15/18

C = 14/18

L = 13/18

M = 6/6

Total = 48/60

Allow about 55 minutes and aim for focused and developed points organised in paragraphs.

Revision essay question

'Despite Atwood's portrayal of Gilead as soulless and destructive, she has nevertheless succeeded in giving the reader a sense of optimism.'

To what extent do you agree or disagree with this statement? Support your answer with reference to the novel *The Handmaid's Tale*.

Prompt!

Focus on the main elements of the question ('portrayal of Gilead as soulless and destructive' and 'sense of optimism') using reference to key scenes.

- Pessimistic vision of Gilead's dystopian world.
- Women resist the oppressive system in admirable ways.
- Flashbacks indicate both Offred's despair and optimism.
- Moments of suffering balanced by friendship and hope.
- Disturbing language and vivid imagery.
- Impact of open-ended conclusion.

key point

- Exam questions are there to be challenged. There is no single 'correct' answer.
- Exemplars illustrate standard and aim to help you to find your own voice.
- Sample essays should not be learned off or recycled in the exam.

Days Without End by Sebastian Barry

Prescribed Single Text for 2021

Prescribed Comparative Study Text for 2021 and 2022

Sample essay

Question

'The insights into love and friendship explored in Sebastian Barry's historical novel, *Days Without End*, are both heart-breaking and life-affirming.'

Based on your reading of the novel, to what extent do you agree or disagree with the above statement? Give reasons for your response, developing your answer with reference to the text.

Sample answer

1   The novel *Days without End* is narrated by an Irish immigrant in America, Thomas McNulty. As a teenager, he survived the famine in the late 1840s and made the journey across the Atlantic Ocean in one of the so-called coffin ships. Thomas eventually travels to Missouri where he accidentally meets up with another young man, John Cole. He describes them as 'two wood-shavings of humanity in a rough world'. Their friendship soon turns to love and they enlist in the army during the so-called Indian Wars and the American Civil War. Although they face many challenges, their deep friendship and love is the basis of their survival and readers are given many different insights into their relationship over the course of the story.

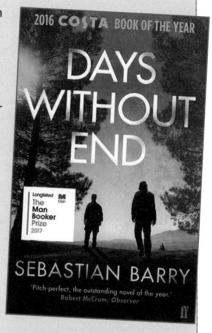

2016 COSTA BOOK OF THE YEAR

DAYS WITHOUT END

Longlisted
The
Man
Booker
Prize
2017

SEBASTIAN BARRY

'Pitch-perfect, the outstanding novel of the year.'
Robert McCrum, *Observer*

> Good overview and basis for addressing the main elements of the question.

2   Thomas meets John by accident – a 'strange and fateful' meeting accidentely under a hedge in the remote mining town of Daggsville. The hedge becomes a symbol of their love, suggesting that it was natural for them to be destined for each other. He remembers it as an 'anonymous hedge', a secret place where they sheltered from the rain. This hedge also signifies their hidden relationship, which they had because of the likelihood of criticism and predjudice against homosexuality at the time. The image helps us understand the couple's lives – and while it was sad that they had to hide their love, their commitment to each other is powerful and life-affirming. They soon become so-called brothers in arms and experience so much together that instantly you are cheering them on, hoping that they survive each new crisis. Thomas often refers to 'Handsome John' as his soulmate.

> Interesting approach to discussing the central relationship.

3   Sebastian Barry keeps emphasising an awareness of the importance of love and friendship. Many of the miners and migrant workers are lonely men. At one stage, Thomas and John work as drag artists dancing in a saloon where they get paid to entertain the local men who miss the company of the opposite sex. The saloon owner named Titus Noone does not allow any actual intimate contact, but just what he calls the 'illusion' of so-called female company. Readers get a sense of the basic natural need for tenderness – even if it is just fantasy.

4   The love between Thomas and John Cole is not the only intense relationship in the novel. Some of the orphaned Indian children are taught by the army commander's wife. Thomas becomes friends with a young girl and names her Winona. Later on, John falls ill and Thomas is discharged along with him. The two men decide to take Winona along with them and make her their servant. Over the next few years, they grow to love her like a daughter and when they eventually 'adopt' her, their happiness is complete. This very unusual group succeeds in challenging all the strict traditions of what is considered an actual accepable family – even though it is not the usual so-called family unit. They all live in an atmosphere of love and security. Readers are given an understanding of the importance and power of human companionship – which is a reassuring lesson throughout the story.

5   Then, they recieve an invitation from one of their old friends from the army, Lige Magan, to join him as workers on his tobacco ranch in Tennessee. After settling on Lige's farm, they meet his housekeeper Rosalee and her brother Tennyson. Sebastian Barry's main point seems to be that friendship and respect are stronger than racial divisions. Sioux Indians and black people were generally disrespected at the time, but not on Liege's watch. Attitudes to friendship vary and not everyone is racist.

> Good ideas but the analysis could be more clearly developed, particularly in paragraphs 5.

6   The loyalty between Thomas, John and Winona is unconditional – an affirming insight that Sebastian Barry emphasises. They are never judgemental and stand by each other in every crisis. However, love can also force them to face very painful personal challenges and commit violent acts. When a soldier named Starling Carlton comes to the ranch, he demands that Winona is returned to her own tribe. She is to be exchanged for a hostage, a young white girl. When John and Thomas refuse, Starling kidnaps her. Thomas then follows them to the army fort and the so-called prisoner exchanges proceeds as arranged. However, the US army do not keep to the agreement and they raid the Sioux camp killing men, women and children. Thomas also takes part, killing Starling Carlton and rescuing Winona.

> Perceptive opening point is well-illustrated throughout paragraph 6.

7   In many ways, this is a very modern novel dealing with themes that are relevant to today's world – including gay rights, racism and gender identity. What is uplifting is the level of tolerence and respect they have for each other. 'We been through many slaughters, John Cole and me. But I am as peaceful and easy now as I ever been.' Many insights into human nature – especially the idea that love and friendship make life worthwhile – and give hope even in times of hatred and war.

> Essay is rounded off relevantly and concisely.

(810 words)

EXAMINER'S COMMENT

GRADE H2

P = 15/18

C = 15/18

L = 14/18

M = 5/6

Total = 49/60

Generally focused on the central elements of the question (i.e. contrasting insights into love and friendship). Perceptive and ranging commentary shows a good working knowledge of the novel and its key themes. The author's 'insights' are suggested through selected language use (e.g. 'awareness', 'sense of', 'understanding', 'lesson', etc). Some useful supportive reference and quotation.

Expression is reasonably clear throughout, but the phrase 'so-called' is overused and there are mechanical errors (e.g. 'accidentaly', 'predjudice', 'accepable', 'recieve', 'tolarence').

Allow about 55 minutes and aim for focused and developed points organised in paragraphs.

Revision essay question

'Sebastian Barry's novel, *Days Without End*, addresses various aspects of identity while challenging readers to reassess their view of America's past.'

To what extent do you agree or disagree with this description of the novel? Develop your answer with reference to the text

Prompt!

- Central characters evaluate their own personal identity over the course of the story.
- Provocative narrative of America – defined by violence and powerful white men.
- Ambivalent depiction of Irish identity and civilisation.
- Disturbing/heartening scenes of 19th-century 'American Dream'.
- Author's thought-provoking portrayal of race and sexuality is realistic/ unrealistic.
- Massacres of Native American Indians undermine myths about the heroic Wild West.
- Positive/negative impact of Thomas McNulty's critical commentary.

- Exam questions are there to be challenged. There is no single 'correct' answer.
- Exemplars illustrate standard and aim to help you find your own voice.
- Sample essays should not be copied or recycled in the exam.

Othello by William Shakespeare

Prescribed Single Text for 2022

Prescribed Comparative Study Text for 2022

> **key point**
>
> For Leaving Cert English Higher Level, a play by Shakespeare must be one of the texts chosen. This can be studied on its own for the 60-mark Single Text section **OR** as one of the three texts for the 70-mark Comparative Study section.

Storyline

Shakespeare's play is **set in 16th-century Venice and also Cyprus**. Othello, a noble black general in the Venetian army, has secretly married Desdemona, daughter of a prominent senator. Iago is furious that Othello has insulted him by promoting an inexperienced soldier, Michael Cassio, to be his lieutenant.

The Duke of Venice sends Othello to Cyprus to lead his forces against an impending Turkish invasion. Desdemona, Iago and Cassio join him there. Iago soon tricks Cassio into getting drunk whilst on guard duty. After becoming involved in a street brawl, **Cassio is demoted by Othello** from his position as lieutenant.

Iago makes Othello increasingly suspicious about his wife's relationship with Cassio. Unaware of this, Desdemona pleads with her husband to re-appoint Cassio – something which only **increases Othello's suspicions** that the pair are lovers.

Iago continues to manipulate Othello who is so enraged with jealousy that he strangles Desdemona as punishment for her apparent infidelity. The truth emerges and **Iago's treachery is exposed**. Othello finally realises his tragic mistake and kills himself.

Using a key scene to answer exam questions

With just 60 minutes to answer the Leaving Cert Single Text section, it's essential to **make use of relevant key scenes** or significant moments to support your discussion points.

Six key scenes

Act 1 Scene 1: **Venice – a street at night time**

On a street in Venice. Iago talks to Roderigo about his hatred for Cassio and Othello. He informs Brabantio that his daughter Desdemona has secretly married the Moor, Othello, a general in the Venetian army.

Act 1 Scene 3: Venice – the Senate council

The Duke of Venice and his senators prepare for war against the Turks. Othello answers Brabantio's accusations of bewitching his daughter and is sent to Cyprus on military duty. Iago initiates his revenge against the Moor.

Act 2 Scene 1: A quayside in Cyprus

Othello, Desdemona and Iago arrive in Cyprus. A storm at sea has destroyed the Turkish fleet. Iago involves Roderigo in his plan to discredit Cassio and replace him as Othello's lieutenant.

Act 2 Scene 3: A hall in the castle

Cassio gets involved in a drunken brawl and loses his position as lieutenant. Iago convinces him that his only hope of reinstatement is to ask Desdemona to plead on his behalf.

Act 3 Scene 3: A room in the castle

Desdemona pleads with her husband to reinstate Cassio. Iago persuades Othello that Desdemona and Cassio are secret lovers. Consumed by jealousy, the Moor is increasingly controlled by Iago.

Act 5 Scene 2: A bedroom in the castle

Othello murders Desdemona in her bed. Emilia reveals the truth about Iago's evil plot. Realising his terrible foolishness, the Moor then kills himself, leaving Iago to be punished by Cassio.

Preparing for the Single Text *Othello* question

It is essential to have a **close knowledge of *Othello*** (particularly the storyline, characters, themes and the main features of Shakespeare's dramatic style). Your written work should show evidence of **effective analysis** of the play. **Support relevant discussion points** with suitable reference to key moments.

Study guide notes are there to be challenged. There is no single 'correct way' to interpret *Othello*. Answers should be clearly based on close reading and supporting evidence.

- Identify the main elements of the question, so that your answer is on target.
- Avoid general narrative or summary.
- Use accurate quotations when appropriate.
- Always express yourself clearly.

Key characters

Othello

As a tragic hero, Othello can be seen as a man of action. The Moor is an army general – and a successful one. Yet he is also a combination of contradictions. At first, Othello seems proud and self assured, but once he falls victim to Iago's influence, he behaves in a most inhuman manner. From the start, there are tensions between Othello's twin roles as dutiful military commander and loving husband. Despite his horrifying treatment of Desdemona, he continues to be an enigmatic figure who divides opinion. We are left considering the extent to which he is a vulnerable victim or a pompous villain. Othello describes himself as an 'honourable murderer' who has acted out of love. Yet his assertion that he was 'not easily jealous' leaves many people asking if he ever really knew himself.

Othello's qualities

- Idealistic, brave and romantic.
- Dutiful, honourable, dignified and trusting.

Othello's faults

- Insecure about his Moorish background.
- Weak-willed, jealous, violent.
- He is a poor judge of character.
- Obsessive, delusional and self-centred.

Iago

Early in the play, Iago declares: 'I am not what I am.' Both his hatred of Othello and natural hypocrisy know no bounds. The vengeful ensign's evil character is revealed through his deceitful behaviour and particularly in his many soliloquies. Filled with resentment, he plots against Othello at every opportunity. Iago is good at manipulating the weaknesses of others. He exploits Roderigo's desire for Desdemona and Cassio's wish to please Othello. He turns Desdemona's kindness to Cassio against both herself and Othello. Iago also uses Othello's obsessive love for Desdemona as the one weak point in the Moor's character. Iago's attitude towards his own wife Emilia typifies his innate disrespect for people in general. Even at the end, he refuses to give anyone the satisfaction of knowing the truth about his villainy.

Iago's qualities

- Clever, inventive and entertaining.
- Observant, witty and convincing.

Iago's faults

- Bitter, cynical, vindictive and racist.
- Insecure, sexist and self-obsessed.

Desdemona

Initially, Desdemona appears strong-willed and independent, but becomes increasingly submissive as the story develops. She falls in love with Othello and elopes with him, challenging Venice's strict social conventions. She also argues convincingly to accompany her husband to Cyprus. Desdemona is naturally well-intentioned and untiring in her kindness to Cassio. Through no direct fault of her own, her goodness is used against her by Iago in his plot to ruin Othello. Even on her deathbed, Desdemona's feelings are unconditional. The victim of a patriarchal society throughout her short life, this 'true and loyal wife' is prepared to take the blame for her husband's actions and meets her death passively. She remains a contradictory figure, but the contradictions in her character suggest that Desdemona's romantic attitudes are both dangerous and destructive.

Desdemona's qualities

- Initially determined, romantic and loving.
- Innocent, compassionate and dignified.
- Forgiving, trusting and faithful.

Desdemona's faults

- Naïve, unrealistic and weak.
- Obedient, passive and self-destructive.

key point

When writing about central characters, consider their development. What is your initial impression? How do they change over the course of the story? What is your final view of each character?

Key themes

Themes refer to issues or ideas that are central to the drama. Shakespeare explores fascinating subjects in *Othello,* including jealousy, deception, race and identity. All of these themes – and many others – are closely interlinked.

Race and identity

Race and identity are central issues throughout the play. Although Othello's actual race is never precisely defined, there is broad agreement that Shakespeare introduced a black hero to explore the **experience of the outsider in a white patriarchal society**. Iago and Cassio also struggle with their own personal sense of identity, and this motivates their decisions. However, most of the focus is on Othello himself whose military status makes him part of Venetian society while his racial background excludes him from that identity.

Othello **initially refers to his race positively**. Indeed, he seems proud – almost boastful at times – about his origins: 'I fetch my life and being/From men of royal siege.' His eloquent speech to the senators stresses the fact that his exotic Moorish history first attracted Desdemona.

Othello's ethnic background is also a cause of underlying tension. For Othello's enemies, black is often associated with wickedness or dishonesty. This negative view is particularly evident in the opening scene when **Iago expresses overtly racist opposition** to Desdemona's elopement with Othello.

Interracial marriage is said to be 'Against all rules of nature'. Bestial images of the 'lascivious' Moor as 'an old black ram' depict Othello as a savage creature. To Iago, Roderigo and Brabantio, the Moor's colour offers **a basis for expressing their personal hatred**. Ironically, such intolerance is likely to make audiences feel greater sympathy for Othello.

On some occasions, the protagonist's colour is less of an issue, especially when Venice itself is under threat. The **Moor seems be held in high esteem** as a 'valiant' army general, recognised by the Duke as 'more fair than black'. Whether this is a genuine compliment or mere flattery designed to encourage Othello's military efforts is uncertain.

All through the play, Othello's sense of self is shaped by others. He soon displays some of the **negative racial characteristics** of which he was first accused, including his superstitious beliefs about Desdemona's handkerchief. At one stage, he turns to 'savage madness' when he viciously strikes his distressed wife in public.

Nevertheless, Othello's successful army career means that he is confident in his role as a soldier. He is **uncomfortable, however, with his identity as a husband.** By Act 5, he is barely recognisable to himself, yet he still clings to the noble image he tried so hard to establish.

Ultimately, audiences are likely to view the tragic drama in relation to Othello's exclusion from Venice. Whether or not he ever fully knows himself or understands the part played by race in his demise remains doubtful. The **racial theme creates much of the play's most compelling drama** and propels the tragic narrative to its horrific conclusion.

Shakespeare's dramatic style

> **key point**
>
> When writing about themes, consider the playwright's viewpoint. How does Shakespeare introduce the theme? How does he treat and develop it over the course of the story? What is his attitude to jealousy, revenge, deception, race and identity?

Imagery

Shakespeare's use of imagery is a key aspect of his dramatic style in *Othello*. The main function of imagery (pictures created by the playwright's use of words) is to aid characterisation. Patterns of imagery (including poison, animals, sea and storms) also help to create distinctive atmospheres and intensify the audience's theatrical experience.

Symbols

Some images have special symbolic significance, e.g. the candle signifies the vulnerability of human life. Symbolism on stage can be achieved through characters, colour, actions, costume and props. Imagery and symbolism are often used together. For example, a storm at sea, which has been described in detail using vivid imagery, could also symbolise chaos or discontent among characters.

Shakespeare makes use of **motifs (recurring symbols) to reinforce key themes**. For instance, there are many references to the word 'monster' in the play. Othello also calls Desdemona's apparent betrayal 'monstrous, monstrous' while he refers to Iago as 'some monster in [his] thought'. The playwright's choice of locations is also symbolic. Venice represents civilisation while Cyprus symbolises the wilderness. Other key symbols are discussed below.

The handkerchief

We first see the embroidered handkerchief just after Othello begins to suspect his wife of being unfaithful. For the Moor, the love-token he gives Desdemona is a treasured family heirloom – **a powerful symbol of the couple's enduring relationship**. Iago, of course, views it as an opportunity for vengeance. Emilia sees the handkerchief as a chance to please her husband.

What begins as a **symbol of fidelity is soon transformed into one of unfaithfulness and betrayal**. Had it not been for the handkerchief, the Moor would not have been convinced of his wife's adultery just as easily. In *Othello*, the playwright explores various themes, including the fragility of marriage – something that is highlighted by the 'light as air' symbol of Desdemona's handkerchief.

The willow tree

In Shakespeare's plays, willow trees are often associated with unhappy love stories. As Desdemona prepares for bed, she recalls a song of 'willow'. The tree is **a poignant symbol of her unhappiness**. Abandoned by Othello, Desdemona sings, 'Let nobody blame him; his scorn I approve'. Although she is entirely innocent, she refuses to condemn her jealous husband. The willow tree song enhances our understanding of Desdemona's selfless character. Her love for Othello is unconditional.

The candle

An equally poignant symbol is the candle, which **epitomises Desdemona's fragile life**. Othello blows out the flame just moments before he strangles his wife, and he himself is aware of the tragic symbolism, 'Put out the light, and then put out the light'. In his deluded state, he acknowledges her beauty and his love for her, but is convinced that he must kill her to cleanse her of her sins. Othello also understands the irreversibility of his decision, 'If I quench tree, thou flaming minister,/I can again thy former light restore'. He knows that he could easily light the candle again, but Desdemona's life will be lost forever.

Othello: Revision of a key scene, Act 3 Scene 3

Summary

Cassio is eager to be reinstated as lieutenant and seeks Desdemona's help. However, as Othello arrives, Cassio leaves because he is too ashamed to face him. Naively, Desdemona persists in persuading her husband. Iago seizes his chance to raise doubts about Cassio's hasty departure. Using subtle hints, he suggests that Desdemona and the lieutenant have something to hide.

Othello now trusts Iago more than his own wife. When Desdemona re-appears, Othello claims to have a headache. In her efforts to calm him, Desdemona accidently drops the handkerchief, her husband's first gift to her. Emilia finds it and shows it to Iago who takes it from her. He intends to place it in Cassio's lodgings as incriminating evidence.

Othello returns, demanding more proof of his wife's infidelity. Iago invents another story about how Cassio revealed his feelings for Desdemona in a dream. Othello's thoughts suddenly turn to revenge and he swears a terrible oath to kill his wife.

Using Act 3 Scene 3 to answer questions

Act 3 Scene 3 can be used successfully in response to a range of examination questions about the play's central themes, characters, relationships and the playwright's dramatic style.

This key scene has significant dramatic functions:

- **Presents the fateful meeting** of Desdemona, Cassio and Emilia.
- Illustrates the opportunistic capabilities and **villainy of Iago**.
- Highlights the **transformation of Othello** from devoted husband to fixated wife killer.
- **Develops themes** of jealousy, revenge, identity, appearance and reality.
- **Effectively uses animal imagery** to inflame, cheating imagery to ridicule, hellish imagery to terrify.
- **Engages the audience** through Iago's clever conspiracies and the grains of truth contained in his cynical views of the world.
- Marks a major **turning point** and intensely ironic moment in the play.

Successful essay writing

How do I approach the question?

'The relentless deception that occurs throughout the play, *Othello*, creates gripping moments of dramatic tension and maintains suspense to the end.'

To what extent do you agree with this statement? Develop your answer with reference to the play.

In this question, you need to:

- Focus on all aspects of the task (relentless deception, dramatic tension, suspense).
- Identify and comment on gripping moments/scenes that support discussion points.
- Adopt a viewpoint or stance by agreeing/disagreeing wholly or in part with the question.

Marking scheme guidelines

Candidates are free to agree and/or disagree, but they should engage with all aspects of the statement, though not necessarily equally.

Possible approaches to answering this question

Approach 1: Viewpoint is in full agreement with the given statement.

All the central characters are tricked and manipulated by Iago. Dramatic scenes of mental anguish and physical suffering involve the audience throughout the play. Tension builds to a horrific climax after which peace is finally restored.

Approach 2: Viewpoint is in partial agreement with the given statement.

Iago deceives everyone else at the start, yet his overwhelming deception of Othello becomes unconvincing at times. Desdemona's naïve passivity also reduces the tension and diminishes the suspense. Some violent scenes are gripping, but the audience is not always engaged.

The Single Text (Higher Level) question is allocated 60-minutes in the exam and worth **60 marks** in total. These are awarded by reference to the **PCLM** criteria for assessment (i.e. 3 x 18 marks for each of P, C and L plus 6 marks for M):

- **P = Purpose:** 18 (30%); Is the answer focused? Does it address the question?
- **C = Coherence:** 18 (30%); Are the ideas and discussion points well sustained?
- **L = Language use:** 18 (30%); Is the candidate's writing style effective?
- **M = Mechanics:** 6 (10%); Are there spelling or grammar errors?

exam focus

- Identify the main elements of the question, so that your answer is on target.
- Avoid general narrative or summary.
- Use accurate quotations when appropriate.
- Always express yourself clearly.

Prompt!

- Relentless pretence, lies, duplicity – real and imagined.
- Moments of revelation and soliloquies affect audience.
- Effect of unexpected developments/plot twists.
- Suspense caused by foreshadowing and irony.
- Extreme violence is compelling/unconvincing.
- Impact of intense/heightened emotional experiences.
- Audience is involved/distanced by tragic/shocking events.

Question

'The relentless deception that occurs throughout the play, *Othello*, creates gripping moments of dramatic tension and maintains suspense to the end.'

To what extent do you agree with this statement? Develop your answer with reference to the play.

Sample essay

1   *Othello* is largely based on deception and self-deception. From the opening scene, the audience is caught up in the complex story of revenge. The play moves relentlessly towards its tragic outcome through a series of intense dramatic moments, which create a heightened state of suspense right up to the terrible conclusion.

> **Clear and succinct overview establishes a definite response to the question.**

2   From the start, Iago operates in the shadows, directing proceedings and causing confusion. The foolish Roderigo openly declares himself to Desdemona's father while the hidden Iago offensively shouts 'an old black ram is tupping your white ewe'. We see Iago play out his double game of informant and loyal follower, 'I must show out a flag and sign of love'. The embittered soldier explains his reasons for hating Othello. He has been passed over for promotion, so he pretends to like the Moor, 'I follow him to serve my turn upon him'. We are aware of Iago's self-centred plan of vengeance, 'I am not what I am'. He deceives everyone else. As a result, we are more informed about his hypocrisy and the tension is all the greater. We want to warn his victims.

3   Iago promises to use Desdemona's decency to destroy his enemies and 'make the net that will enmesh them all'. But Desdemona has also practised deception. She hides her relationship with Othello from her father by eloping. Her intentions were probably good, she wished to spare her father anguish. But in doing so, she deceives herself. When Brabantio finds out, he warns the Moor, 'She has deceived her father and may thee'. Iago uses this later to discredit her with Othello and plant suspicion in his mind, 'She did deceive her father marrying you'. This creates unease in the audience. We wonder if Desdemona can be fully trusted. Later on, she lies to Othello when he asks for her handkerchief, telling him 'I have not it with me'. She compounds the lie by declaring 'I have not lost it' even though she has. Again, she is acting out of good intentions, wishing to spare her husband grief because he values the handkerchief so highly. Unlike the audience, she is not aware at this time of how suspicious Othello has become or the full impact of her deceit.

> **Very good use of detailed reference shows close knowledge of and engagement with the play.**

4   This leads to the final dramatic scene where Desdemona tells another lie. Just before her unfortunate death, she seeks to pursue blame for her own murder. It was 'Nobody; I myself'. This desperate effort to keep hurt from her guilty husband could result in sending her soul to 'burning hell'. Desdemona practises deception, both on others and herself in an effort to spare those she loves grief. The irony of this has a distressing effect and we sense the tension. Desdemona's naivety prevents her from realising the terrible outcome. All will be revealed to rebound on her. No matter what she does to try and protect her husband. She will soon pay a terrible price.

> Focus is well-maintained, with the emphasis now placed on Desdemona.

5   It is only in the play's last lines that the truth about 'honest' Iago is revealed by Emilia. She dramatically accuses her husband of a 'wicked lie' if he told Othello that Desdemona was 'false' with Cassio. But Iago excuses himself by saying that he just offered his opinion. If Othello chose to believe it, that was the Moor's own fault. Othello acted out of his inherent insecurity, 'that he found himself most apt and true'. From this point, however, Iago refuses to explain the true motives for his evil actions. The playwright succeeds not only in creating suspense until the conclusion of the play but beyond it. The audience is left to wonder what Iago meant by his cryptic statement, 'you know what you know'. What exactly do they know?

6   Shakespeare concludes this scene's shocking and compelling plot twists in Othello's final soliloquy. The Moor has gained some self-knowledge. He recognises himself as the 'dolt' and 'gull'. But, like Desdemona, right to the end, he deceives himself.

> Insightful point about how suspense is maintained to the end.

He demands that he 'must' be spoken of as 'one who loved not wisely but too well'. We are left to evaluate what he has done. Othello was fully aware of the gravity of his action, that he cannot give 'vital growth' back after he has 'plucked the rose'. As the play reaches its climax, he murders Desdemona. We are shocked that he could not 'see' what was before him, his beautiful innocent wife. Instead, he 'sees' the distorted image Iago placed before him, a 'strumpet', a 'lewd minx'. So, the playwright maintains suspense, asking the audience to consider whether it is really true that Othello loved 'too well', thereby increasing the dramatic tension to the play's heart-breaking end.

7   Through gripping moments of dramatic tension that force the audience to re-examine previous events in light of the tragic ending, Shakespeare succeeds in maintaining suspense to the conclusion and beyond.

> Effective conclusion rounds off the essay with confidence.

Othello is a tense and disturbing play which explored the practice and horrific consequences of relentless deceit.

(820 words)

EXAMINER'S COMMENT

GRADE H1

- Sustained and assured focus on 'deception', 'tension' and 'suspense'.
- Well-supported and developed analysis throughout the essay.
- Paragraph 3 makes an interesting point about Desdemona's impact.
- Apt quotations are integrated effectively into the critical discussion.
- Overall, expression is impressive – although slightly awkward at times, e.g. in paragraph 4.
- Some impressive vocabulary (e.g. 'compounds', 'inherent insecurity', 'compelling plot twists').

P = 10/18
C = 17/18
L = 16/18
M = 6/6
Total = 57/60

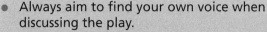

- Always aim to find your own voice when discussing the play.
- Exam questions are there to be challenged.
- There is no single 'correct' answer.
- Exemplars of paragraphs and essays illustrate different standards of answering.
- Sample essays should not be learned off or recycled in the exam.

Revision essay question

'Over the course of the play *Othello*, Shakespeare presents a morally confused world where hatred and love can be seen as equally destructive forces.'

Discuss this view, developing your answer with reference to the text.

Prompt!

- Iago is an amoral character who controls events for most of the play.
- Othello and Desdemona's questionable feelings lead to obsessive tragedy.
- Love and hatred are confused by lack of communication and misunderstanding.
- As an outsider, the Moor is unable to cope with the moral values of Venice.
- Hatred is/is not the more dominant force in the story.
- Desdemona's unconditional love for Othello is self-destructive.
- Othello never gain a full understanding of right and wrong.

Allow about 55 minutes and aim for focused and developed points organised in paragraphs.

The Picture of Dorian Gray by Oscar Wilde

Prescribed Single Text for 2022

Prescribed Comparative Study Text for 2021 and 2022

Overview

Genre

Wilde's moral fantasy of youth, beauty and corruption is often categorised as late Victorian Gothic fiction. The novel can also be classified as philosophical and a comedy of manners. There are melodramatic parallels with the medieval legend of Faust who sold his soul to the Devil in exchange for unlimited knowledge and worldly pleasures.

Setting

The Picture of Dorian Gray is set in London, England, during the late 19th century. The story takes place in the height of the Decadent artistic movement, which celebrated aesthetic pleasure and sensual experience.

Storyline

Dorian Gray is the impossibly beautiful young man who becomes the subject of a portrait by the fashionable society painter, Basil Hallward. The artist becomes infatuated with his model, and introduces the 'young Adonis' to Lord Henry Wotton. Dorian is immediately attracted to Henry's devotion to pleasure. Under his influence, he lives a life of self-indulgence and depravity in the seedy underworld of Victorian London's opium dens.

Dorian wishes that the painting, and not his body, would show the effects of ageing. His wish is granted and he remains youthful. Free to lead a double life of outward respectability while secretly living for pleasure, Dorian acts on his every desire, denying himself nothing and committing unspeakable acts. However, as time passes, the painting becomes disfigured and repellent.

After destroying the lives of various friends and lovers, Dorian decides to reform. In frustration, he plunges a knife into the picture, thus breaking the magic. This causes time and immorality to catch up with the real Dorian. He is found dead at home, horribly decrepit while the portrait reverts to its original beauty.

Characters

Dorian Gray

The novel's protagonist is a contradictory character. To a large extent, he represents the ideal of artistic beauty and innocence. Dorian Gray's body remains young and beautiful, yet his portrait alters to reflect his age and guilty conscience.

Dorian is impressionable and well-meaning – at least until he becomes corrupted by vanity and the influence of Henry Wotton. Worshipped for his good looks, Dorian becomes terrified of ageing – to such an extent that when he sees the portrait Basil Hallward has painted of him, he yearns that it would grow old instead of him. Inexplicably, Dorian gets his wish and stays forever young, while the painting of him reveals the signs of the immoral acts he commits. Narcissistic and self-destructive, he becomes more and more cruel throughout the novel.

Yet Dorian struggles with his immorality and eventually seeks redemption from his sins. By destroying the extraordinary portrait which 'embodies his moral sense', he 'decides to kill his conscience'.

The picture reflects the degradation of his soul, suggesting that his strange life really does become art. Dorian Gray leaves a trail of corruption, broken hearts and dead bodies behind him. In the end, readers are left to judge him on his actions – and to what extent he is a tragic hero, an evil villain or a pitiful victim.

Henry Wooton

One of the most entertaining characters in the novel, Lord Henry Wooton, idles away his time in London's fashionable society, using his razor-sharp wit to ridicule and charm everyone around him. He hypnotises people with his humour and intellect, and his cynical philosophies about life.

Lord Henry is famous for his epigrams: '"Men marry because they are tired, women because they are curious," he sighs. "Both are disappointed."' Or the old favourite: 'The only way to get rid of a temptation is to yield to it.'

Henry sees Dorian Gray as a challenge – another innocent person to corrupt. Over the course of their friendship, he holds a hugely negative influence over young Dorian, encouraging him to pursue instant gratification.

Although Henry is a self-proclaimed hedonist who promotes the pursuit of both moral and immoral pleasure, he himself lives a jaded, selfish life. A symbol of London's decadent and irresponsible society, he is a shallow, manipulative character with little regard for his friends. His callous attitude to the poor is particularly evident when he casually dismisses Sibyl Vane's suicide.

At the end of the novel, when Dorian tries to reform, Henry mocks him, convincing him to remain true to his indulgent life. He ridicules Dorian's attempts to change his evil ways and makes him feel like it is a futile exercise. To the end, Lord Henry typifies the Gothic villain, tempting and corrupting his youthful victims.

Sibyl Vane

Dorian Gray's first love is a beautiful and impoverished young actress who performs Shakespeare's heroines for a living. Sibyl Vane captivates Dorian, but their relationship is based on fantasy. Because Dorian values artistic beauty so much, he confuses his feelings for Sibyl's art as an actress with a love for Sibyl herself.

Their romance ends tragically when Sibyl is unable to act well because of her intense feelings for Dorian. He is embarrassed publicly by her poor theatrical performance as Juliet – and abandons her in a fit of rage. In desperation, Sibyl explains that her experience of true love in real life makes her realise the falseness of imitating emotions onstage.

Having lost out in love and art, Sibyl is heartbroken and commits suicide. Her death is Dorian's first experience of tragedy and he refuses to take responsibility. This marks a major turning point in Dorian's life – prompting the beginning of his downfall. Sibyl Vane remains a significant symbolic figure, pure and vulnerable, embodying artistic perfection.

Basil Hallward

As one of the few characters with a sense of right and wrong, Basil Hallward seems slightly out of place in this novel. His modesty and lack of interest in self-promotion is in striking contrast to most of the other male characters.

Basil is a talented artist who is primarily interested in creating and capturing beauty. He becomes obsessed with Dorian after meeting him at a party, believing that he possesses an exceptional beauty. This inspires him to reach a new level of artistic expression in the portrait he paints. The result is his masterpiece – a pure and angelic image of Dorian Gray.

Unfortunately, Basil's strong feelings for Dorian leave him vulnerable – particularly since they are not returned. As a result, he is filled with deep disappointment and longing.

Although Basil himself is a static – and somewhat dull – character, he tries to protect Dorian from the corrupting influence of Lord Henry. In an otherwise cruel world, his natural decency reflects his genuine love and concern for those he loves.

Key themes

Beauty

Oscar Wilde believed that art existed primarily to provide beauty. Indeed, the idea of beauty symbolises purity and perfection in the novel. Ugliness signifies corruption. Dorian appears to be the definition of beauty and he is widely admired because of his attractive appearance.

Sibyl Vane falls in love with him because he is good-looking. Most of his friends associate beauty with youth – particularly Lord Henry. Yet the degradation of Dorian's portrait shows that corruption of the human soul is hideous.

Dorian's obsession with beauty leads to the ill-fated wish that ultimately destroys him. When he realises that he will keep his youthful appearance regardless of whatever immorality he indulges in, he considers himself free to do whatever he likes. His mistaken faith in the value of beauty is the cause of his downfall. The story may be read as a moralistic tale – a stark warning of the dangers of vanity while neglecting one's conscience.

Within London's fashionable social circles, beauty is invariably on the surface. It is a means to escape life's harsh realities and satisfy people's senses. Dorian immerses himself in the appreciation of beautiful things – particularly artwork, jewellery and tapestries. For a time, he is popular and superficially happy, but he soon begins to worry about losing his handsome looks.

Ironically, Dorian learns the hard way that beauty and eternal youth can be dangerous illusions. Although they remain important right to the end of the story, the portrait indicates that they come at a very high price. In Dorian's case, his immortal soul.

Art

Wilde's novel explores the role of art by examining the relationship between a work of art and its viewer. Over the course of the story, Dorian's portrait reminds him that he will age and eventually lose his beauty.

The author's personal philosophy regarding art has its origins in aestheticism, the appreciation of beauty. Indeed, Wilde maintained that art had no real purpose other than to be beautiful. This idea is encouraged by Henry Wotton who believes in the hedonistic pursuit of new experiences in life. Dorian is greatly influenced by Henry, but he eventually becomes aware of the moral consequences of his behaviour.

Basil Hallward is an artist who is constantly reflecting on the relationship between appearance and reality. The picture takes on a dangerous power of its own by capturing Dorian's spirit. Staring at his decaying portrait, Dorian is fascinated by the contrast between the degradation depicted in the painting and his flawless innocence reflected by his own handsome image in the mirror.

Two works of art dominate the story – Basil's portrait and the yellow book that Henry gives Dorian. Both have a negative effect, encouraging years of pleasure-seeking immorality. The author seems to be saying that tragedy will follow when any individual surrenders to another person or to a work of art.

The more that Dorian and Basil become involved in art, the closer they come to death or destruction. Dorian spends much of his double life surrounded by art and it is hardly surprising that he ends up stabbing his own painting because the truth is mirrored in the portrait. Indeed, it is the constant pressure of art – and of almost being a piece of living art himself – that destroys Dorian Gray.

key point

In any discussion about the themes in a text, there is always some overlap; art, beauty and friendship are obvious examples in *The Picture of Dorian Gray*.

Preparing for *The Picture of Dorian Gray* Single Text question

- It is essential to have a **close knowledge** of the novel.
- **Check the plot summary** to revise how the story develops.
- Your written work should show evidence of **effective analysis**.
- You should **support relevant points** with suitable reference to key moments.

Using a key scene to answer exam questions

With just 60 minutes to answer the Leaving Cert Single Text section, it's essential to make use of key scenes or significant moments to support your discussion points.

Reference to **relevant key scenes** can be useful in responding to questions on:

- characters and relationships
- themes
- narrative techniques.

Extract, Chapter 7

He rubbed his eyes, and came close to the picture, and examined it again. There were no signs of any change when he looked into the actual painting, and yet there was no doubt that the whole expression had altered. It was not a mere fancy of his own. The thing was horribly apparent.

He threw himself into a chair, and began to think. Suddenly there flashed across his mind what he had said in Basil Hallward's studio the day the picture had been finished. Yes, he remembered it perfectly. He had uttered a mad wish that he himself might remain young, and the portrait grow old; that his own beauty might be untarnished, and the face on the canvas bear the burden of his passions and his sins; that the painted image might be seared with the lines of suffering and thought, and that he might keep all the delicate bloom and loveliness of his then just conscious boyhood. Surely his wish had not been fulfilled? Such things were impossible. It seemed monstrous even to think of them. And, yet, there was the picture before him, with the touch of cruelty in the mouth.

Cruelty! Had he been cruel? It was the girl's fault, not his. He had dreamed of her as a great artist, had given his love to her because he had thought her great. Then she had disappointed him. She had been shallow and unworthy. And, yet, a feeling of infinite regret came over him, as he thought of her lying at his feet sobbing like a little child. He remembered with what callousness he had watched her. Why had he been made like that?

Commentary

The extract provides valuable insight into Dorian's thoughts and feelings shortly after breaking off his engagement with his fiancée, Sibyl Vane. When Dorian returns home, he finds that his portrait has reacted to his actions. As he studies the painting closely, he notices a 'touch of cruelty in the mouth'.

However, Dorian dismisses the thought that he had been unkind to Sibyl. Since coming under the influence of Lord Henry, it is evident that he no longer takes responsibility for his behaviour towards others. Indeed, his sense of regret about Sibyl's tragic death is short-lived and he soon blames her entirely.

Dorian's picture reflects his private self and enhances our understanding of his inner struggles. It also serves as a symbol, allowing readers to reflect on the age-old conflict between right and wrong. In Dorian's case, he is governed entirely by self-regard and has no moral filter. He can only see himself as a pitiable victim.

Some key quotes

'As a rule, he is charming to me, and we sit in the studio and talk of a thousand things. Now and then, however, he is horribly thoughtless, and seems to take a real delight in giving me pain.' (Chapter 1)	Basil describes the young Dorian who has not yet become ruined by vanity. Yet there are signs of a dark side to his character.
'If it were I who was to be always young, and the picture that was to grow old! For that – for that – I would give everything!' (Chapter 2)	Dorian's fateful wish will change many lives forever. While he remained young and free from the effects of time, he paid for this with his life.
'There is no such thing as a good influence, Mr. Gray. All influence is immoral.' (Chapter 2)	Lord Henry reveals his own philosophy that all individuals are responsible for themselves. Ironically, Henry exerts a huge, and negative, influence on Dorian.
'A strange sense of loss came over him. He felt that Dorian Gray would never again be to him all that he had been in the past.' (Chapter 6)	Basil Hallward knows his relationship with Dorian has been changing since Lord Henry began influencing Dorian. He is left with a deep sense of loss.
'I have never searched for happiness. Who wants happiness? I have searched for pleasure.' (Chapter 17)	Dorian has no interest in happiness as a goal. He is completely unconcerned that he exchanged true contentment for eternal youth and beauty.
'He seized the thing, and stabbed the picture with it.' (Chapter 20)	Unable to cope with what the portrait represents, Dorian destroys it. The painting returns to its original state and the servants find the aged and decrepit body of Dorian with a knife in his heart.

exam focus

- Identify the main elements of the question, so that your answer is on target.
- Make sure to avoid unfocused narrative.
- Use reference to key scenes in your discussion.
- Always express yourself clearly.

Sample essay on *The Picture of Dorian Gray*

Question

'In depicting Dorian Gray as a flawed character who is easily influenced by others, Wilde provides a highly critical commentary of the society of his day.'

To what extent do you agree or disagree with this statement? Develop your answer with reference to the novel *The Picture of Dorian Gray*.

Sample answer

1   From studying Oscar Wilde's novel, it is clear that one of Dorian Gray's greatest flaws is that he is a naïve sort of privileged character who is so easily influenced for the worst by manipulative people like Lord Henry Wotton. As a result, Dorian drifts into a life of evil, losing all sense of right and wrong. Wilde's story is based around immorality and hypocrisy among London's upper classes during the 1890s. He leaves us in no doubt that the faults of his characters reflect the corrupt society of his day.

> Clear introduction focusing on the key elements of the question.

2   Early on, Dorian's friend, the artist Basil Hallward, sees the good in Dorian and captures this in his beautiful portrait. When he sees his youthful beauty in the picture, Dorian swears he would give anything – even his soul – to stay as he is seen in the painting by his friend. Because he is so shallow and completely egotistical, he makes his choice, such a terrible life-changing mistake. After then exchanging his soul for eternal youthful beauty, his behaviour slowly becomes cruel and twisted.

> Good contextual point, but expression is laboured.

3   Lord Henry Wotton is a charismatic character whose ideas charm the impressionable Dorian. However, his influence is damaging. Dorian himself gets so self-centred that he soon becomes obsessed with losing his youth and handsome looks. He imitates his witty new mentor, living a really heedless hedonistic life. He soon discards any sense of morality. This corrupt lifestyle is geared to seeking instant gratification and pleasure without any thought of responsibility. Henry takes full advantage of Dorian's immature personality to show how hedonism can corrupt.

4   Under Henry's influence, Dorian begins to affect others, encouraging them to be just like himself in wanting to be 'filled them with a madness for pleasure'. He even corrupts Lady Gwendolyn, Henry's sister. Before they became close friends, we are told that 'not a breath of scandal had ever touched her'. What is interesting is that Dorian is so arrogant that his advantaged social position will offer him protection. Victorian society trusted wealthy aristocrats as decent people who automatically deserved to be respected.

> Good discussion point well-illustrated.

5 Indeed, most of the author's criticism is directed at the immoral lifestyles of England's privileged classes. Dorian's bad conscience – the dark side of his personality – is represented by his portrait. In another sense, the picture also symbolises Victorian hypocrisy and upper-class corruption. Dorian frequents 'dreadful houses' and visits 'the foulest dens in London'. He escapes reality by taking drugs. After he murders Basil, for example, he goes to an opium den so that 'the memory of old sins could be destroyed'.

6 Dorian's selfishness becomes more evident when close friends around him are no longer as important as the beauty they can create. Dorian indirectly causes the death of the young actress who loves him, Sibyl Vane, but his murder of Basil Hallward is much more calculated. His awful deviousness is seen in the way he covers up his violent crime and then blackmails a former friend, Alan Campbell, to dispose of the body.

> Important point deserving of a more developed analysis.

7 The division between rich and poor in social classes is characterised by Lord Henry and Sibyl's brother, James Vane. With his inherited wealth, Henry typifies the wealthy upper class. He spends his time socialising, amusing himself by spreading scandal and idle gossip and ridiculing his friends. Wilde makes it clear that Henry wants the unequal society to stay exactly as it is – 'I don't desire to change anything in England except the weather'. In complete contrast, James Vane is used to poverty and hardship, but is forced to accept social inequality. He becomes a sailor just to get away from the corruption in London.

8 Wilde uses contrasting locations to highlight class inequality and injustice. Selby Royal is grand and could not be more different from Dorian's secret world in the seedy backstreets of London. Wilde writes about lavish parties, witty conversations and sunny days at Selby. But on two occasions, the disturbing reality shows up the corruption in high society. When Dorian is picking flowers, he collapses in a faint after seeing the face of James Vane, spying on him from the conservatory.

> Perceptive commentary, very well-supported.

9 Later while hunting, a working man is shot accidentally. He is one of the beaters hired to drive the hares into open fields. Henry shows no sympathy for the victim, and only calls off the hunt because it 'would not look well to go on'. Dorian is equally unconcerned for the dead man or his family and automatically assumes that money will solve the problem. However, he is uncomfortable that such unpleasantness occurred on his country estate and says, 'Death walked there in the sunlight'. Evil and wrong-doing is expected in run-down slums and opium dens, but not in the fresh country air of Selby Royal.

> Effectively illustrated and focused discussion.

10 To a large extent, Wilde's novel is a stark reminder of the two worlds in 1890s England. For all the talk of art and beauty, the story clearly shows that mass poverty, injustice and corruption are all by-products of a highly advanced society and sophisticated civilisation.

> Succinct conclusion rounds off the essay with confidence.

(830 words)

EXAMINER'S COMMENT

Thoughtful response that addresses the three aspects of the question throughout. Dorian's character flaws and the effects of influence on his behaviour are teased out. This is followed by some interesting and sustained analysis of Wilde's critique of Victorian society – particularly in paragraphs 7 and 9. The essay shows close engagement with the novel and points are supported effectively with accurate textual reference. Overall expression is good, although slightly awkward in paragraph 2.

GRADE H1

P = 18/18

C = 17/18

L = 17/18

M = 6/6

Total = 58/60

Revision essay question

'Wilde inspires varying degrees of shock, outrage and compassion in his unsympathetic presentation of Dorian.'

Allow about 55 minutes and aim for focused and well-argued points organised in paragraphs.

To what extent do you agree or disagree with this statement? Develop your answer with reference to the novel *The Picture of Dorian Gray.*

Prompt!

Focus on the main elements of the question ('shock, outrage and compassion' and 'unsympathetic presentation of Dorian') using reference to key moments in the novel.

- Effect of Wilde's depiction of Dorian on readers.
- Dark disturbing vision of English society.
- Basil and Sibyl are sympathetic characters.
- Incidents of crime, murder, suicide and injustice shock readers.
- Gothic and supernatural elements affect our response.
- Dorian can be viewed as a tragic victim of circumstances.
- Impact of the melodramatic conclusion.

- Exam questions are there to be challenged. There is no single 'correct' answer.
- Exemplars illustrate standard and aim to help you to find your own voice.
- Sample essays should not be copied or recycled in the exam.

A Doll's House by Henrik Ibsen

Prescribed Single Text for 2022

Prescribed Comparative Study Text for 2022

Sample essay

Question

'Nora Helmer has often been described as a feminist heroine, but she is essentially a victim of a patriarchal society.'

To what extent do you agree or disagree with this view? In your response, you should address all aspects of the statement, developing your answer with reference to the play.

Sample answer

1 Although written around 1889, *A Doll's House* challenges a lot of misunderstandings about women. Over the course of the play, Nora Helmer develops into a strong character with great inner strength. She does not seem very feministic at the beginning. In the first act, we are introduced to Nora as an 'extravagant little person' and a 'sweet little spendthrift'. This suggests that she will be just another female caricature. The patronising language used by Torvald her husband reflects his insulting view of his wife as a 'sweet little skylark', The adjective 'little' emphasises his superior attitude. The more Torvald uses such compliments, the more we can see that he is actually condescending and takes Nora for granted, clearly indicating that she is a victim of a patriarchal society.

> Solid introductory overview that takes on the question.

2 From the start, Nora is depicted as being almost childlike. She is lacking in the ways of the real world outside of her luxury home. She does posess some secret experience, however, and this is evident in her small acts of rebellion that indicate that she is not quite as innocent or happy-go-lucky as she comes across at the start. Nora eventually realises her passive role in her marriage and finds in herself the strength to leave her selfish husband.

3 Nora isn't permitted to have her own views or opinions. Her husband controls her life a lot of the time. We gradually suspect that her feminist instincts are growing inside her as she leads this unfulfilled life of giving the outward impression of being in a happy marriage – all to please others and do what society expects. Deep down she is intensely discontented. Even her role as a mother is unreal. She does not act like a normal mother to her three children but just plays with them, as if she continues playing with dolls.

> Interesting discussion of the uneven relationship between Nora and Torvald.

4   A lot of other characters in the play, especially Nils Krogstad and Dr Rank, do not take Nora very seriously. Even though they could of shown her more respect. But she accepts this and even encourages it, sometimes calling herself 'little Nora'. Nevertheless, there are signs that she is not complitly happy with her restricted life as a wife and mother. We see this when she admits the secret of how she borrowed money to pay off a family debt and protect Torvald. Nora claims that it was fun to be in charge of money, 'almost like being a man'.

5   Kristine Linde can be seen as a contrast to Nora. When Nora learns that Kristine is a widow with no children, she says: 'So you are quite alone. How dreadfully sad that must be.' Her attitude is a mixture of self-satisfaction and pretence. It's the kind of attitude expected of rich middle-class women at that time back in the 1890s. Nora was expected to have children as if that on its own meant she was living a fulfilled and happy life. In reality, she is clearly a sad victim of her times because she is putting on a performance.

6   Mrs Kristine Linde is an old friend and a woman who enjoys being financially independent without giving up family life. Earning her own money and being independent has not harmed Mrs Linde. She enjoys her work but also longs for the role of being a loving mother and wife. It could be argued that Kristine's life with Krogstad can be seen as offering hope for Nora and Torvald's marriage.

Good idea here, but the analysis could be more clearly developed.

7   *A Doll's House* exposes the injustice which women like Nora suffered. This was a key part of the culture of the male-dominated society of Norway in the late 1890s. To me, Nora represents a call for justice, particularly to women. Even though Nora is just an ordinary housewife, it is undeniable that she does in fact posess some 'greatness', making Nora a modern tragic heroine.

8   Questions remain as to whether or not Nora should have left her family. When she announces that she is leaving Helmer, he accuses her of neglecting her 'sacred duties' towards her husband and children. But Nora rejects this and tells Torvald of her duty towards herself, 'I believe that I am first and foremost a human being – like you'. She finally realises she has changed a lot and cannot continue playing the role of a carefree, slightly silly mistress of the Helmer 'doll house'. What makes Nora a heroic feminist is that she challenges the state of marriage and the double standards of society which restrict individuality and personal development.

Insightful discussion that maintains solid focus on the question.

9   The play's final image of Nora is of an embittered yet intelligent and newly empowered woman, freeing herself from the oppression of an unfulfilled life – as a doll, a possession whose sole purpose is to entertain her husband. Unfortunately, to become an independant individual, she has to leave her young children and risk being blamed for causing a scandal. This is what makes her a tragic victim as well as a feminist heroine.

Good conclusion which rounds off the whole essay clearly.

(820 words)

EXAMINER'S COMMENT

Sustained overall focus on the question (i.e. feminist heroine, victim of a patriarchy). Insightful points about Nora's private and public life, well-supported by textual reference, both general and detailed. Some close personal engagement with the play (e.g. in paragraph 7). However, the contrast between Nora and Kristine deserved more consideration. Expression was generally clear – apart from overuse of 'a lot' plus some mechanical errors (such as 'could of', 'posess', 'completly', 'should of', 'independant').

GRADE H2

P = 15/18

C = 14/18

L = 14/18

M = 5/6

Total = 48/60

Revision essay question

'The effectiveness of the imagery and symbolism in Henrik Ibsen's play, *A Doll's House,* heightens the play's dramatic impact.'

Allow about 55 minutes and aim for focused and developed points organised in paragraphs.

To what extent do you agree or disagree with this description of the play? Develop your answer with reference to the text.

Prompt!

- Title reflects Nora's compelling role as a 'trophy wife' – passive, beautiful, helpless.
- Child imagery highlights Nora's apparently innocent, frivolous character.
- The Christmas tree – needs to be decorated – powerful symbol of Nora's role in the household.
- New Year's Day – ironically, a time of dramatic new beginnings for the Helmer family.
- The tarantella dance illustrates Nora's conflicted situation – passionate, objectified.
- Macaroons – guilty pleasure representing Nora's engaging disobedience and deceit.
- Birds – poignant representation of Nora's caged life, treated as a delicate and beautiful bird.

key point

- Exam questions are there to be challenged. There is no single 'correct' answer.
- Exemplars illustrate standard and aim to help you find your own voice.
- Sample essays should not be copied or recycled in the exam.

5 Paper 2: The Comparative Study

aims
- Identifying and understanding the four comparative modes.
- Developing successful comparative responses to question.
- Revising key prescribed comparative texts.

The Leaving Cert Comparative Study section is worth **70 marks** – the second most important question on the exam paper.

In this section, novels, plays and films are all referred to as **texts**.

A **mode** of comparison is simply a basis or framework for exploring a text.

The prescribed Higher Level modes for 2021 are:

- Cultural context
- General vision and viewpoint
- Theme or issue

The prescribed Higher Level modes for 2022 are:

- Cultural context
- General vision and viewpoint
- Literary genre

exam focus

You will need to study at least **two of the three** prescribed modes.

key point

In the Comparative Study section, a mode is a way of studying a text.

key point

Note that cultural context, and general vision and viewpoint, are prescribed modes for both 2021 and 2022.

Students can check details about prescribed texts with their teachers or by accessing www.education.ie for circulars regarding prescribed material.

Note:

- There will be questions on two of the three prescribed modes in the examination.
- Each mode on the exam paper will offer a choice of two questions.
- Candidates must choose one mode and answer one question.

EITHER	OR
A **single essay** question comparing **three** prescribed texts (70 marks) (Aim for at least 900 words) Time: 70 minutes	A **two-part** question: • **Part (a)** requires discussion of **one** prescribed text (30 marks) (Aim for at least 400 words) • **Part (b)** requires comparison of **two** other prescribed texts (40 marks) (Aim for at least 500 words) Time: 70 minutes

When answering comparative questions, candidates may compare and/or contrast, i.e. address similarities and/or differences in both the subject matter and style of their chosen texts.

In your answer you may not use the text you have answered on in **Section I** – The Single Text.

> The modes and texts used in the study notes and sample answers that follow are all prescribed for both the 2021 and 2022 examinations.

Cultural context

Prescribed mode for 2021 and 2022

• Studying texts by examining the 'world' of the story.
• Understanding how aspects of cultural context shape characters and events in texts.

The cultural context is often described **as the society or 'world' of the text**. It refers to the social setting, values, attitudes and day-to-day practices. Our understanding of a text is enriched by knowing about the culture in which the story is set.

key point

Various aspects of cultural context, such as social class and identity, are likely to overlap at times.

Analysis of cultural context

Family	How does family impact on characters and their actions? Does it nurture or restrain characters? (Obedience, love, duty, guilt, confidence, etc.)
Society/class structure	How does the type of society affect the characters and their actions? Does it empower or restrict characters? (Power, money, status, education, etc.)

key point

Cultural forces can have a positive or negative impact on characters.

Men/women	Who has power, men or women? (Patriarchy, matriarchy.) How does this influence the central character's life?
Religion	Is religion a comforting or inhibiting force? (How does it affect marriage, sex, social change, the happiness of characters?)
Violence	Is the violence physical, emotional or intellectual? Who is the offender and who is the victim? What is the impact of violence on society and individuals?
Poverty	How does poverty affect the progress of characters? (Lack of opportunity, helplessness, disease, honour, pride, etc.)

Making comparisons

First text: drama	Second text: novel	Third text: film
Philadelphia, Here I Come! **Brian Friel**	*Room* **Emma Donoghue**	*Unforgiven* **Clint Eastwood**
Who has power or influence?		
Older men, the Church	Old Nick, society	Violent men
Is power used responsibly or abused?		
Abused	Abused	Abused
Choose a scene that illustrates how power is used.		
The tea-time scene between Gar and his father S. B. He longs for S. B. to make 'one unpredictable remark' to bridge their tragic communication gap.	Old Nick switches off the electricity and stops bringing food.	In a brothel, a cowboy slashes a woman's face because she mocks how he looks.
Outline what happens as a result.		
No change in relationship occurs. Gar and his father hold precious memories of their shared past (fishing trip, wee sailor suit) but they are unable to express their true feelings.	Ma decides they must escape (pretends Jack is dead). Police catch Old Nick who gets sent to prison for 25 years to life with no parole.	The sheriff treats it as a minor matter. The women of the brothel employ William Munny, a hired killer, to take revenge.
Cultural context impact		
Has Gar succeeded in overcoming his oppressed cultural context?	Have Ma and Jack succeeded in overcoming their restrictive cultural context?	Has the rule of law succeeded in overcoming violent lawlessness?

Responding to texts

How individuals react to their problems within the confines of their different worlds is of great interest today. We have to learn how to co-exist. We have to be aware of differing points of view. Yet what one person perceives as a threat may be viewed by another as admirable.

Different personalities react in distinctive ways to unexpected challenges in their lives. Do they act or do they remain passive? Are the odds overwhelming? By examining the responses of individual characters as they conform to (or rebel against) the forces of class, money, privilege, dreams and expectations, we gain important insights into life.

For example, when challenges are met with courage, **we can learn what adds to a character's feeling of self-worth.** Authors and film directors often want us to think about an aspect of the human condition and to question our opinions and beliefs. In turn, we can re-evaluate what real success means and the importance of genuine friendship.

Comparative study texts broaden our understanding of what it means to be a human being. They allow us to experience (at a safe distance) the struggles of others as they seek to find a resolution to their difficulties. We all need to know ourselves, to distinguish between reality and appearance, growing up, taking responsibility for our decisions, understanding the corrosive effects of hatred as well as the redeeming power of love and to ultimately face the finality of death.

Developing a personal response

Check the graphic below to aid your understanding of **the impact of cultural forces** on a character in a text. The forces which influence an individual are those on the left. They will either help or hinder the central character as he or she tries to achieve their goal in life.

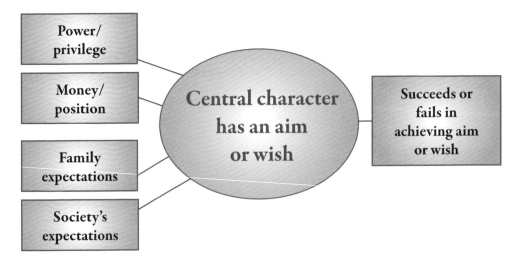

Cultural and social forces in any particular place or time shape the lives of people as they conform to (or sometimes rebel against) the pervading forces of class, money, privilege, dreams and expectations.

Cultural context in *Philadelphia, Here I Come!*

Overview

- Brian Friel's play is set during the early 1960s in the small Donegal village of Ballybeg just before Gar O'Donnell emigrates to America.
- Gar finds it difficult to live in such a claustrophobic environment.
- The play reflects the conservative structure of society during this period.
- Emphasis was on the family unit and religion was at the centre of family life.
- Traditional male/female roles are strongly defined.
- The dominant influence of State and Church provided moral and social leadership for the people.

Negative cultural influences			
Religion	**The Irish State**	**Education**	**Patriarchal society**
Canon Mick O'Byrne represents the Church.	**Senator Doogan** represents the Irish State.	**Master Boyle** represents education and scholarship.	**S. B., Gar's father,** represents the patriarchy.
Parish priest, spiritual leader in the community, local school manager – he **has immense influence** in society. **Represents conservatism** in the Catholic Church. **Remote and self-regarding,** he has no words of comfort for Gar about leaving home or for S. B. who will miss his only son.	**Wealthy establishment figure,** local politician. Wants his daughter Kate to marry **a university graduate** rather than Gar. Epitomises **middle-class snobbery** and class prejudice. Conservative symbol of power and **high social standing.**	Gar's teacher is a **drunken failure** who quarrels with the Canon. **Unsuccessful suitor** to Gar's mother, Maire. **Self-interested fantasist** who dreams of important teaching post in Boston.	**S. B. is a prominent respectable citizen.** Tragically, **unable to communicate** with Gar. **Personal tragedies** – Gar's mother dies giving birth. **Willing to accept societal norms,** servile attitude to the Canon.
Cultural impact			
The Canon demonstrates how religion is **no longer relevant.** He **does not support Gar's emotional needs** or spiritual life.	Skilled speaker who confuses and **discourages Gar.** The senator amplifies and **exposes Gar's sense of inferiority.**	Although Boyle has some regard for Gar, **he insults him:** 'You're young and strong and of average intelligence'.	Cannot express his feelings. **Gar is devastated** when S. B. misses his chance to discuss his memory of the blue boat fishing trip.

Positive cultural influences

Madge, housekeeper to the O'Donnell family, plays the traditional female role; central figure, mediator and surrogate mother to Gar.	Kate Doogan is Gar's lost love – she belongs to a wealthy family and represents the privileged middle class.	Ned and the 'boys' are Gar's male friends – they symbolise the constricted lifestyle of most young Irish people during the 1960s.	Con and Lizzy, American relations (Lizzy's sister was Gar's mother) who want Gar to return to America with them – they represent a possible escape for Gar.
Madge has **genuine affection** for Gar hidden by horseplay and rough language, 'you brat you'. She is **important to Gar**, 'I think I love you more them any of them'. A **mediator** – attempts to break the silence between father and son. **Loyal** to S. B. – 'Just because he doesn't say much doesn't mean he hasn't feelings'. **Disapproves of the 'boys'** – 'couldn't even come here to say good-bye to you on your last night'. Allows audience **to see things as they really are** – S. B. and Gar are 'as like as two peas'.	Kate is **inventive** – tries to circumvent her father's opposition to her marrying Gar (S. B.'s 'supposed' retirement). **Assertive** – tries to make a man out of an adolescent – tells Gar that their future is 'entirely up to you'. **Mature** – makes the best of a situation, such as marriage to Dr King, 'I hear no complaints'. **Caring** – calls to say goodbye to Gar and wishes to maintain friendship. **Sensitive** – tells Gar, 'Your father'll miss you'. **Dignified farewell** – 'Good-bye Gar'.	**Ned, Joe and Tom have difficulty communicating their feelings** – Madge 'asked' them to call to see Gar. **Immature** – they live in fantasy land, 'Any volunteers for a big booze-up and a couple of women?' **Dependent financially on parents** – 'I meant to buy you something good, but the aul fella didn't sell the calf to the jobbers'. Ned has **genuine affection** – 'flings belt' as a gift to Gar – 'If any of them Yankee scuts try to beat you up'. **Encourages Gar** – 'You'll make out all right over there'.	**Lizzy is emotional** – but also sentimental, impulsive, vulgar, dissatisfied and misses having children of her own. **She is also over-protective** towards Gar – 'we'll offer him everything we have'. Lizzie can be **cruel** – sarcastic nickname for her husband, 'Rudolph Valentino', famous Hollywood screen lover. **Gar has reservations** about her – 'She'll tuck you into your air-conditioned cot every night'. **Con and Lizzy glorify the 'American Dream'**, unlike their friend Ben Burton who says 'it's just another place to live'.

Bittersweet memories			
Gar fails to communicate his feelings about Madge and is left with the bittersweet memory, 'Watch her carefully … this is a film you'll run over and over again'.	After losing Kate, **Gar fails to communicate** his love for her and is left with feelings of regret, 'sweet Katie Doogan … my darling Kathy Doogan'.	**Gar is aware of his friends' flaws** – 'ignorant bloody louts' and has nostalgic memories of 'foolish, silly fun and foolish silly laughing … precious, precious gold'.	**Gar rashly decides to emigrate** – he wants to associate himself with the 'laughing, crying, impetuous' family of his mother – but has he made the right choice?

Gar's two 'worlds'

Exterior world

The playwright allows Gar Public to interact with his everyday world.

Interior world

The audience can also see into Gar's mind through Gar Private who comments on events, actions and characters, including himself. By retreating into fantasy, Gar Private blocks what his public self finds unpleasant in the exterior world.

Cultural references in the play

In addition to Irish heritage, Gar inherits fragments of **Anglo-Irish, European and American culture.**

- Gar repeatedly quotes from a speech by the Irish commentator Edmund Burke: 'It is now sixteen or seventeen years since I saw the Queen of France, then the Dauphiness, at Versailles.'
- Burke celebrates an idealised past which is contrasted with an unhappy present.
- Gar also refers to American cowboys forging forward new frontiers: 'let's git that li'l ole saddle bag opened and let's git packin'.'
- He listens to European music, particularly Mendelssohn's 'Violin Concerto', representing beauty.
- Gar also enjoys Irish music, 'She Moved through the Fair', possibly reflecting his inability to find his own voice.

What significance do these cultural references have for Gar?

- Do they suggest that Gar is a dreamer or a realist?
- What does Gar Private's 'life' reveal about the cultural values of Ireland in the 1960s?
- How have the negative and positive aspects of the cultural context shaped Gar's personality?
- Do they enable or prevent him from making good choices in order to achieve his dreams?

In Part (a) 30-mark questions on one text, no comparison is necessary. Discuss the mode only.

- Allow about 30 minutes and aim for 400 words approximately.
- Organise your answer into clearly defined paragraphs.
- Support your opinions with quotations and references from the text.

Sample 30-mark question

'Central characters can successfully or unsuccessfully challenge aspects of the cultural context in texts.'

Discuss the extent to which at least one main character challenges successfully or unsuccessfully at least one aspect of the cultural context in **one text** on your comparative course. Support your answer with reference to the text.

Prompt!

Refer to the mode and the question in your answer.

The purpose of the question:

- to show evidence of understanding the cultural context of the text (focusing on the mode);
- to discuss the behaviour of one or more central characters who challenge (or conform) to the world of the text;
- to examine the degree of success achieved.

Decide on your opinion:

- Gar needs to challenge the establishment figures of Senator Doogan and S. B., who represent the power, wealth and traditional values in Ballybeg, in order to achieve his dreams of independence and love. He fails to do so.

Make a short plan of your key points:

- Gar must confront Senator Doogan for permission to marry Kate, but he lacks the courage to do so and gives up.
- Gar has to make his father aware that he resents the way he is being treated. However, he fails to communicate with him.
- Gar fails to challenge restrictive aspects of the cultural context of his world and this prevents his pursuit of happiness and fulfilment.

Sample answer

1 In *Philadelphia, Here I Come*, Gar responds weakly to the challenges of rural Irish society in the 1960s. Society is tightly ruled mainly by older men through wealth and class. However, Gar's lack of courage in challenging these social values leads to his ultimate defeat.

2 Gar wants to marry Kate, the daughter of the local lawyer, Senator Doogan. Kate is a realist who knows the objections her father will raise against Gar. The senator is busy engineering a 'suitable' match for her with Dr Francis King. But time is running out. So she creates the false impression that S. B. is about to retire and Gar will take over. She insists Gar meet her father, 'You talk to Daddy, Gar'. But Gar panics, 'they'll wipe the bloody floor with me'. Kate reminds him, 'It's up to you'. But Gar fails to fight for his love.

3 Doogan also uses class superiority to belittle Gar. The Kings all went to university, 'his father and I were class-fellows school', 'later at university when he did medicine and I did law'. The culture of the time makes Gar inferior, so he lacks the confidence to marry Kate. He failed to seize his opportunity away from the restrictions of Ballybeg. Gar now also fails to seize the opportunity Kate had created for him. Private Gar immediately blames her, 'the aul bitch'. He criticises Public, 'you look a right fool standing there'. Gar has defeated himself, 'I think I'd better move on'. He has lost Kate.

4 Gar also blames his failure on his father, S. B., 'I'm twenty-five and you treat me as if I were five'. He complains that he cannot order a 'dozen loaves' without his father's permission. S. B. confides to his son that his business is going down, 'I mind the time when I got through a couple of dozen a week'. It is obvious that the business needs a young man with modern ideas. But Gar again displays a lack of courage and cuts his father off, 'Better get these pills and then try to get a couple of hours sleep'. Gar does not confront S. B. about his low pay, 'you pay me less than you pay Madge'.

5 While Gar bitterly complains about Ballybeg as 'a backwater, a dead-end', Kate disagrees, 'It isn't as bad as that'. Gar is blaming his failure in life on a place, not on his own decisions and lack of action. Gar conforms to his society not because of tradition, but because he lacks the moral strength to claim his rightful place in Ballybeg's society.

(425 words)

EXAMINER'S COMMENT

Generally focused response to the question. Clear understanding of some cultural aspects prevalent in Ballybeg and Gar's failure to challenge them. Key points are well-supported with relevant textual reference and suitable quotation. Language use is reasonably good apart from some repetition and note-like expression (e.g. paragraph 2). Discussion is rounded off effectively.

(24/30 marks)

Cultural context in *Room*

Overview

- Emma Donoghue's novel is set mainly in a secluded, sound-proofed garage. Captive Ma and her son Jack live there, visited by Ma's captor, Old Nick.
- Only environment Jack has known, having spent five years thinking that he's in this small world with his mother and that outside there's just outer space.
- Objects in Room are the child's friends, e.g. Lamp, Toothpaste.
- Jack believes that all he reads in books or sees on TV is fiction, 'Mountains are too big to be real'.
- Discovery that they are prisoners shatter his worldview when Ma starts 'unlying'; 'what we see on TV is ... it's pictures of real things'.
- After the escape to Outside, Jack finds it difficult to believe everything around him is real, 'I've seen the world and I'm tired now'. He has little idea of boundaries or acceptable behaviour.
- Ma and Jack return only once and the child realises that he has outgrown Room: 'Has it got shrunk?' With help and support, he begins to navigate the outside world. 'I look back one more time. It's like a crater, a hole where something happened.'

Negative cultural influences			
Violence	**Media**	**Family**	**General public**
Old Nick, Ma's captor, rapist and Jack's biological father. He exerts absolute power over Ma and Jack.	**Paparazzi and TV interviewer with 'puffy hair'** represents the media's primary interest in 'getting a story'.	**Grandpa**, Ma's father, represents strict conservative views. He is an unsupportive and distant character.	**Some members of the general public** are voyeuristic and don't consider how they might hurt someone vulnerable.
Cultural impact			
Old Nick is deceptive – lured Ma, aged 19, to truck with story of a sick dog, and imprisoned her for seven years. **Controlling** figure – holds the code to the lock of the sound-proofed shed.	**Paparazzi act like 'vultures'** surrounding Ma and Jack as they exit the police car. Media sensationalise story – Headline: 'HOPE FOR BONSAI BOY'.	**Grandpa is an unsympathetic figure,** divorced from Grandma because she refused to believe Ma was dead. Grandpa 'wants (Jack) not born'.	**Sales associate and co-workers gawk** at Jack when he explains he is a 'rap star' and ask for his autograph.

Negative cultural influences
Cultural impact *contd.*

Sees himself as a benefactor, bringing food: 'Plenty girls would thank their lucky stars for a setup like this.' **Vindictive** – turns off heat and electricity for days. **Bully** – physically hurts Ma, leaving purple marks on her neck. **Old Nick, the 'monster' caught** and will probably 'get twenty-five to life' in jail. Jack's bravery and Ma's resilience overcome Old Nick's powerful control.	Puffy haired interviewer asks **invasive questions,** e.g. if Ma experienced Stockholm syndrome, how she felt about 'deceiving' Jack. **Ma answers bravely** that she wants to shine a light on 'people, locked up in all sorts of ways'. The interviewer has a **damaging effect on Ma** who subsequently tries to commit suicide. Media is **a powerful negative force for** victims who are repeatedly worn down.	**Cannot accept child born of rape.** He puts his own interests first and abandons family responsibilities by flying back to his home in Australia. **Grandma is unsure** about how to respond to what has happened. **Shocked** that her Book Club ladies saw photos of Jack. Sometimes **indifferent** to Jack's needs. Ma and Jack are **rejected** by Grandpa.	**Pilar, Dr Clay's assistant,** accidentally lets Jack see himself and Ma on TV: 'The malnourished boy, unable to walk, is seen here lashing out.' **Ma and Jack suffer more because of** thoughtless people and sensational media.

Positive cultural influences

Mother	Professionals	Family	General public
Ma, Jack's mother, abducted by Old Nick. She is a tough and resilient supporter for her five-year-old son.	**Caring professionals, Officer Oh and Dr Clay** support both Jack and Ma to make the stressful transition to Outside.	Supportive family, **Grandma and Steppa** (Step-Grandad Leo) help Jack and Ma adjust to their new life.	**Ajeet** is a kind stranger who encounters Jack trying to escape. He calls the police and sets rescue in motion.

Cultural impact

Ma never regrets having Jack – even though she is **traumatised** by abduction.	**Officer Oh is patient** – spends time eliciting the story of how Jack and Ma 'did a trick' so that Ma can be rescued.	**Grandma is loving** – never stops hoping for return of her daughter.	**Ajeet – a responsible stranger**.

Positive cultural influences

Cultural impact *contd.*

Genuine affection – keeps Jack healthy through 'Phys Ed' and teaches him to read, write and understand right and wrong. Uses TV as linguistic tool. **Honest** – Ma has to tell Jack there is a world outside Room. **Protective** of Jack – faces down negative forces of Outside (media, etc.) **Enables Jack to develop** – stops breastfeeding and helps him to accept the loss of Bad Tooth.	**Caring** – calls media 'vultures'. **Competent** – arrests Old Nick. **Dr Clay is also supportive** – organises medical examinations, sun protection, etc. **Empathetic** – carefully listens to Ma's concerns and tries to help Ma move on, 'It's not just the two of you anymore, is it?' **Encourages** Ma and Jack to get DNA testing to prevent Old Nick getting 'let off on technicality'.	**Accepts Jack** as grandson despite birth circumstances. **Pragmatic** – looks after Jack when Ma is suicidal. **Steppa/Leo** – kind, gentle, good sense of humour, he teaches Jack to play Lego. **Intervenes helpfully** – when Jack yells at Grandma because she did not return with a promised soccer ball, Steppa picks him up yelling and screaming and sits with him on Jack's mattress until he calms down.	**He is concerned** about Jack's behaviour when Nick lifts him, so he confronts him and calls the police. Ajeet **threatens Old Nick** that he has the number of his truck 'magic numbers' which causes Nick to drop Jack and run away. **Effective** – if Ajeet had not intervened the escape plan may not have worked.

Overall influence

Positive Enables Jack to make transition to Outside.	Positive Helps Jack and Ma to adjust to Outside.	Positive Always supportive of Jack and Ma.	Positive Intervenes to allow Jack to escape.

The two 'worlds' of *Room*

Interior world

Room, where Ma and Jack are held captive, is Jack's entire world for five years. It is claustrophobic, yet cosy. Jack feels safe there. All the familiar objects in the room are capitalised, i.e. Lamp, Toothpaste, because Jack sees them as his friends. Everything on TV is 'fake'. Jack is not sure he wants to leave, but Ma insists. He is aware of famous singers, such as Kylie Minogue, Lady Gaga, Kanye West, Rihanna, Eminem and Hannah Montana.

Jack plays lots of games with Ma and they sometimes watch old adventure movies on television. He likes TV shows, including *Dora the Explorer* and *Spongebob*, which help connect him to 'real' kids. He is also fond of children's books, *Dylan the Digger, Alice in Wonderland* as well as stories from the Bible. Old Nick brings provisions and Sunday treats. During these visits, Jack is hidden in Wardrobe while Ma is raped.

Exterior world

Ma gets Jack to escape to Outside by a pretending he is dead. Overwhelmed and curious by new experiences and people, he is unable to understand personal boundaries. He touches Bronwyn inappropriately and wants Grandma to share a bath. Ma, delighted at first, becomes brittle and angry at how many adjustments still have to be made despite her best efforts in Room. She overdoses after a nasty TV interview, but is saved. Jack is critical of Outside, 'In the world I notice persons are nearly always stressed and have no time'.

How have the negative and positive aspects of the cultural context in *Room* shaped Jack's personality?

- Has the constrictive, sometimes violent, environment of Room negatively impacted on Jack's ability to cope with Outside?

- Have Ma's loving efforts to support and protect her son enabled him to make a successful transition between Room and Outside?

- Have the negative forces of Outside (the media and intrusive, thoughtless strangers) a more or less powerful impact on Jack than the positive forces (caring professionals, loving family, responsible strangers)?

Sample 30-mark question

'Identify at least one type of behaviour considered to be unacceptable within the world of one text on your comparative course. Explain why such behaviour is considered unacceptable in this cultural context and discuss the response or responses of society to such behaviour.'

Support your answer with reference to the text.

In Part (a) 30-mark questions on one text, no comparison is necessary. Discuss the mode only.

- Allow about 30 minutes and aim for 400 words approximately.

- Organise your answer into clear, defined paragraphs.

- Support your opinions with quotations and references from the text.

Prompt!

Refer to the mode and the question in your answer.

The purpose of the question:

- to show evidence of understanding the cultural context of the text **(focusing on the mode)**;
- to discuss the unacceptable behaviour of one or more characters in the text;
- to explore the response or responses of society to that behaviour.

Types of behaviour considered unacceptable:

- Violent or criminal acts.
- All forms of dishonesty e.g. lying, cheating, stealing, etc.
- Forming relationships considered inappropriate within society.

The response of society to such behaviour:

- Various punishments including prison or execution.
- Social ostracisation, stigmatisation/loss of face/social standing.
- Withdrawal of rights.

Decide on your opinion:

- Old Nick, Pilar and Jack behave in unacceptable way within the 'world' of the text; violent criminality, thoughtlessness, not recognising social boundaries. They are punished by society.

Make a short plan of your key points:

- Old Nick abducts Ma, imprisons her for seven years, rapes her, has two children with her. Society sends him to prison for 25 years to life.
- Pilar lets Jack see the unpleasant coverage of himself and Ma on TV. She is criticised by Dr Clay and has to apologise.
- Jack does not understand the ways of the outside world. He steals a book in the mall and throws a tantrum when he doesn't get a promised gift. He is chastised gently.

Sample answer

1 In Emma Donoghue's novel, *Room*, several characters behave in objectionable and offensive ways. There are times when Pilar, Jack and Old Nick are thoughtless, ignorant and evil, respectively in their actions and they are all punished accordingly.

2 Pilar, Dr Clay's assistant in the psychiatric hospital where Ma and Jack are being treated, thoughtlessly allows Jack to see himself and Ma on TV. 'The malnourished boy, unable to walk, is seen here lashing out.' The reporting is sensational and very negative. Jack starts to call out to his mother who is inside with Dr Clay. This type of invasive media coverage of the boy's case will only prove damaging to Jack, adding to the suffering he has already

endured. Doctor Clay emerges and 'he says mad things to Pilar'. She loses face and has to apologise to the doctor. Her reputation has been damaged.

3 Jack has spent his life in Room with Ma. He has no idea of the social boundaries of the outside world. Deana, Ma's sister-in-law takes Jack and her daughter Bronwyn to the toilet when on a trip to the mall. Deana sits Bronwyn down on the toilet and Jack reaches out to touch her. Deana hits him, scraping his hand. He has no idea of a simple social norm of keeping his hands to himself. Everyone ends up upset.

4 When in a book store in the mall he sees his favourite book, *Dylan the Digger*, and shoves it into his Dora bag. He has no concept of property and then is quickly reprimanded. The young boy crosses social boundaries unknowingly and is punished, although the adults are only beginning to realise how much Jack doesn't fully understand about the outside world.

5 Steppa, when Jack throws a tantrum because he did not receive a promised soccer ball, handles the boy differently. He firmly removes him and sits quietly with him until he calms down and then offers pie and to watch a game. Although childless himself, he understands the need for the young confused boy to express himself.

6 Old Nick commits terrible crimes. He abducts Ma when she is only nineteen and imprisons her for seven years. He rapes her constantly, resulting in a stillborn child he buries in the garden and Jack. He is sadistic, turning off the electricity to punish them. In the end, Old Nick gets what he deserves for his terrible abuse of acceptable behaviour: imprisonment for 25 years.

7 Society responds differently to characters who transgress its rules, Pilar is roundly criticised and loses face for thoughtless behaviour, Jack is punished for his ignorance while Old Nick gets the full sentence of the law for his crimes.

(445 words)

EXAMINER'S COMMENT

Overall, well-focused on the question, showing a good understanding of the cultural context mode. The response is effectively organised in paragraphs. A range of suitable illustrations from the novel support the discussion throughout – some of which include apt quotation. Expression is reasonably good except for occasional awkwardness (e.g. paragraphs 4 and 5).

(25/30 marks)

Cultural context in *Silas Marner*

Overview

- *Silas Marner* by George Eliot is set during the early 19th century in England at the start of the Industrial Revolution.
- The weaver, Silas Marner, leaves his Calvinist congregation of Lantern Yard, a slum street in Northern England, for the seclusion of the traditional village of Raveloe.
- Silas has rejected one community and isolates himself from another.
- Social class divisions are clearly evident in Raveloe.
- The novel emphasises the importance of living in harmony with one's community to forge a sense of identity and belonging.
- Emphasis is on redemption, love and a belief in God's goodness.
- Traditional aggressive male/nurturing female roles are strongly defined.
- The dominant influences of community and God provide moral and social leadership for the people.

Negative cultural influences

Lantern Yard – 'narrow religious' Calvinist sect, represents harsh and puritanical aspects of religion. The **church dominated** everyday life and Silas is a victim of its strict authority.	**Squire Cass and family of Red House, Raveloe** represents the powerful class of wealthy landowners. **Squire** is 'the greatest man in Raveloe' but only has 'a tenant or two'.	**Raveloe** represents a rich world of plenty, 'orchards looking lazy with neglected plenty'. Yet its **inward-looking society** is suspicious of strangers but also a place of lazy plenty: pints at the local inn and a carefree religion.

Negative cultural influences

Proximity to jail, **'Prison Street', suggests rigid restrictions** and lack of individual freedom.

Silas Marner is a well-respected member of the chapel, 'a young man of exemplary life and faith'.

His **cataleptic fits are treated with suspicion** – interpreted as visits from the devil by friend William Dane, another member of the religious community.

Silas has staunch religious belief – even after William and other chapel members accuse him of stealing a bag of church money – 'God will clear me'.

Suspended from chapel membership until he confesses and repents, Silas calls off his engagement to Sarah who marries the hypocritical William 'in little more than a month'.

Silas loses hope and renounces his faith, 'there is no just God that governs the earth righteously'.

– he leaves town for Raveloe.

Many years later, Silas returns to Lantern Yard with Eppie to **resolve questions of his youth.**

Everything has changed. The Industrial Revolution has swept away all traces of strict religious life, 'Lantern Yard's gone ... see that big factory ... It's all gone.'

The Red House – dark uninviting, masculine world – 'decorated with guns, whips and foxes' brushes' – suggesting every man for himself.

Squire Cass – wealthy landowner able to keep his sons at home in idleness.

Dunstan – 'a spiteful jeering fellow' who blackmails his brother Godfrey into 'borrowing' money from their father over Godfrey's secret marriage.

Later he steals Silas's gold.

Godfrey – 'good-natured' but with a dark secret – married to opium addict Molly Farren, fathered a child, Eppie, whom he disowns.

Moral coward – Godfrey allows Silas to raise Eppie in humble circumstances in order to marry Nancy whose 'principles' will not permit her to adopt a child.

Eventually, Godfrey comes to reclaim his abandoned child – he believes he did 'a father's duty' by paying Silas for Eppie's upkeep.

The Cass family characterise the decadence of England's landed gentry, focusing attention on the sharp differences in social class in the village of Raveloe.

Raveloe offers seclusion and sanctuary to Marner who is 'stunned by despair' after events in Lantern Yard – he finds security in Raveloe and is paid five guineas for creating table linen for Mrs Osgood.

There has been **little change in Raveloe** from generation to generation, 'how was a man to be explained unless you at least knew somebody who knew his father and mother'.

Country villages are suspicious of outsiders – some folk also considered weavers as '**aliens**', seeing this trade as repulsive and dehumanising – even regard Silas as a piece of machinery, 'a crooked tube, which has no meaning standing apart'.

Marner is regarded by local boys with '**half-fearful fascination**'.

Silas's attempt to help Sally Oates's dropsy with herbal foxglove treatment is misunderstood as 'charms', so local people became **apprehensive** about his so-called magical powers.

The community is wary of a reclusive man who 'never strolled into the village to drink a pint at the Rainbow Inn' – nor does Silas attend the local church.

Jem Rodney reported **strange sight** of Silas in a cataleptic fit, solid as stone, 'superstition easily clung round every person or thing that was at all unwonted'.

Changes course of Silas's life

Rigidity of chapel **has deprived Silas of friends, community and faith,** 'cut off from faith and love'. The inward-looking, self-righteous, **restrictive sect** whose reliance on Chance to prove innocence or guilt is the bad seed which produces bad fruit. Silas's question ('Why?') will never be answered, 'I shall never know whether they got at the truth o' the robbery'.	**Dunstan's actions changed Silas's life** – robbery of gold leaves him 'like a forlorn traveller on an unknown desert' and forces him to go to villagers for help. **Godfrey**'s rejection of Eppie leaves Silas in position to claim her – 'I should have thought your affection for Eppie would have made you rejoice in what was for your good, even if it did call upon you to give up something.'	Initially, Silas becomes like **an unthinking spider,** an 'insect-like existence', in Raveloe. His isolated life centres around his work – **weaving and accumulating money.** He hoards his gold coins which he regards 'as if they had been unborn children'. **Silas loves the gold for itself,** not for what it can buy, 'How the guineas shone!'

Positive cultural influences

Eppie, the abandoned daughter of opium addict Molly Farren and moral coward Godfrey Cass, is responsible for Silas, her adoptive father's redemption.	**Dolly Winthrop** befriends Silas after he adopts Eppie – she helps him become part of the Raveloe community.	**The local people of Raveloe** generously accept Silas – 'when a man had deserved his good luck, it was the part of his neighbours to wish him joy'.
Eppie symbolises innocence, **unconditional love** and hope – in contrast to the gold that Silas hoarded. She **replaces Silas's sense of value in life** from material objects – 'instead of the hard coin with the familiar resisting outline, his fingers encountered soft warm curls'. The child's presence **brings calm and contentment** to the old weaver. Eppie unlocks Silas's heart and **re-establishes connection with a community,** integrating him into society – 'the little child had come to link him once more with the whole world'.	**Dolly is a valued friend** – she offers generosity sensitively – baby clothes 'patched and darned, but clean and neat'. **She advises Silas** on disciplining the pretty two-year-old with golden hair and blue eyes, 'a fine capacity for mischief'. Dolly regards religion as a **'mystery'** – puts IHS on buns without understanding the meaning – 'they're good letters else they wouldn't be in the church'. **She encourages Silas to go to church** at Christmas, – 'you could put your trust i' Them as knows better nor we do.'	Silas seeks help at the Rainbow Inn after his gold is stolen. He accuses an innocent man, Jem Rodney, without proof (similar to his own case in Lantern Yard) – but **the locals turn to the law,** rather than cast lots to solve the crime. Unlike the brethren in Lantern Yard, the people of Raveloe **treat Silas with due respect.** Over the years, **the villagers have changed their attitude** towards Marner – who was first regarded as 'a poor mushed creatur'.

Positive cultural influences

Eppie is also **associated with nature**, 'robin', 'sunshine', 'buttercups' – and makes Silas interested in simple natural objects, 'the old winter-flies that come crawling forth in the early spring sunshine'. **She cares for Silas** – plans garden, will only wed Aaron if she can stay with Silas. Over time, Lantern Yard is rejected as 'a dark ugly place' – **freeing Silas from his unhappy past.**	**Dolly helps Silas come to terms with the past** and the truth about the robbery, 'There are many things we'll never know. It's God's will'. Her son Aaron weds Eppie, agreeing to live with Silas and take care of him.	Having observed Silas take Eppie with him while he delivered his linen, he is now **greeted with kindness** – 'open smiling faces and cheerful questioning'. Raveloe is **a close-knit vibrant community** with regular social events and traditional celebrations, such as the New Year's Eve ball in Red House. **Silas adopted the communal customs** and values of Raveloe through 'seeking what was needful for Eppie'.

Redemption

Silas shows true love by allowing Eppie to choose between him and Godfrey – 'I'll hinder nothing'. **Eppie rejects Godfrey** – 'I can't feel as I've got any father but one'. Silas finds **renewed belief in love** and the goodness of others.	After losing Kate, **Gar fails to communicate** his love for her and is left with feelings of regret, **Mrs Winthrop plays an important role in helping Silas recover his humanity and his faith** – 'that doesn't hinder there being a rights, Master Marner, for all it's dark to you and me'.	**The weaver is embraced into the community** – Raveloe society concluded that Silas 'had brought a blessing on himself by acting like a father to a lone motherless child'. This enabled him to blend his unhappy past with his happy present.

Silas's two 'worlds'

Lantern Yard

Austere industrial town with 'whitewashed walls', 'little pews' and an 'unquestioned doctrine'. Silas is a valued member of the chapel community where the people are strictly religious and puritanical, but not particularly friendly. When Silas is accused of robbery, 'any resort to legal measures' was 'contrary to the principles' of Lantern Yard. The chapel elders are superstitious – they draw lots which declare Silas guilty. He leaves in despair. Many years later when he returns to clear his name, the place has disappeared.

Raveloe

Secluded rural village; 'nestled snug in a well-wooded hollow' – pre-industrialisation. The local people are less pious – they 'keep a jolly Christmas, Whitsun and Easter tide'. Raveloe has clearly defined class divisions. Silas is an outsider and is regarded with suspicion at first. The villagers are sociable and less religious than those in Lantern Yard. They rely on law when Silas's gold is stolen. Silas is gradually drawn into the community when they see him take care of Eppie, an orphan. He eventually becomes a valued member of the community.

Cultural references in the novel

- Early 19th century England – a time of change.
- Industrial Revolution – factories, urbanisation, materialism.
- Contrasting religious practice – harsh and charitable.
- Different attitudes to punishment and reward.
- Rural areas changing traditions.
- Class divisions – Cass family wealthy landed gentry, unskilled village workers.
- Nature's regenerative power, morality, importance of loving relationships.

How have the contrasting aspects of the cultural context in the novel shaped Silas Marner's life?

- What impact has the strict, puritanical, judgemental community of Lantern Yard had on Silas?
- How has the traditional, practical, easy-going nature of the Raveloe community changed Silas?
- Which environment made the greater impact on Silas?

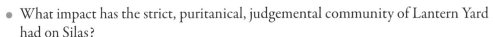

Sample 30-mark question

'The relationships between characters can be deeply revealing about the cultural context of a text.'

With reference to the above statement, compare the extent to which **at least one central relationship** in **one** of your comparative texts helped influence your understanding of the cultural context of that text. Support your answer with reference to the text.

In Part (a) 30-mark questions on one text, no comparison is necessary. Discuss the mode only.

- Allow about 30 minutes and aim for 400 words approximately.
- Organise your answer into clearly defined paragraphs.
- Support your opinions with quotations and references from the text.

Prompt!

Refer to the mode and the question in your answer.

The purpose of the question:

- to show evidence of understanding the cultural context of the text (focusing on the mode);
- to discuss at least one central relationship in the text (focusing on the question);
- to examine how it influenced your understanding of the cultural context.

Decide on your opinion:

- Silas Marner has to change and adapt to survive the negative world of Lantern Yard and to thrive in the more positive world of Raveloe.

Make a short plan of your key points:

- Silas is betrayed in Lantern Yard, resulting in his suspension from the community; this reveals a cold, rigid society.
- In Raveloe, Silas is loved by his adopted daughter, Eppie, who helps him come to terms with the past and embrace the future.
- Silas is helped by Dolly Winthrop in raising Eppie and recovers his belief in human goodness, revealing a supportive moral society.

Sample answer

1   In George Eliot's *Silas Marner*, the central character learns to change his own life through relationships, so that he can survive negative experiences. At first Silas was a respected member of his faith community in Lantern Yard, 'a young man of exemplary life'. But his so-called friend William begins to undermine Silas's reputation. He describes Silas's cataleptic fit as 'a visitation from Satan'. When a robbery is blamed on Silas and he is 'suspended from the church, William does not leap to his friend's assistance but states, 'I can do nothing but pray for you'.

2   Silas's blind faith, 'God will clear me', is shattered. Silas calls out William that he 'stole the money' and concludes 'there is no just God'. The unforgiving religious community 'shudder at this blasphemy'. This changes Silas's peace of mind completely. Lack of Christian compassion loses Silas his social position and his faith, changing everything. His unfortunate relationship with William and the cold rigid world of Lantern Yard has totally changed the course of his life.

3   After moving to the remote village of Raveloe, Silas lives like a miserly recluse until he accidentally becomes the guardian of Eppie, an abandoned child. His relationship with Eppie brings happiness and love into his life, 'the child was come instead of the gold'. He is accepted by the welcoming community of Raveloe who had previously regarded him as 'a poor mushed creature'. The simple villagers are true Christians who believe 'he had brought a blessing on himself by acting like a father to a lone motherless child'.

1   Silas also has a supportive neighbour in Dolly Winthrop who assists him in raising Eppie. Dolly is typical of the local community spirit, doing practical things to help the old weaver take care of Eppie and constantly bringing them lard cakes. She also helps him get back his faith and take part in Raveloe's traditional celebration of Christmas when her son sings the carol, 'God rest you merry gentlemen'. Dolly's honesty and practical help encourages Silas to accept that he cannot change the past. She advises him to leave things be, 'It's the will o' Them above as a many things should be dark to us'.

5   Through these relationships, Silas Marner learned to deal with two very different worlds, strict Lantern Yard and friendly Raveloe. He turns from his totally unhappy past and faces into a bright future with Eppie and the good people of Raveloe. In the end, Eppie sums up their lives together when she says 'what pretty home ours is! I think nobody could be happier than we are'.

(430 words)

EXAMINER'S COMMENT

High-grade response. The three relationships range widely, engaging well with the novel. Includes some interesting discussion on key aspects of the contrasting worlds of Lantern Yard and Raveloe – but a little more direct focus on cultural context would be welcome. Expression is clear, overall – although there is some repetition (e.g. paragraph 2). Points are aptly supported by relevant reference and quotation.

(24/30 marks)

Cultural context in *Unforgiven*

Overview

- Western movie directed by Clint Eastwood set in Big Whiskey, Wyoming, in the early 1880s.
- This is a dangerous patriarchal world filled with gunfighters whose taming forged America's identity.
- The main business in town, the brothel, is run by Skinny Dubois, who regards the sex workers as 'property' rather than human beings.
- After Delilah Fitzgerald is disfigured by cowboys, her fellow brothel workers offer a reward for the guilty men's murder.
- Opportunists look for easy money. William Munny, Ned Logan and the Schofield Kid arrive in town to collect the bounty.
- English Bob also wants the reward. He has a ruthless reputation as a killer of Chinese railway workers.
- Sheriff Little Bill Daggett is keen to implement the law, but is more concerned with property rights than an individual's rights.
- Male supremacy and order are enforced by routine violence.
- The Wild West is depicted as an impoverished and often unheroic man's world.

Negative cultural influences

Law	Violence	Local business
Little Bill Daggett, sheriff of Big Whiskey, represents the authority of the law in the town.	**The Schofield Kid** and **English Bob** represent violent assassins.	**Skinny Dubois and the exploited sex workers who work for him** are an important part of business life in the town.
Little Bill, former gunslinger, trying to become an honest man – but even his nickname is false. **Efficient lawman** – determined to keep crime away from his town – 'violence isn't the answer'. **A mediator of the peace** – the centre of authority, but detached. **Fails to enforce law justly,** puts business first – accepts Skinny's argument that sex workers are 'property' and concludes the cowboys were not 'bad men' but 'just two hard-working boys that was foolish'. **Sadistic** – beats English Bob senseless for having a firearm, 'I'll have that 32, Bob'. Crowd stand mute at the savagery with which he enforces the law. **Little Bill abuses power** – beats Munny for having a gun, forces him to crawl from saloon – also beats to death Ned Logan whose mutilated body is put on display in a coffin outside salon with warning sign 'This is what happens to assassins'.	**The Schofield Kid** is not a skilled gunfighter, but a brash kid full of bluster who takes his name from his gun. **Desperate** to get the $1,000 bounty. **He taunts** Munny – 'You don't look like no rootin' tootin' son of a bitchin' cold blooded assassin'. **He also dismisses Will** – 'He ain't nuthin' but a broken-down old pig farmer'. **The Kid is morally blind** – thinks murder is no big deal and being an outlaw is cool. **English Bob** – a British-born gunfighter is eager for the bounty. **He has an old association with Little Bill** – 'It's been a long time'. **He is disarmed by Little Bill** who expels him from town as an example to others.	**Skinny** is owner of Greely's Saloon and regards sex workers as 'stupid bitches'. He thinks that 'women can lie' and are untrustworthy. **He sees sex workers not as people**, but as 'a contract that represents an investment of capital'. **Skinny is pragmatic** – 'nobody's gonna pay good money for a cut-up whore' – and agrees to sheriff's 'no fuss' solution. **Strawberry Alice**, leader of the sex workers, tries to excuse Delilah's naivety about the attack. **Wyoming is a patriarchal world** – 'she didn't know no better'. **But Alice also demands stern justice** – 'you gonna hang 'em, Little Bill?' **She organises a generous $1,000 bounty** for assassins and is outraged, 'by God we ain't horses'. **Acceptance would equate them with horses**. Both Bill and Alice make the same mistake, equating a person with financial worth.

Negative impact

Unjust enforcer of the law – Munny kills him in revenge for Ned's brutal death. **Daggett believes he was right** – 'I don't deserve to die like this.' He wanted to be a member of the community – but doesn't achieve his dream of sitting on his porch watching the sunset. **No redemption** – 'I'll see you in hell.'	The Schofield Kid is also **unmasked** – not a real killer. **Suffers breakdown** – 'I ain't like you, Will.' **English Bob** – disgraced and exposed as a killer of Chinese workers on the railroads – 'You run out of Chinamen?' **Status of legendary gunfighter deflated** when the truth is revealed.	Skinny is killed by Munny although 'unarmed'. **Strawberry Alice** – morally inferior, morally wronged. **Lacks independence** in a man's world and is driven by vengeance rather than justice. **Alice's thirst for vengeance threatens all civilised life in town.**

Positive cultural influences

Friend	Wife
Ned Logan, friend to Will Munny and former notorious gunslinger, now married and a successful farmer.	**Claudia Feathers**, deceased wife of William Munny, reforms the notorious gunslinger into a sober farmer with two children, a son and daughter.
Ned is also in 'retirement' as a farmer, joins Will to break monotony of farm life; tempted to relive his glory days when they 'were young and full of beans'. **Shows his age** – and is not used to living rough, 'I sure do miss my bed'. **Close confidant to Munny** who discloses, 'I ain't the same, Ned … I just need the money, get a new start for them youngsters.' **Consoling influence** – 'Easy, partner, easy'. **Loyal** – 'I don't kill nobody without him.' **Rejects life of violence** – gives Will his rifle.	**Claudia frames the story** – opening shot of Munny digging wife's grave; she died from smallpox, 'a comely young woman and not without prospects'. **Will acknowledges the supportive role Claudia played** in reforming him – 'your departed mother, God rest her, showed me the errors of my ways.' **Respect** for his wife's memory makes Will decline Delilah's offer of a 'free one'. **Claudia's guidance helped Will** – 'I ain't had a drop in over ten years. My wife, she cured me of that, cured me of drink and wickedness.' Will **hopes to give his children a better life** – needs the money to get a new start for 'them youngsters'.

Overall influence

Positive	Positive
Ned Logan encourages Will – 'We ain't bad men no more'. **Gives an honourable reason** for killing – 'if you was mad at 'em … If they'd done you wrong, I could see shooting 'em'.	**Claudia brings out the best in Will** – she saw good in 'a known thief and murderer' and had forgiven him. The former gunslinger's life was changed by 'the love of a good woman'.

Positive cultural influences

Overall influence *contd.*

Agrees to killing because a woman was attacked – 'I guess they had it coming'.	**Her influence** continues to grow after her death – she makes him realise that 'It's a hell of a thing, killin' a man'.
Becomes a substitute version of Claudia, reminding Will – 'you wouldn't be doing this if Claudia was alive'.	**Claudia's moral voice** is reinforced by Ned's friendship and is personified by soft guitar tune.
Ned's death – a motive for Munny's killing of Little Bill, 'And I'm here to kill you, Little Bill, for what you did to Ned'.	Munny, the angry spirit, the 'Angel o' Death', terrifies others into doing what is right – in the end, he has become a **force of redemptive violence**.

Past and present in *Unforgiven*

The past haunts William Munny. He is traumatised by memories of savage killings he committed and he is deeply influenced by his wife Claudia. Her goodness led him to reform his wicked ways and develop a strong moral sense.

The present is difficult to negotiate for the reformed gunslinger. Will fails at farming and his family is short of money. He is tempted to return to his old ways to solve his problems, but struggles, he cannot hit a coffee tin. His friend Ned enables him to find a path by adapting his violence for a good cause, righting a wrong.

How have the negative and positive aspects of the cultural context in *Unforgiven* shaped Munny's personality?

- Has he reverted back to the indifferent violent killer of 'women and children' of his past?
- Has he changed under the influence of Claudia and Ned to become a violent force for the restoration of good?
- Is Munny able to achieve his goal of providing a better life for his children at the film's conclusion?

Sample 30-mark question

'The opening scene (or scenes) of a text can reveal valuable insights into the impact the cultural context of a narrative is likely to have on the outcome of the story.'

Discuss this view in relation to your study of one text on your comparative course.

In Part (a) 30-mark questions on one text, no comparison is necessary. Discuss the mode only.

- Allow about 30 minutes and aim for at least 400 words.
- Organise your answer into clear, defined paragraphs.
- Support your opinions with quotations and references from the text.

Prompt!

Refer to the mode and the question in your answer.

The purpose of the question:

- to show how the opening scenes reveal aspects of the world of the text **(focusing on the mode)**;
- to discuss how these insights into the world of the text impact on the outcome of the story in the text;
- to show the initial impact of setting/atmosphere on characters and events;
- to prove that cultural aspects of opening scenes often foreshadow tragic developments.

Decide on your opinion:

- Harsh setting encourages characters to focus on survival through money and violence.

Make a short plan of your key points:

- Impoverished farmer buries wife; unsuccessful in providing for family.
- Sex worker has face slashed by angry cowboy for insult.
- Law is reduced to unsavoury business transaction, rather than justice.
- Violence and money lead to tragic outcome.

Sample answer

1   The first scenes of Clint Eastwood's revisionist Western, *Unforgiven*, reveals a world of economic deprivation and violence. Money is needed to survive in this scenically beautiful but harsh world of the Wild West of America where law and order is enforced through savage violence.

2   Early on, Will Munny is silhouetted against an orange sunset. His broken-down cabin symbolises the harshness of rural life. A scrolling message fills in the back story. This 'thief and murderer' is digging a grave for his wife Claudia who has died of smallpox. This is a result of the unforgiving life of the frontier. Mournful music, 'Claudia's Theme', adds to the mood, depicting the harsh reality of life.

3   The second scene takes place two years later in 1880 in the frontier town of Big Whiskey. Heavy rain pelts against the night scene of Greely's Saloon. The camera moves inside to where sex is for sale. Quick camera shots expose a savage scene. A woman's face is slashed by an angry cowboy customer as punishment for laughing at him as he undressed. A sharp click stops the attack as Skinny Dubois, the brothel owner, pulls a gun on the cowboy. Delilah is Skinny's 'property'. She has been damaged.

4   In the third scene, Skinny complains. He tells Sheriff Little Bill Daggett that his 'investment' is in danger. It's because 'nobody' gonna pay good money for a cut-up whore'. Little Bill represents law and order. He agrees to treat the attack as a property issue. He just fines the two cowboys seven ponies. Strawberry Alice speaks up for the sex workers. She wants more. She protests loudly, 'It ain't fair, Bill'. But the sheriff has already decided that the cowboys were 'hard-working boys who was foolish'.

5   These scenes shatter the myth about the Wild West which was really a place where money and male violence ruled. Rather than fairness and justice rule. The angry sex workers are driven to raise $1,000 to get justice for Delilah by hiring assassins to kill her attackers. It results in Munny, the hard-up pig farmer, being tempted. The outcome is many deaths and a town plunged into even more lawlessness.

6   Munny restores some order, but it is achieved through vicious actions and threats, 'better bury Ned right, better not cut up or otherwise harm no whores. Or I'll come back and kill everyone of you sons o' bitches'. Violence and poverty, seen in the opening scenes, reveal important lessons into the impact the cultural context of *Unforgiven* has on the story's violent conclusion.

(415 words)

EXAMINER'S COMMENT

Impressive introductory paragraph focused on cultural context and a sustained overall response to the question. Evidence of understanding of aspects – particularly violence, justice and patriarchy – prevailing in 1880s America. Discussion points are effectively supported by relevant reference and apt quotation. Language use is reasonably good apart from some note-like expression (e.g. paragraph 4). The commentary on the mode is also rounded off successfully.

(25/30 marks)

The part (b) question

In the 40-mark part (b) Comparative Study question, you are asked to compare aspects of the cultural context mode in two of the prescribed texts.

The language of comparison requires you to respond in blocks of paragraphs, interweaving comparative points.

Useful comparative phrases include:

- In a similar way ...
- The opening scene is distinctive ...
- By contrast ...
- This is not the case in ...
- Both texts are alike ...

- In a slightly different way ...
- This is mirrored in ...
- On the other hand ...
- The conclusions differ significantly ...
- This is evident in all three stories ...

Sample part (b) question (40 marks)

'Understanding who holds the power and who is powerless helps to reveal the cultural context in texts.'

Compare how the distribution of power within two of the texts on your comparative course helps to reveal the cultural contexts in these texts.

Prompt!

Respond to the question by taking a comparative approach and referring closely to the mode.

The purpose of the question:

- to address the three key elements (question, mode, comparison);
- to point out the similarities and differences (**comparison**);
- to show how the distribution of power helps to reveal (**question**);
- to examine the cultural context (**mode**) in two texts.

Decide on your opinion:

- Wealth and influence are two aspects of power which impact on characters positively/negatively and expose the cultural context of texts.

Make a short plan of your key points

- *Philadelphia*: Gar, Ned and Madge are powerless while S. B., Senator Doogan, the Canon and Master Boyle all have positions of power. Gar is unable to break free.
- *Room*: Ma and Jack are powerless victims. Old Nick is in a position of power. In contrast to *Philadelphia*, a kind stranger, caring professionals and Ma's family are supportive.

Sample answer

1   The cultural contexts in *Philadelphia, Here I Come* and *Room* are revealed as we become aware of who is powerful and who is powerless, and why. Friel's play has three powerless characters; Gar, Ned and Madge. They are financially dependent on older men – which inhibits their actions. S. B. O'Donnell, Senator Doogan, the Canon and Master Boyle hold power in business, politics, religion and education respectively. None of them use their power compassionately. In the novel, Ma and Jack are held captive by Old Nick. They're completely dependent on him. However, in this text, some caring professionals, a kind stranger and loving family enable Ma and Jack to overthrow Old Nick and become powerful.

2   Gar depends for money on his father. His only independent means is £1 a month from an egg trade that S. B. 'knows nothing about'. Ned can't buy Gar a decent going away present because 'the aul fella didn't sell the calf to the jobbers'. Madge has to use the money she had saved in order to give Gar something to mark his emigration. She is powerless to intervene between father and son as she is their paid housekeeper. None of these powerless characters feel free to express their frustrations openly.

3   Jack and Ma in *Room* are also financially dependent. Old Nick brings 'Sunday treat' and food. 'Plenty girls would thank their lucky stars for a setup like this, safe as houses'. Cruelly he cuts off their electricity when he becomes displeased. He threatens that 'he'd go away' and Ma would become 'hungrier and hungrier till I died'.

4   Friel's play shows how those in power intimidate the powerless. Master Boyle insults his former pupil, 'of average intelligence'. Senator Doogan confuses Gar and stops him from asking permission to marry his daughter. The Canon fails his congregation and ignores Gar's approaching emigration. Gar Private knows that the Canon fails to 'translate all this loneliness' into 'Christian terms' so that life might be 'bearable' for S. B. and himself. S. B. does not 'hear' Gar when he mentions a childhood memory of a fishing trip on a blue boat. Gar has no support in Ballybeg to enable him to break free. He remains powerless.

5   But Jack and Ma are more fortunate. Ajeet, a stranger, challenges Old Nick and calls the police when he sees Jack's distress, a stark contrast to the Canon in Ballybeg. Officer Oh listens patiently, unlike S. B., to Jack's story of 'a trick' he and Ma did on Old Nick, which leads to the release of Ma. Dr Clay encourages Ma's confidence and Grandma minds Jack while Ma recovers after attempting suicide. All these supports enable Ma and Jack to escape the clutches of their evil predator and help end their powerless existence as his victims.

6   Examining powerful and powerless characters led me to a better understanding of the contrasting worlds in each text. Money and position made powerful characters in *Philadelphia, Here I Come*. Money and position also made powerful characters in *Room*. But Gar just swapped one prison for another when he emigrated, 'She'll tuck you into your air-conditioned cot every night' because those in power abused that power. In contrast Jack and Ma said goodbye to Room helped by those who used their power to support them.

(540 words)

EXAMINER'S COMMENT

Solid mid-grade response that shows reasonable engagement with the two texts. Some good use of supportive quotation integrated into the commentary. The observations in paragraph 3 lack development. Elsewhere, other discussion points need to focus more directly on the social norms and prevailing values in both texts. Paragraph 5 includes some effective comparison. Expression is functional, overall – but repetitive and note-like at times.

(29/40 marks)

Sample part (b) question (40 marks)

'Aspects of cultural context affect the extent to which a character can be happy or successful within the world of a text.'

Identify a central character in two of the prescribed texts on your comparative course. Compare the aspect/s of the cultural context in each of these texts that, in your opinion, most affects/affect the extent to which your chosen characters are happy or successful.

You may refer to the same or different aspects of cultural in each of your chosen texts.

Support your answer with reference to the texts.

Prompt!

Respond to the question by taking a comparative approach and referring closely to the mode.

The purpose of the question:

- to address the three key elements (question, mode, comparison);
- to point out the similarities and differences (**comparison**);
- to examine aspects of the cultural context (**mode**);
- to reveal impact on the happiness or success of two characters from two texts (**question**).

Decide on your opinion:

- Money, justice and community influence Will Munny and Silas Marner's chances of achieving happiness and success.

Make a short plan of your key points:

- *Unforgiven*: A Wild West town's patriarchal community reacts unjustly to violence against a woman. Will Munny is lured by a bounty to take revenge and achieves some fulfilment in the end.
- *Silas Marner*: Lantern Yard's strict religious community reacts unjustly to a theft of money which negatively influences Silas's chance of happiness. He eventually achieves fulfilment in the more compassionate rural community of Ravaloe.

Both Silas and Will eventually overcome the negative forces in their communities.

Sample answer

1 Will Munny, a 'broken down old pig farmer' and former notorious gunslinger, is the central character in Clint Eastwood's Western, *Unforgiven*. Silas Marner, a miserly weaver, 'stunned with despair', expelled from his community for stealing, is the central character in George Eliot's novel *Silas Marner*. Both characters are negatively impacted by the attitude to money and justice in their respective social worlds and redeemed by the positive influence of good friends.

2 Silas Marner's troubles begin with a false accusation that he had stolen a bag of church money. Silas, 'a young man of exemplary life and faith' really believed 'God will clear me'. The Lantern Yard community had no 'resort to legal means' because it was 'contrary' to their principles. So they drew lots and Silas was expelled. He declared 'there is no just God that governs the earth righteously'. Silas left his home to seek contentment elsewhere. Lantern Yard's injustice, its refusal to work with the agency of the law and their attitude to wealth negatively impact Silas's chance of happiness.

3 Similarly, Will Munny in the film *Unforgiven* is also prevented from securing happiness because of an absence of money. His pigs are sick, he has no income to provide for his two children. So he is lured by the prospect of a $1,000 bounty put up by sex workers who feel they have been treated unjustly by the law. They, like the community of Lantern Yard, seek justice outside the authorized guardians of the law. He, like Silas, leaves his home. Munny, like Silas, has been deprived of money and is dealing with a society which does not obey the recognised rule of law.

4 Silas has his beloved gold replaced by an orphaned girl, Eppie. Through her he learns to live in a more tolerant community, 'the little child had come to link him once more with the whole world'. He makes a new friend, Dolly Winthrop, who helps him raise the child and encourages Silas to live well by going to church at Christmas, 'you could put your trust i' Them as knows better nor we do'.

5 Will also has a good friend, Ned Logan, who encourages him not to revert back to his violent past where he indifferently killed 'women and children'. Ned points out that killing should only be done for a just cause, 'If they'd done you wrong, I could see shooting 'em.' Will Munny kills Little Bill in retribution for the torture and death of Ned, 'I'm here to kill you, Little Bill, for what you did to Ned'. He killed Skinny Dubois because he used the corpse of Ned to 'decorate his saloon'. Silas and Will have replaced their focus on money to a focus on doing what is right, thanks to the influence of good friends.

6 Two men were impacted negatively by the lure of money and injustice. Two men were set on a path of redemption through love and friendship, so Will Munny and Silas Marner achieved a level of contentment.

(500 words)

70-mark question

In the 70-mark Comparative Study question, you are asked to compare aspects of the cultural context mode in three of the prescribed texts.

Sample 70-mark question

'Moments of crisis for central characters can be crucial in revealing the cultural context of a text.'

Compare how aspects of the society in your **three** comparative texts are revealed by the response of central characters at a crucial point in their story.

Prompt!

Respond to the question by taking a comparative approach and referring closely to the mode.

The purpose of the question:

- to address the three key elements (comparison, question, mode);
- to compare and contrast (**comparison**);
- to examine the response of central characters to moments of crisis (**question**);
- to reveal the cultural contexts in three texts (**mode**).

Structuring the answer

Make a short plan of your key points:

- **Intro:** Name your three comparative text choices and their authors. State whether you agree, disagree or partially agree with the statement in the question. Outline the cultural context points you are going to discuss.

- Allow about 65–70 minutes and aim for at least 900 words, organised into paragraphs.
- Focus on the cultural context mode.
- Develop comparative points with suitable reference to the three texts.

- *Philadelphia*: Gar fails to marry Kate Doogan, reflecting the oppressive class divisions and stagnation of Irish rural life in the 1960s.
- *Room*: Jack escapes from Room, freeing himself and Ma from Old Nick, their captor. This highlights the positive power of family love to overcome evil in a dangerous world.
- *Unforgiven*: Will Munny succeeds in avenging wrongs for honourable reasons, revealing a violent patriarchal world.
- **Conclusion:** Sum up central arguments and overall response to the question.

Sample answer

1   The worlds created in my three comparative texts, *Philadelphia, Here I Come* by Brian Friel, *Room* by Emma Donoghue and *Unforgiven* directed by Clint Eastwood, are revealed through the decisions made by the central character in each text at a moment of crisis. Gar's failure to take action exposes the stagnating environment of rural Ireland in the 1960s. Jack's 'Scaredybrave' action in *Room* reveals how love for his mother enables him to overcome the daunting obstacles of their imprisonment. Will Munny overcomes the challenges of moral corruption and mindless violence in the Wild West of the 1880s, like Jack, through love for his deceased wife, his children and his friend, Ned.

2   In Friel's play, Gar has to face Senator Doogan to ask permission to marry Kate. She has done all she can to bolster Gar's case inventing a fictitious salary of £20 a week, £5,000 in the bank and a story about S. B.'s impending retirement. Gar lacks confidence, 'they'll wipe the bloody floor with me'. Kate presses him, 'it's up to you entirely'. However, Senator Doogan, the polished politician, is intent on putting this upstart in his place. He uses hints and innuendo, introducing a rival for Kate, Francis King, who is in line for 'the new dispensary job'. He pulls the class card, King's 'father did medicine and I did law' and they hung around together. Gar rashly judges Kate as an 'aul bitch', totally accepting the older man's 'version' of events. He excuses himself, 'I think I'd better move on'. He, financially dependent on his father with no income, who left university after one year, ignored by the Canon and belittled by his former teacher for being 'of average intelligence', cannot find the courage to fight for Kate, despite her love for him. The negative conditioning of Ballybeg has paralysed him.

3   Jack, the five-year-old in *Room*, also has to make a crucial decision. Ma, like Kate, prepares him for this. Jack has to make the 'Great Escape' from 'Room' to save them both. Jack, like Gar, is scared and vows 'I won't do it not ever and I hate you'. Ma gently explains 'Scared is what you're feeling. Brave is what you're doing'. Jack's feelings of not wanting to disappoint his Ma are greater than his fear, 'you said you were going to be my superhero'. Jack, unlike Gar, will break free of his constrictive environment. Jack's 'dizzy' but he succeeds in rolling out of Rug when he is placed in the back of Old Nick's truck who thinks he is dead. He fights off Old Nick raising Ajeet's concerns so that the police are called. He manages to explain

to the patient Officer Oh about the 'cunning trick' he and Ma pulled on Old Nick, and to show his note and explain how Room is 'not on any map'. His refusal to submit to the constricting force of Old Nick, unlike Gar who is overcome by Ballybeg, results in his and Ma's freedom so that they can do 'anything now'.

4 Will Munny, like Gar and Jack, also has to make an important decision. An alcoholic gunslinger who 'killed women and children' is now reformed due to a woman's influence. Claudia, his deceased wife, like Kate and Ma, has tried to influence. Munny is reformed, 'I don't touch that stuff no more'; he no longer kills, 'I ain't no angry killin' fool'. But he like Gar and Jack is in a restricted environment, a struggling pig farmer with two children to rear and not enough money. He like Gar feels a failure, he can't mount his horse, can't shoot a coffee tin off a tree stump. Although he starts on his journey to resume killing for a bounty, everything changes with a significant event. His friend Ned, who had been bullwhipped to death by the sheriff and placed in a coffin outside Greely's Saloon with a sign, 'This is what happens to assassins around here', awakens in Munny a motive of grim moral revenge.

5 A sharp click in the foreground signals Munny's arrival in Big Whiskey. He kills Skinny Dubois, the saloon owner for daring to enter his saloon 'with my friend'. He, unlike his actions in the past, does not kill indiscriminately. He issues a warning, 'Any man don't want to get killed better clear on out the back'. When the fatally wounded sheriff complains, 'I don't deserve this', Munny replies, 'Deserve's got nuthin' to do with it'. All anybody deserves is the opportunity to go after what they want to become, they must earn the right to get what they are after. Munny's redemptive violence has removed a sadistic sheriff who abused his power. He rides out of town in the teeming rain, issuing a warning to the locals to mend their ways, 'you better bury Ned right. You better not cut up nor otherwise harm no whores' otherwise he vows to return to kill everyone. Munny, like Jack, has defeated the forces of evil corruption by violent confrontation and both earn a hopeful future. Munny, according to the scrolling writing at the film's conclusion is 'rumoured' to have settled in San Francisco with his children and to have 'prospered in dry goods', thereby achieving his aim of securing a better future for his children.

6 The three central characters in my comparative texts reacted in different ways to their moment of crisis. Gar, defeated by the oppressive society of Ballybeg, fails to rise to the moment, preferring to blank out reality. Jack, in contrast, bravely rises to the occasion and frees himself and Ma. Munny also rose to the occasion, swapping mindless violence for righteous vengeance.

(940 words)

Checklist

○ Identify all key elements within the question.

○ Discuss cultural context mode throughout.

○ Avoid unfocused narrative summary.

○ Use the language of comparison.

○ Develop personal opinions on how the cultural context shapes your understanding of texts.

○ Practise making plans for past paper questions to prepare effective responses.

General vision and viewpoint

Prescribed mode for 2021 and 2022

> • Studying texts by examining the 'broad outlook' on life that is presented.
> • Understanding the overall impact of a particular text on the reader or viewer.

The general vision and viewpoint mode refers to the **broad outlook** of a particular text.

For example, if a writer is critical of a society, events or central characters, the vision of the text is likely to be dark and **negative**. If the outlook in the text is **positive** and life-affirming, the author might well be showing the courage and resilience of characters as they overcome or come to terms with problems and circumstances.

Texts can usually be described as:

- **optimistic** – bright, hopeful, favourable, inspiring
- **pessimistic** – dark, hopeless, critical, cynical

> • You are not required to make a distinction between vision and viewpoint.
> • Both terms refer to the overall impact of a text.

- **realistic** – credible, accurate, truthful
- **ambiguous** – unresolved, unclear, contradictory, etc. (or any combination of these)

The **ending** of a story is very important in determining the viewpoint. Whether happy or sad (or a mix of both), the central conflict must be resolved, and the ending has to be believable within the 'world' of the story.

Readers and audiences will ultimately form their own views about the outlook of the text.

Responding to the author's treatment of a theme

An optimistic outlook can be reflected by:

- the resilience of characters who have developed and matured
- some sense of redemption at the end; friendships endure, etc.

The viewpoint is pessimistic or tragic because:

- the plot focuses on suffering and failure
- an author's views are bitter and cynical
- the 'world' of the text is unjust, oppressive, violent
- language use and symbols add to the negativity.

The reader/audience may interpret the text as being balanced and realistic:

- if the future is not likely to be bleak for every character
- if death is a release for some characters
- if comic moments compensate for some of the unhappiness
- if we are given a realistic insight into a particular time and place
- if lyrical/descriptive language adds beauty
- if the ending is credible within the context of the story.

> **key point**
>
> Modes overlap. For example, the culture influences the general vision and viewpoint of a text.

Vision and viewpoint is dark/negative

The author presents obstacles and challenges which prevent a central character becoming fulfilled.

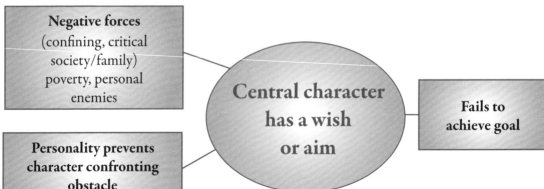

Negative forces (confining, critical society/family) poverty, personal enemies

Personality prevents character confronting obstacle

Central character has a wish or aim

Fails to achieve goal

Vision and viewpoint is bright/positive

The author presents supports and encouragement which help a character become fulfilled.

Positive forces (caring, compassionate society/family) money, good luck, personal friends

Central character has a wish or aim

Succeeds in achieving goal

Personality enables character to confront obstacle

How authors establish vision and viewpoint			
Drama	**Novel**	**Novel**	**Film**
Philadelphia, Here I Come! **Brian Friel**	*Room* **Emma Donoghue**	*Silas Marner* **George Eliot**	*Unforgiven* **Clint Eastwood**
What mood is established by the setting of the text?			
1960s fictional Irish town, Ballybeg, Co. Donegal, eve of Gar's emigration to America. His dreary routine existence is marked by lack of opportunity and provincial suffocation. Blurring of reality and fiction. Overpowering sense of oppression and claustrophobia. **Mood is downbeat.**	Modern times, modern city, 11 ft by 11 ft garden shed with skylight. Ma and Jack are cruelly imprisoned. Their solitary existence isolates them from the outside world. They fear violence. Limited opportunities. **Mood varies –** claustrophobic and bleak yet secure.	1800s Industrial Revolution, England. Opening urban setting Lantern Yard, a puritanical religious sect. By contrast, the secluded setting of idyllic village Raveloe offers friendship and hope. **Mood varies** – initially dark, but turns optimistic.	1880s American Wild West. Beautiful natural landscapes. Sordid, forlorn frontier town of Big Whiskey. Violent, desolate, male-dominated, morally corrupt. Harsh environment, difficult to make honest living. **Dominant mood** is unforgiving and dark.

How authors establish vision and viewpoint

What is the central character's aim/wish/dream?

Gar wishes to **escape** oppressive small-town life by emigrating to America, land of opportunity. He also wants to be told to stay.	Jack and Ma are desperate to **escape** the cruel confinement of Room to find freedom to live independently and without fear.	Ageing farmer Will Munny plans to **escape** his failing life. He hopes for a better future by becoming a bounty hunter.	Silas Marner **wants to escape** the injustice and disappointment he experienced in Lantern Yard. He aims to make money weaving.

What are the obstacles preventing this aim?

Gar's personality is **deeply conflicted**. Aunt Lizzy's overpowering personality.	Tyranny of their **cruel captor** Old Nick. Predatory media attention.	**Will's promise** to his deceased wife to reform. Corruption of the forces of law.	**Silas thinks gold brings happiness**, but his coins are stolen and replaced by an orphaned child.

Has the main character supporters or enemies who help or hinder?

Supporters – Madge, Kate, Ned. **Enemies** – Senator Doogan, Master Boyle, Canon O'Byrne, S. B.	**Supporters** – Ajeet, Officer Oh, Dr Clay, Grandma, Steppa. **Enemies** – Old Nick, the media and public's curiosity, Grandpa.	**Supporters** – Eppie, Dolly Winthrop, Raveloe villagers. **Enemies** – William Dane, Dunstan and Godfrey Cass, Lantern Yard community.	**Supporters** – Claudia, Ned Logan, Delilah and sex workers. **Enemies** – Little Bill, the community in Big Whiskey.

What is the critical decision made by the main character?

Fails to ask Senator Doogan's permission to marry Kate; fails to communicate with father.	Jack and Ma agree on a daring plan, which enables them to escape from Room.	Everything changes for the better when Silas willingly adopts a young orphaned girl, Eppie.	Will Munny resumes his old violent lifestyle as a gunslinger to claim the $1,000 bounty.

Is the conclusion optimistic/pessimistic or realistic/unresolved?

Unresolved	**Optimistic overall**	**Realistic**	**Optimistic overall**
Gar physically escapes his unhappy life in Ballybeg. He has lost Kate, however and is already preparing to relive memories.	Ma and Jack escape, Old Nick caught. But the security of Room is gone for Jack who is beginning to realises that it will always be a part of him.	Will Munny has changed; he no longer kills thoughtlessly but for honourable reasons. But righteous revenge, while moral, is still brutal.	Symbolised by the fairytale wedding of Eppie and Aaron. Silas has to leave behind past injustice unsolved. Industrial changes are coming.

How authors establish vision and viewpoint

Is the conclusion optimistic/pessimistic or realistic/unresolved? *contd.*

Gar's future is uncertain – he doesn't fully understand why he is leaving home.	Ma and Jack's strong mutual love ensures a positive conclusion.	Will's rumoured new life in San Francisco points to redemption of sorts.	Silas and Eppie's enduring love, highlights the redemptive ending.

General vision and viewpoint in *Philadelphia, Here I Come!*

Sample part (a) question (30 marks)

'Our personal beliefs and values can influence our sense of the general vision and viewpoint of a text.'

With reference to one text on your comparative course, explain how your sense of the general vision and viewpoint was influenced by at least one of your personal beliefs. Support your answer with reference to the text.

Prompt!

Refer to the mode and the question in your answer.

The purpose of the question:

● to show evidence of understanding the general vision and viewpoint of the text (**focusing on the mode**);

● to discuss how a personal view or belief can affect the reader's sense of the general vision and viewpoint of the text (**question**).

Decide on your opinion:

● My sense of general vision and viewpoint is influenced by my belief that the play's final scenes were open-ended and reflected the conflicted views emigrants have about leaving home.

Make a short plan of your key points:

● Gar's uncertainty about leaving;

● lasting memories of home;

● future in America is unclear.

In Part (a) 30-mark questions on one text, no comparison is necessary. Discuss the mode only.

● Allow about 30 minutes and aim for at least 400 words.

● Organise your answer into clear, defined paragraphs.

● Support your opinions with quotations and references from the text.

Sample answer

1   My sense of the general vision in Brian Friel's *Philadelphia, Here I Come* was coloured by the extent to which I found the conclusion ambiguous. Gar did get to escape Ballybeg by emigrating to the land of opportunity that is America. But I felt he brought Ballybeg with him because of his tortured divided personality, Public and Private Gar. I believe he will be unlikely to follow Master Boyle's advice, 'be 100 per cent American'. Whether or not he will be happy there is questionable.

2   Although Gar found his hometown 'a backwater, a dead-end', it provided him with memories of 'precious, precious gold'. He is aware the 'boys' are all talk but he recalls 'there was fun and there was laughing'. Similarly, he will remember Madge. He gives instructions to himself as if he were a film director, 'watch her carefully... for this is a film you'll run over and over again'. He will be in America physically, but I imagine his heart and mind will be in Ballybeg. It's likely that this must be a common attitude young emigrants have and I believe this affected my sense of an uncertain viewpoint in the play.

3   Gar made a sudden decision to emigrate because his Aunt Lizzy invited him on a particularly vulnerable day. Kate, his former girlfriend, was getting married and his father had failed to share his childhood memories of fishing in a 'blue boat'. Aunt Lizzy accused him of being like his father 'an O'Donnell – cold-like'. I wondered if Aunt Lizzy was going to eventually treat Gar with the same disrespect which she treated her husband with. I believe Gar will find her controlling. He already fears she will treat him as the child she never had. The play's conclusion has Gar Private asking what I wanted to know, 'why do you have to leave?' It ends with the unsatisfactory response, 'I don't know'. This is why I believe the outlook in this play to be ambiguous.

4   Madge regarded Gar to be very like S. B., 'as like as two peas'. Each person lived in their own minds presenting a false public persona. I think Gar will live for a while like S. B. in his memories of his past even though he is in America which 'doesn't give a curse about the past'. Yet there is always a chance that he will make a better life for himself. In summary, my personal views on emigrants like Gar make me believe that that Friel's play is ambiguous.

(415 words)

EXAMINER'S COMMENT

Focused high-grade response to the task and the text with a sustained emphasis on how personal views influence the sense of general vision and viewpoint. A range of interesting points are cited based on apt references to significant scenes. These are well-supported by relevant quotation. Expression is clear – though slightly awkward in paragraph 3 and there is overuse of the verb 'believe' throughout.

(26/30 marks)

General vision and viewpoint in *Room*

Sample part (a) question (30 marks)

'Relationships between central characters can shape our sense of the general vision and viewpoint of texts'.

Discuss the extent to which your sense of the general vision and viewpoint of one text on your comparative course is influenced by one (or more) central relationship(s) in the text.

Support your answer with reference to the text.

In Part (a) 30-mark questions on one text, no comparison is necessary. Discuss the mode only.

- Allow about 30 minutes and aim for at least 400 words.
- Organise your answer into clear, defined paragraphs.
- Support your opinions with quotations and references from the text.

Prompt!

Refer to the mode and the question in your answer.

The purpose of the question:

- to show evidence of understanding the general vision and viewpoint of the text (**focusing on the mode**);
- to discuss the impact of one or more relationships between central characters in shaping our sense of the broad outlook of the text.

Decide on your opinion:

- Ma and Jack's loving relationship transforms a sordid, ugly story into one of hope and inspiration.

Make a short plan of your key points:

- Ma's careful nurturing of her son Jack, despite the horrific circumstances leading to his birth.
- Jack's incredible bravery in carrying out their plan for escape because of his love for Ma.
- Ma's selfless gesture in agreeing to return one last time to Room so that Jack can transition into Outside.

Sample answer

1 The loving relationship between Ma and Jack in Emma Donoghue's novel, *Room*, transforms an ugly, brutal violent situation into an uplifting story about the redemptive power of true love. After a cruel seven-year imprisonment, their escape shows the triumph of their determination despite terrible odds. Ma's love for her little son changes her life, Jack's brave actions save his beloved Ma and himself from Old Nick, and Ma's generous gesture to allow both of them to revisit Room one last time allows them both to put the past behind.

2 19-year-old Ma cried incessantly, stayed in bed and neglected her hygiene in the early years of her captivity before Jack 'zoomed in'. But 'seeing Jack was everything. I was alive again'. Now she had a purpose. She nurtured Jack diligently. They sang, 'Row, row, row your boat', read stories, watched TV sparingly. She made sure Jack had 'dazzling' teeth not like her own neglected which were 'pretty rotted'. Ma is Jack's world, even though he is five she breastfeeds him, 'have some', to give him comfort.

3 When Ma realises they are in danger because Nick has lost his job and may also lose his house and so could kill them to prevent his secret being discovered, she starts to prepare her little son for Outside by 'unlying'. She encourages Jack to accept plans for their 'Great Escape'. They practise Jack pretending to be dead. Jack is 'dizzy' when he thinks about Old Nick carrying him wrapped up in Rug to the truck. He is terrified, 'I'm too scared', but his love for Ma makes him determined not to disappoint her and so he becomes her 'superhero'. This great act of courage on the part of five-year-old Jack is inspiring.

4 Ma performs one more tremendous selfless act of love for her son. Jack longs to return to Room. The trauma of revisiting the site of her captivity was too much for Ma. But she followed Jack into Room. When he complains that it's 'got shrunk', she reassures him that it was always really like that. She encourages Jack to say 'good-bye' to everything that is still left in Room. Her bravery is allowing Jack to transition to Outside by accepting that Room happened but that it is right to leave it behind. Her wisdom is shown by Jack's acceptance that Room was 'a hole where something happened'.

5 Ma and Jack's selfless mutual love transformed a bleak, horrific nightmare into a redemptive story about the wonderful power of love.

(420 words)

EXAMINER'S COMMENT

Good introductory overview of the central storyline, stating how Ma and Jack's close relationship shaped the novel's positive outlook ('uplifting', 'redemptive'). Paragraph 3 touches on mode ('inspiring') while paragraphs 2 and 4 include a great deal of detailed but unfocused narrative. Expression is clear throughout and the succinct conclusion responds to the task, focusing on vision and viewpoint effectively.

(20/30 marks)

General vision and viewpoint in *Unforgiven*

Sample part (a) question (30 marks)

'Authors make effective use of a range of techniques to dramatically heighten the impact of the general vision and viewpoint.'

Discuss the technique(s) used to dramatically heighten the impact of the general vision and viewpoint of one of the texts you have studied for your comparative course.

Support your answer with reference to the text.

In Part (a) 30-mark questions on one text, no comparison is necessary. Discuss the mode only.

- Allow about 30 minutes and aim for 400 words approximately.
- Organise your answer into clear, defined paragraphs.
- Support your opinions with quotations and references from the text.

Prompt!

Refer to the mode and the question in your answer.

The purpose of the question:

- to show evidence of understanding the general vision and viewpoint of the text **(focusing on the mode)**;
- to discuss one or more techniques used to increase the dramatic impact of the vision.

Decide on your opinion:

- Eastwood's use of three techniques creates tension and adds to the ambiguous vision in the film.

Make a short plan of your key points:

- Music, 'Claudia's Theme', symbolises redeeming power of love; adds poignant beauty.
- Low-key lighting increases the tense anticipation of dark deeds.
- Imagery of guns highlights violence and the wrongs in a corrupt society.
- All three techniques intensify the ambivalent picture of life in the Wild West.

Sample answer

1 In *Unforgiven,* Clint Eastwood effectively uses the techniques of music, lighting and imagery. These increase the audience's awareness of the film's ambiguous vision and viewpoint which exposes not only the brutality of violence but also its sense of redemption.

2 'Claudia's Theme' opens and closes the film. It reinforces the all-powerful influence of Will Munny's deceased wife on the former gunslinger's outlook on life. A lone guitar gently picks out the slow, melancholy tune. Munny, a widowed father and a failed farmer, is burying his wife who died of smallpox. The music increases poignancy to the film's dark view of struggle and death. At the film's conclusion, Munny is at his wife's grave again. He has broken his promise to her who 'showed me the errors of my way'. He has killed again, but not indiscriminately but to give their children a better life, to set right a brutal wrong and to avenge his friend, Ned's, death. Is the director suggesting that Munny has indeed reformed? Yet we are left wondering if this is a redemptive vision.

3 The director uses low-key lighting to suggest the dark, ambivalent message of his film. In the scene where Delilah has her face brutally slashed, extreme dark shadows are cast across the actors' faces. This increases the dramatic tension of this harrowing scene. Similar lighting is also used in the shooting scene in Skinny Dubois's saloon. Here it increases the sense of ominous danger. Munny has returned to avenge those who used his dead friend, Ned, to 'decorate' their saloon. This dark lighting emphasises the vicious natures of those in the bar. As the final action unfolds, contrasting bright light on Munny's face suggests, his determination to retaliate the death of his friend. This technique is used to increase the director's dual view of the times as a mix of sordid brutality and righteous revenge.

4 The imagery of guns is used as a symbol of masculinity. Little Bill emasculates his town by his no gun law and increases his own authority by brutally enforcing this law. He bends English Bob's Webley Bulldog .32 to symbolise the weakness of the bounty hunter. Both Ned and The Kid hand over their guns to Munny because both are reluctant killers, 'I'm never gonna use it again'. But Munny has regained his skill with a gun and cleanses a town of a corrupt law officer.

5 Eastwood presents us with the ambivalent view that civilisation is only safe when it is violently defended by flawed killers, 'Deserve's got nuthin' to do with it'.

(420 words)

EXAMINER'S COMMENT

Clearly focused response based around three interesting stylistic features that accentuate the film's ambivalent outlook. The commentary on music (paragraph 2) is particularly impressive. Good expression, overall – although slightly repetitive ('increase', 'brutal'). Discussion points are aptly supported by relevant reference and quotation.

(28/30 marks)

General vision and viewpoint in *Silas Marner*

Sample part (a) question (30 marks)

'A variety of factors in texts can change or reinforce our initial impression of the general vision and viewpoint.'

Discuss the main factor(s) in one of your texts on your comparative course that changed or reinforced your initial impression of the general vision and viewpoint in the text.

Support your answer with reference to the text.

In Part (a) 30-mark questions on one text, no comparison is necessary. Discuss the mode only.

- Allow about 30 minutes and aim for 400 words approximately.
- Organise your answer into clear, defined paragraphs.
- Support your opinions with quotations and references from the text.

Prompt!

Refer to the mode and the question in your answer.

The purpose of the question:

- to show evidence of understanding the general vision and viewpoint of the text (**focusing on the mode**);
- to discuss one or more factors which changed or reinforced our initial impression of the vision.

Decide on your opinion:

- Eliot's revelation of the character of Silas Marner taking responsibility for his actions and choosing to develop relationships has positive impact on our vision.

Make a short plan of your key points:

- Dark outlook expressed in opening chapter.
- Silas's decision to adopt Eppie alters initial viewpoint.
- Fairytale ending heightens sense of optimism.

Sample answer

1 The introduction of a miserly weaver illustrates a dark vision in George Eliot's *Silas Marner*. The author highlights not only the importance of taking personal responsibility for actions, but also the importance of reaching out to develop personal relationships. Our growing knowledge of Silas changes from an impression of pessimism to an impression of optimism for the future.

2 Flint introduces the dead personality of her central character in the novel's opening chapters. He is one of the 'itinerant weavers' who are regarded by the inhabitants of Raveloe with suspicion because they believe their strange trade comes with 'the help of the Evil One'. Silas's backstory adds to the oppressive viewpoint; he was betrayed by his best friend, and lost both his love, Sarah, and his faith, 'God of lies'. Eliot uses bleak imagery to reinforce this point of view. Silas, a 'spider', lived an 'insect-like existence' weaving 'from pure impulse without reflection'.

3 When Silas is forced to seek help from the community because his gold has been stolen, the vision changes. He calls for help, 'I've been robbed. I want the constable'. The community comes to his aid and two villagers accompany him to the constable. This is in sharp contrast to events in Lantern Yard. Now Silas is taking a pro-active step to get justice rather than passively accepting the chance verdict of the drawing of lots to expose the truth. He is taking personal responsibility for his actions. This is how the vision in the novel changes.

4 The perspective is further brightened when Silas discovers 'his own gold' is replaced by the 'soft curls' of an orphaned child. He refuses to let her go 'to the parish'. Silas insists that 'it's a lone thing – and I'm a lone thing'. His choice of name for Eppie not only references his mother and sister's name but also his feelings for her, Hepzibah, 'my delight is in her'. Eppie calls 'him away from his weaving' in order to find joy in the most ordinary sights, 'old winter-flies' emerging into the spring sunshine.

5 The novel concludes with Eppie's fairytale wedding. Silas's future is now secure because, 'now she says she'll never leave me, I think I shall trusten till I die'. Silas has reclaimed a place in a community. He took personal responsibility for his actions and he made the effort to develop human relationships. The stance in the novel has radically changed from pessimism to optimism, 'nobody could be happier than we are'.

(410 words)

EXAMINER'S COMMENT

Addresses the question directly throughout, showing a close understanding of the changing outlook in the novel. Discussion points are well-supported with relevant textual reference and accurate quotation. Language use is generally good apart from slight awkwardness in paragraphs 1 and 4. Discussion is rounded off effectively.

(27/30 marks)

The part (b) question

In the 40-mark part (b) Comparative Study question, you are asked to compare aspects of the general vision and viewpoint mode in two of the prescribed texts.

Useful comparative phrases include:

The language of comparison requires you to respond in blocks of paragraphs, interweaving comparative points.

- In a similar way ...
- The opening scene is distinctive ...
- By contrast ...
- This is not the case in ...
- Both texts are alike ...
- In a slightly different way ...
- This is mirrored in ...
- On the other hand ...
- The conclusions differ significantly ...
- This is evident in all three stories ...

Sample part (b) question (40 marks)

'Our view of the personal integrity of a central character can help shape our impression of the general vision and viewpoint of a text.'

Compare the extent to which your view of the personal integrity* of one central character, in two of the texts on your comparative course, helped to shape your impression of the general vision and viewpoint of your chosen texts. Develop your answer with reference to your texts.

Note: * integrity can be taken to mean honesty, decency, loyalty, character, reliability, honour, etc.

Prompt!

Refer to the mode, question and comparison in your answer.

The purpose of the question:

- to address the three key elements (mode, comparison, question);
- to explore the extent to which (**comparison**);
- to examine your view of the personal integrity of central characters (**question**);
- to help shape your impression of the broad outlook in two texts (**mode**).

Decide on your opinion:

- the ability/inability of Gar or Will Munny to behave with integrity in adversity influences the viewpoint;
- the conclusions of the texts revealing the integrity of Gar and Munny shape our impression of the vision.

Make a short plan of your key points:

- *Philadelphia*: Gar lacks integrity in the scene with Canon O'Byrne and at the play's conclusion, influencing a bleak viewpoint.
- *Unforgiven*: Will Munny shows integrity in saloon shoot-out and at film's conclusion, shaping a dark outlook.

Sample answer

1 My comparative texts, *Philadelphia, Here I Come* by Brian Friel and *Unforgiven* directed by Clint Eastwood, both have pessimistic viewpoints. Their two protagonists, Gar and Will Munny, contrast in personal integrity. Munny, 'known thief and murderer', is honest and righteous, yet this will end up forming a bleak outlook in the film. While Gar, although courteous and considerate, is morally weak, and this also forms a gloomy outlook in the play.

2 Gar is presented as a divided personality, Public Gar and Private Gar. Private's voice is witty, eloquent and energetic. When the Canon appears for his nightly game of draughts with S. B., Private's internal voice savagely mocks the cleric by anticipating his clichéd conversation, 'how's the O'Donnell family tonight?' He exposes the Canon's failure to perform his Christian task, 'you could translate all this loneliness … into Christian terms that will make life bearable'. But the Canon doesn't 'say a word'. And neither does Gar, either Public or Private! Instead he diverts himself with a silly song, Screwballs, Screwballs, give me your answer do!' This dishonesty on Gar's part, criticising someone else for what he himself is doing, contributed to the dark vision in the play.

3 In contrast, Will dares to openly confront Little Bill. He is a man on a mission – to avenge the murder of his friend Ned. When Skinny identifies himself as the killer, Munny shoots him point blank. The sheriff attempts to disempower Will by outing his criminal past, exposing him as a killer of women and children. But Munny owns his past, unlike Gar who runs away from his. He cooly acknowledges, 'I've killed just about everything that walked'. He knows exactly why he is executing Little Bill, 'I'm here to kill you, Little Bill, for what you did to Ned'. He is the honest outsider who rides into town to take out the corrupt lawman. In the face of adversity Munny's integrity is on full display, but it exposes a pessimistic vision. Righteous killing is brutal, messy and often carried out by professional killers.

4 The conclusion of Friel's play heightens our sense of a bleak outlook because we witness doubt and uncertainty which is so different from the focused gaze of Munny. Private asks the question the audience wishes to

know, 'why do you have to leave?' Public replies, 'I don't know'. This exposes Gar's lack of honesty and conviction. Unlike Will Munny who acted out of a firm sense of purpose. This conclusion reveals a lack of personal integrity in Gar which reinforces the bleak vision in the text.

5 Munny departs like Gar but, unlike Gar, he clearly tells the townsfolk what he wants, 'better bury Ned right' and not harm any sex workers otherwise he'll 'come back and kill every one of you sons of bitches'. Will's personal integrity is highlighted by the American flag in the background. This is a society based on violence, drenched in blood yet which defends the rights of the individual.

6 Both texts reveal a dark outlook, Munny through his bloodthirsty vengeance and Gar though his inability to communicate.

(510 words)

EXAMINER'S COMMENT

Solid high-grade response that engages well with both texts. Clear introduction addresses the question. Sustained comparative approach and some well-supported developed discussion – particularly in paragraphs 2 and 3. Interesting point about the symbolism of the flag in paragraph 5. Expression is reasonably good, overall.

(32/40 marks)

Sample part (b) question (40 marks)

'The general vision and viewpoint of a text can be interpreted by a reader's response to key scenes or significant moments in that text.'

With reference to two of the prescribed texts on your course, compare how key scenes or significant moments shaped your personal response and helped you interpret the general vision and viewpoint in these texts. Develop your answer with reference to your texts.

Prompt!

Respond to the question by taking a comparative approach and referring closely to the mode.

The purpose of the question:

- to address the three key elements (question, mode, comparison);
- to identify the general vision and viewpoint in each text (**mode**);
- to compare how key moments in each text (**comparison**);
- to show how these moments shaped the general vision and viewpoint (**question**).

Decide on your opinion:

- Contrasting key moments in each text left me both uplifted and appalled, and with an ambivalent vision and viewpoint.

> **Make a short plan of your key points:**
> - *Room*: Jack's interview with Officer Oh created an inspirational vision while Ma's TV interview was shocking and pessimistic.
> - *Silas Marner*: A sense of optimism surrounded Dolly's visit to Silas. However, Godfrey's indifference towards his daughter resulted in a dark outlook.
> The general vision and viewpoint in both texts is ambivalent.

Sample answer

1 I found the vision in my comparative texts, *Silas Marner* by George Eliot and *Room* by Emma Donoghue, ambivalent. Both texts had moments which made me feel at times optimistic and pessimistic. Donoghue's novel revealed Officer Oh's patience was similar to Dolly Winthrop's kind attitude to Silas. This created a bright outlook in these texts. But the coldness of the interviewer towards Ma in *Room* was mirrored by the indifference of Godfrey in *Silas Marner*. This led me to form a pessimistic outlook. Overall, the texts presented an indecisive vision which is true of real life where nothing is completely black or white.

2 In *Room*, Ajeet's 911 call summoned Officer Oh. She refuses to give up on the boy despite her partner's insistence that they call 'Child Protective Services' because Jack communicate in a strange way. Her breakthrough comes when she bets Jack that he is great at telling stories. The boy opens up to reveal that he and Ma 'did a trick' to escape. Jack describes Room and explains that there is a skylight. Satellite images are brought up and the location is worked out. I found it inspiring when Officer Oh returned to the car with Ma at her side. However, Jack sobbed when told he would not be returning to the security of what he had known. This threw a shadow on an otherwise bright vision.

3 In Eliot's novel, Dolly Winthrop helps an awkward individual. Like Jack, Silas had reached out to the community for help. Robbed of his gold, Silas went to Rainbow Inn to seek justice. Dolly is patient like Officer Oh. She visits the weaver with a present of 'lard-cakes baked with 'letters pricked on 'em' which were on the 'pulpit-cloth at church'. Like Oh, she gently coaxes, suggesting that the recluse 'go to church'. Although Silas is grateful, he is like Jack just wants to return to the security of what he knows, to 'weave again and moan at his ease'. Like the key scene in *Room*, an optimistic event is overcast.

4 In the significant moment of Ma's TV interview, the author makes the reader aware that media sensationalism is responsible for making the lives of survivors of tragedy even more difficult. The interviewer puts words in Ma's mouth, 'you said ... it was "easier to control" Jack when you were in captivity'. Ma corrects her, 'control things'. The consequence of this exploitation was that Ma had a 'Gone' day when she attempted suicide. This scene revealed the pessimistic view that the media actually exploit victims to boost ratings.

5   The interviewer's cold indifference to Ma's trauma is similar to Godfrey's indifference to the plight of his own child. He is more concerned that if he speaks up, his secret marriage to Molly will be revealed and he will lose his chance to marry Nancy, 'throwing away his happiness'. In both these scenes from *Room* and *Silas Marner*, the reader is shocked at the lack of empathy for the victims. This reveals a bleak outlook in each text.

6   Through the key moments of Jack's interview with Officer Oh, Ma's TV interview, Dolly's visit and Godfrey's refusal to acknowledge his child, ambivalent viewpoints are revealed. Kindness and cold indifference exist side by side.

(535 words)

EXAMINER'S COMMENT

The ambivalent vision in the two comparative texts is clearly introduced in the opening paragraph. This is then well-illustrated and developed in the follow-up paragraphs, indicating a close knowledge of both stories and the general vision mode. The comparative approach is sustained throughout the discussion. Expression is good, overall – though slightly repetitive (e.g. the overuse of 'like' in paragraph 3).

(34/40 marks)

70-mark question

In the 70-mark Comparative Study question, you are asked to compare aspects of the general vision and viewpoint mode in three of the prescribed texts.

Sample 70-mark question

'The way in which characters are presented in texts can offer interesting insights into the general vision and viewpoint of these texts.'

With reference to three texts on your comparative course, compare the ways in which the presentation of characters in each text offered interesting insights into the general vision and viewpoint of these texts. Support your answer with reference to your chosen texts.

Prompt!

Respond to the question by taking a comparative approach and referring closely to the mode.

The purpose of the question:

- to address the three key elements (comparison, question, mode);
- to compare and contrast (**comparison**);
- to show how characters are presented in three texts (**question**);
- to offer interesting insights into the vision and viewpoint in these texts. (**mode**).

Structuring the answer

Make a short plan of your key points

- **Intro**: Name your three comparative text choices and their authors. State whether you agree, disagree or partially agree with the statement in the question. Outline the insights into the general vision and viewpoint you are going to discuss.
- *Philadelphia*: Passive role of women (Kate and Madge); type of hero, Gar; losing to powerful establishment figure, Senator Doogan; advances a negative vision in the play.
- *Unforgiven*: Oppressed role of women (Claudia and sex workers); Will Munny triumphs over powerful establishment figure, Little Bill; creates a darkly optimistic viewpoint in the film.
- *Silas Marner*: Positive female role (Dolly and Eppie); Silas Marner prevails over powerful establishment figure, Godfrey Cass; contributes to the novel's optimistic outlook.

exam focus

- Allow about 65–70 minutes and aim for at least 900 words, organised into paragraphs.
- Focus on the general vision and viewpoint mode.
- Develop comparative points with suitable reference to the three texts.

- **Conclusion**: Sum up central arguments and overall response to the question.

Sample answer

1 The way in which women, men and powerful establishment figures are presented in my three comparative texts posed thought-provoking insights into the general vision and viewpoints of those texts. Brian Friel in *Philadelphia, Here I Come* introduces two female characters, Madge and Kate, who fail to affect change, and a tortured hero Gar O'Donnell who fails to challenge and an influential establishment figure, Senator Doogan. All contribute to the play's bleak outlook. Clint Eastwood in *Unforgiven* presents women who succeed in overturning society's norms and an improbable hero who challenges a corrupt law enforcer. These portrayals offer a darkly optimistic vision. George Eliot in *Silas Marner* creates two nurturing female characters, another unlikely hero and an amoral landowner who is justly punished. The novel's outlook is broadly optimistic.

2 In Friel's pessimistic play, Gar's girlfriend Kate is well aware of her father's overbearing smugness and her tormented boyfriend's lack of confidence. She uses all her ingenuity to by-pass her father's obstacles to a marriage between herself and Gar. She creates a fictional income and a £5,000 account in the bank and a fictional story about S. B.'s 'supposed' retirement. She is attempting to make a man out of an adolescent boy when she insists to Gar that it is 'entirely up to you'. But Gar just cannot make the leap of courage needed to secure their happiness, 'I think I'd

better move on'. He is intimidated by the overbearing Senator Doogan who is keen for Kate to marry someone of her own class.

3 Even Madge, the housekeeper, fails to lighten the gloomy mood. She tries to break the long silences between father and son with sarcastic comments, 'The chatting in this place would deafen a body'. But neither man seizes the moment. S. B. clumsily reinforces Gar's financial dependence, 'I suppose you'll be looking for your pay'. Both Madge and Kate tried in vain to help Gar break the stranglehold of small-town Ireland. However, Gar is a tormented figure who is unable to rise to the occasion. These character portrayals produced a sombre pessimistic viewpoint in the play.

4 In Eastwood's film, two contrasting visions of women are presented: the mercenary sex workers and the saintly deceased wife, Claudia. In turn, Will Munny is a flawed hero, 'a known thief and murderer', but he reforms because his wife believed in him, 'she 'cured me of drink and wickedness'. When two cowboys mutilate the face of one of the sex workers, Munny takes the job of bringing them to justice. Will is strengthened by becoming the righteous bearer of vengeance. The reluctant hero is able to summon up the moral courage to right several wrongs. He overcomes the corrupt establishment figure, Little Bill and issues a stern warning to the town to clean up its act, 'or I'll come back and kill every one of you sons o' bitches'. Will's steely-eyed purpose and triumph is in stark contrast to the divided personality of the unfortunate Gar O'Donnell. The scrolling screen writing at the film's conclusion reinforces the darkly optimistic viewpoint of the film. Munny is thought to have gone to San Francisco with his kids and was rumoured to have 'prospered in dry goods'.

5 Silas Marner is a most unlikely hero, 'withered and yellow', a reclusive miser who lived alone for the sole purpose of weaving and hoarding. Two female characters greatly impacted his life, Dolly Winthrop and an abandoned child, Eppie. Like the women in the other two texts, they provided a focus for goodness, bringing out Silas's human qualities. Dolly not only helps Silas to raise his adopted daughter, but encourages him to forget about unsolved matters from his past, like the robbery in Lantern Yard, 'There are many things we'll never know. It's God's will'. She invites the old weaver to become part of the Raveloe community, adding to the novel's cheerful vision.

6 But it is Eppie, like Claudia, who truly redeems Silas. Not only does she integrate him back into society, 'the little child had come to link him once more with the whole world', she rekindles his interest in the natural world, 'the old winter-flies'. Eppie is presented as a symbol of childhood child. She is closely associated with nature and renews Silas. Over the years, Silas sees more of his world through Eppie's eyes, remembering childhood days when he himself felt carefree and happy. She replaces the selfish materialism in Silas' life and offers him a brighter future by promising to stay with him after her marriage top Aaron.

7 Unlike Gar whose love for his 'darling Katie Doogan' was not strong enough to give him the courage to stand and fight, Silas's love for his adopted daughter instils him with the courage to confront the local landowner, Godfrey Cass. He was Eppie's biological father and he arrived 'to own Eppie as my child'. But Silas withstands pressure from Godfrey, 'your affection for Eppie would have made you rejoice in what was for her good'. He dares to challenge Cass, 'why didn't you say so sixteen year ago?' Silas, like Munny, has a very clear understanding of what is morally right and wrong. Like Munny, he defeats the powerful establishment figure. Once again, a broadly optimistic viewpoint is established through the character portrayals in the novel.

8 My three comparative texts provided me with interesting insights into their vision and viewpoint through the authors' presentation of their characters. The varied influence of women, different types of heroes and the defeat or triumph of powerful establishment figures contributed to the play's gloomy outlook, the film's darkly optimistic viewpoint and the novel's broadly bright vision.

(935 words)

EXAMINER'S COMMENT

Effective top-grade response, beginning with a clear overview. This comparative essay generally addresses all aspects of the question, focusing on how vision is shaped by the way particular characters are presented and developed. Discussion points are well-focused on the vision and viewpoint mode, and supported by apt reference. Although a slightly formulaic approach limits some of the discussion, there is impressive evidence of engaged literary thinking – particularly in paragraphs 4, 5 and 6. Apart from occasional repetition (e.g. in paragraph 2), expression is well-controlled.

GRADE H1

P = 20/21

C = 19/21

L = 18/21

M = 7/7

Total = 64/70

exam focus

40-mark and 70-mark Comparative Study questions require a different approach than questions in the Single Text section.

- Keep a strong emphasis on the comparative mode when referring to key moments or scenes in texts.
- Respond to all the aspects of the question you have chosen.
- Use comparative language throughout, pointing out similarities and differences between texts.

Checklist

- ○ Identify all key elements within the question.
- ○ Discuss general vision and viewpoint mode throughout.
- ○ Avoid unfocused narrative summary.
- ○ Use the language of comparison.
- ○ Develop personal opinions on how the general vision and viewpoint context shapes your understanding of texts.
- ○ Practise making plans for past paper questions to prepare effective responses.

Comparative Study Appendix 1
Theme or issue

Prescribed mode for 2021

A theme or issue refers to the central idea or message in a text. The theme should not be confused with the plot or storyline. It's likely that there will be a number of significant themes in most texts.

Popular themes include:

- isolation
- relationships
- identity
- injustice
- good and evil

- change
- power
- conflict
- social class
- appearance and reality, etc.

Why has a theme special meaning for you?

The author's presentation of a theme or issue often challenges the reader or audience to think about human nature and to distinguish between right and wrong. We learn that struggling to do what is right can be difficult.

How do we respond to the author's treatment of a theme?

Comparing how different authors treat a theme broadens our understanding of that theme or issue and can sometimes help us deal with difficulties that we face in life.

When we engage with characters in their efforts to overcome obstacles such as growing up, learning to be independent, responding to crises, etc.

Key theme: Isolation

Isolation can have a significant impact on a character's sense of identity.

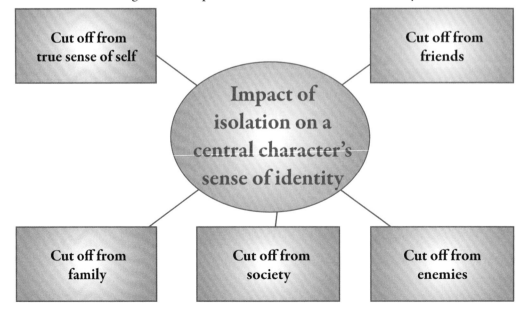

Writing about the theme of isolation in Comparative Study texts

Drama	Novel	Novel	Film
Philadelphia, Here I Come! **Brian Friel**	*Room* **Emma Donoghue**	*Silas Marner* **George Eliot**	*Unforgiven* **Clint Eastwood**
Isolation			
Gar O'Donnell's voluntary withdrawal from the world is due to emotional turmoil.	Jack and Ma's involuntary confinement in Room is due to imprisonment by Old Nick.	Silas withdraws voluntarily from former life due to personal hurt and seeks seclusion in Raveloe.	Will Munny leaves his violent past behind for quiet farm life – but his isolation does not last.
Family			
Negative	**Mostly positive**	**Supportive, positive**	**Supportive, positive**
Gar's sense of isolation is primarily caused by his inability to communicate with his father. S. B. is equally lonely and misses the opportunity to breach corrosive silence between himself and Gar.	Throughout their confinement, unconditional mutual love is crucial for Jack and Ma – except for Ma's unhappy 'Gone' days. Loving support from Grandma amplified by Steppa.	Silas has fond memories of his mother and sister which comfort him in times of solitude. His adopted daughter Eppie and the Raveloe villagers rescue him from unhappy isolation.	Deceased wife, Claudia, is a good moral influence; helps Will cope with loneliness and isolation. Responsibility to provide for his children ultimately saves Will, rehabilitating him into society.
Friendships and support			
Some friends support Gar, but without success. Gar's girlfriend Kate and his friend Joe try to support him but their efforts fail. Gar remains conflicted and socially isolated. **Negative impact.**	**No friends, only caring professionals.** Jack's imprisonment has prevented him from making any friends. He has difficulties socialising after escaping Room. **Negative impact.**	**Friends and community support Silas.** Dolly Winthrop helps to socialise Silas. She provides support in rearing Eppie and in making him part of the Raveloe community. **Positive impact.**	**Some friends support Silas.** Ned Logan, Will's former partner in crime, remains a loyal friend, accompanying Munny on the bounty hunt. **Positive impact.**

Writing about the theme of isolation in Comparative Study texts

Enemies

Enemies increase isolation.	Enemies increase isolation.	Enemies increase isolation.	Enemies fail to increase isolation.
Senator Doogan intimidates Gar, the Canon ignores him and Master Boyle belittles his ex-pupil. **All of them reinforce Gar's isolation.**	Old Nick prevents Ma and Jack communicating with the outside world. Media relentlessly intrudes on their personal privacy. **All add to isolation.**	William Dane, false friend in Lantern Yard, betrays Silas. Dunstan Cass steals Silas's gold, leading him to despair. Godfrey Cass tries to reclaim Eppie as his daughter. **They all add to Silas's isolation.**	Little Bill Daggett, sheriff of Big Whiskey, fails to enforce law justly, but Will Munny challenges him and triumphs. **Will becomes less isolated – but remains a remote figure.**

Character's relationship with society

Outlook bleak for future role in community.	Outlook promising for future role in community.	Outlook bright for future role in community.	Outlook promising for future role in community.
Little sign that Gar will change. Private blocks out what is unpleasant, retreating into fantasy. He seems likely to remain confused and anxious, looks set for desolate solitude in Philadelphia.	Outside world is challenging. However, Ma and Jack seem able to adjust and function well. Helped by caring professionals, they should soon claim their place in society. Segregation is at an end.	Rejected in Lantern Yard, Silas is looked on with suspicion in insular rural Raveloe initially. After adopting Eppie, however, society rallies to Silas, accepting him as a valued part of the community.	Will abandons isolated farming life and restores order to a corrupt town. He makes a new life with his children in San Francisco. The outsider finally claims his rightful place in society.

exam focus

- Discuss how a theme is first established in a text.
- Then trace how the author develops this theme.
- Identify turning points or moments of crisis.
- Finally, comment on how the theme is resolved at the end.

Comparative Study Appendix 2
Literary genre

Prescribed mode for 2022

Literary genre refers to the techniques authors use to tell stories and convey the text's message. Appreciation of a text is increased by being aware of the author's choice of literary techniques.

Key literary techniques

- **Characterisation** is a key feature of literary genre. Our response to how a central character is presented and developed shapes our understanding of a text. Authors create characters in different ways. This can be done realistically (three-dimensional character with credible characteristics) or as a stereotype (one-dimensional figure, such as an obvious hero or a villain).
- **Narrative structure**. The structure or shape of a story, whether chronological and linear (presenting consecutive events as they happen) or using flashback (moving back into the past), increases our appreciation of why the plot (storyline) is unfolding in a particular way.
- **Symbols and images** enrich our engagement with a story.
- **Titles** excite our interest about what will happen in the text. Titles can be ironic and include a deeper meaning.
- **Genre** (the type or category of the narrative) raises expectations. In Shakespearean tragedy, the central character will die after gaining self-knowledge. In modern tragedies, the characters might not achieve self-knowledge. A socially realistic text often shows evil defeating good. Comedies usually have a happy ending.
- **Setting** is used to make the story credible and can highlight the atmosphere within the text.
- **Dialogue** adds to the authenticity of a story. It not only conveys the personality of central characters but also their socio-economic status. Soliloquies increase our understanding of a character's internal emotional struggles.
- **Conflict, tension and climax** involve readers and audiences in the story's development and outcome.
- The **resolution** (whether the conflict is resolved happily, unhappily or is left open-ended) strengthens the reader's engagement. Has the story concluded as expected?

Developing a personal response through literary genre

Check the graphic below to aid your understanding of how key literary genre techniques can affect a central character. The techniques on the left are common to most texts. Those on the right are specific to a particular type of text. The techniques used shape our response towards themes, characters and their 'worlds'.

Title

Camera (film)

Plot

Genre

Symbolism/ Imagery

All these literary genre features contribute to the reader/ audience's sympathetic or unsympathetic engagement with central characters and story.

Irony

Dialogue

Characterisation

Descriptive writing (novel)

Setting

Stage directions (play)

Using literary genre to make comparisons

Drama	Novel	Novel	Film
Philadelphia, Here I Come! **Brian Friel**	*Room* **Emma Donoghue**	*Silas Marner* **George Eliot**	*Unforgiven* **Clint Eastwood**
Title			
From popular song, represents Gar's hopes but lyrics then read, 'right back where I started from', suggests ominous outlook.	Four letters (Room) represent five-year-old Jack's whole world. He and Ma are captive in an 11 ft by 11 ft room. This is both Jack's prison and his security.	Full title is *Silas Marner, The Weaver of Raveloe*, focusing on work and the central character's role in community.	Sets up series of intriguing questions: Who is unforgiven? Why? Is forgiveness possible? Who can forgive?
Presentation of central character			
Complex personality: Public Gar is quiet, unassuming, polite while Private is witty, energetic, and critical – Private comments honestly.	Complex personality of five-year-old narrator, Jack, who has a limited unique perspective of world. Jack is mature, devoted to Ma, incredibly brave.	Simple weaver, ordinary imperfect human going about day-to-day works. Extraordinary events. Unlikely kind-hearted hero who triumphs.	Complex flawed hero, clumsy, ageing, Failed farmer, former killer. Haunted, ambiguous. Triumph of male violence to establish order and justice.

Using literary genre to make comparisons

Presentation of central character *contd.*

Extraordinary hero/victim. Engages some sympathy. **Ends in confusion.**	Extraordinary hero. Engages sympathy. **Ends in redemption.**	Engages sympathy. **Ends in redemption.**	Engages some sympathy. **Ends in redemption of sorts.**

Genre

Tragic-comic drama, stream of consciousness (continuous flow of thoughts, feelings, reactions). Gar is caught in whirlwind of his thoughts; **he fails to adapt.**	Modern psychological novel. Thoughts, feelings, motives of Jack are of equal interest to external narrative. **Jack adapts to survive.**	Victorian novel of manners; pastoral fiction (rural setting, romantic fairytale ending). Silas **transforms his life** to achieve happiness.	Revisionist Western film challenges the traditional Western. Morally questionable world where people must adapt to survive. **Will changes for the better.**

Viewpoint

Audience placed outside story, observing, **objective viewpoint**. Story unfolds through plot, setting, stage directions and dialogue to create dramatic experience.	First-person limited point of view. Reader only knows what Jack knows, learns as Jack learns. **Personal viewpoint.**	Omniscient (all-knowing) third-person describing what characters are feeling, thinking, seeing. **Judgemental viewpoint.**	Camera is omniscient narrator, influencing audience's reactions to characters and events. **Judgemental viewpoint.**

aims

● Identifying and understanding a poet's key themes and use of poetic language.
● Developing successful personal responses to poems.

The Unseen Poem (20 marks)

In the Unseen Poem 20-mark question, you will have **20 minutes** to read and respond to a short poem that you are unlikely to have already studied. Targeted reading is essential. Read over the questions first to focus your thoughts and feelings.

In your **first reading** of the poem, aim to get an initial sense of **what** the poet is writing about and **why** the poet is focusing on that particular subject.

● What is happening in the poem? Who is involved?
● Who is speaking – the poet or another character?
● Is the poet describing a scene or an incident?
● Is there a strong sense of place or atmosphere?
● What, in your opinion, is the main theme or message?

In your **second reading**, look more closely at **how** the poem is written.

● What do you think of the poet's choice of title?
● Are there any noteworthy details or images?
● Can you find any interesting ideas or viewpoints?
● Are there any changes in tone or atmosphere?
● Did anything in the poem surprise you?

exam focus

Avoid wasting time worrying about any words that you don't understand. Instead, focus on what makes sense to you.

key point

Engage with the poem honestly. How does it make you feel? Trust your own reaction.

Practice exercise 1

Read the following poem by Norman MacCaig and answer the question that follows.

November Night, Edinburgh

The night tinkles like ice in glasses.
Leaves are glued to the pavements with frost.
The brown air fumes at the shop windows,
Tries the door, and sidles past.   sidles: *creeps*

I gulp down winter raw. The heady
Darkness swirls with tenements.   tenements: *apartment blocks*
In a brown fuzz of cotton wool
Lamps fade up crags, die into pits   crags: *rock faces*

Frost in my lungs is harsh as leaves
Scraped up on paths. – I look up, there,
A high roof sails, at the mast-head
Fluttering a grey and ragged star.

The world's a bear shrugged in his den.
It's snug and close in the snoring night.
And outside like Chrysanthemums
The fog unfolds its bitter scent.

                    Norman MacCaig

Question 1

Discuss the effectiveness of the poet's use of language and imagery throughout this poem. Refer to the text in support of your answer.   (20 marks)

Sample answer 1

The effectiveness of the poet's use of language and imagery is very good. He is talking about the icy roads and the weather in November. He describes the fog very well using images. The brown air fumes are fuzzy and it is hard to even breath it is so dense. There are images of lamps in windows back in the old days before electric light.

It says in the poem that the frost is so bad that it almost gets into his throat. Norman protrays his walk home as a challenging. Slipping on the ice and not being able to see where he is going half the time. His language shows that it is a tough night to be out in and he describes the winter as 'raw winter'. His language is very negative in the poem as the raw weather is not so easy to be out in on a November night. Especially as he would be much more happier to be at home snug like a bear snoring away in comfort instead of being out in the dark icy roads. He is comparing the outside with the inside at the end of the poem and it is pretty obvious that Norman prefairs the snug homestead.

EXAMINER'S COMMENT

- Much more emphasis needed on the poet's language.
- Little focus on the effectiveness of language use.
- Some reasonable comment on descriptive details.
- Flaws in mechanics ('protrays', 'it says in the poem', 'more happier', 'prefairs').
- Basic response.

MARKS AWARDED: 6/20

Improving the answer:

- Focus more directly on examples of the poet's language, e.g. the image in line 1.
- Comment on this opening comparison and what the simile might suggest, e.g. a party atmosphere.
- Discuss the sounds, e.g. the sharp 'k', 'c' and 'r' effects in the first two lines.
- Look for metaphors and personification, e.g. the fog prowling like a thief in the night.
- Work through the poem, searching for examples of interesting imagery in all stanzas.
- Take care with spelling, so as to avoid errors ('portrays', 'prefairs').
- Instead of using the poet's first name, refer to 'MacCaig', 'Norman MacCaig' or 'the poet'.

Sample answer 2

The poem's opening lines are highly atmospheric. MacCaig creates a powerful impression of a freezing November night that 'tinkles like ice in glasses'. While sibilant alliteration suggests the shrill sound of winter wind, there is also an unexpected sense of celebration in the simile. The first stanza is filled with detailed description of the cold outdoor scene. Personification is effectively used to convey the intrusive fog – 'brown air fumes at the shop windows'. The dense air is depicted as a threatening figure, trying to break into houses before it 'sidles past'.

MacCaig's metaphorical language continues in stanza two as the poet expresses experiencing 'winter raw'. The harsh weather is depicted as something that must be endured, to 'gulp down'. Yet the windswept darkness 'swirls' around the buildings. The dynamic verb adding to the dramatic mood. Dull lights 'fade' and 'die' in the murky streets.

As he continues his walk, the poet's feelings of isolation are evident, 'Frost in my lungs is harsh' – sharp 'r' sounds emphasise the chilling night air. MacCaig compares the high gable walls to 'roof sales', suggesting that he is at sea. Despite the coldness, he seems exhilarated – close to nature and excited by the harsh beauty of the 'ragged star'.

The poem ends on this ambiguous note. While the rest of the world is 'snoring' like a hibernating bear in his den, the poet is energised and acutely aware of the natural world. He is experiencing the fog's scent which is 'bitter' and yet unfolds like a delicate chrysanthemum.

Throughout the poem, MacCaig has captured the harsh and exciting mood of a bitterly cold night in Edinburgh's foggy streets. Vivid sensual images convey the severe weather, but there is also an appreciation of how the poet feels invigorated by his experience.

EXAMINER'S COMMENT

- Addresses the question successfully by focusing on the poet's language.
- Good focus also on the effectiveness of language use.
- Impressive range of stylistic techniques discussed.
- Excellent use of examples of sound effects, comparisons, personification, etc.
- Response is organised into paragraphs and expression is clear throughout.
- Confidently written top-rate standard.

MARKS AWARDED: $\frac{20}{20}$

key point

There is no single 'correct' reading of the poem.

Practice exercise 2

Read the following poem by Brian Patten and answer the question which follows.

First Love

Falling in love was like falling down the stairs
Each stair had her name on it
And he went bouncing down each one like a tongue-tied lunatic
One day of loving her was an ordinary year
He transformed her into what he wanted
And the scent from her
Was the best scent in the world
Fifteen he was fifteen
Each night he dreamed of her
Each day he telephoned her
Each day was unfamiliar
Scary even
And the fear of her going weighed on him like a stone
And when he could not see her for two nights running
It seemed a century had passed
And meeting her and staring at her face
He knew he would feel as he did forever
Hopelessly in love
Sick with it
And not even knowing her second name yet
It was the first time
The best time
A time that would last forever
Because it was new
Because he was ignorant it could ever end
It was endless

Brian Patten

Question 1

Discuss the effectiveness of the poet's use of language throughout this poem. Your answer should refer closely to the text. (20 marks)

Prompt!

- Dynamic opening image – literally falling in love.
- Run-on lines and breathless rhythm reflect mood of excitement.
- Repetition of 'scent' and 'Each' emphasise emotions.
- Evocative comparisons: 'like a stone', 'century'.
- Change of tone: dread of rejection ('Hopelessly', 'Sick').
- Final sense of reality ('ignorant it could ever end').
- Short lines reflecting shock.

exam focus

Always quote from the poem to support your main discussion points.

Checklist

- ○ Study the wording of questions to identify the task or tasks that you have to do.
- ○ Express points clearly.
- ○ Include and supportive reference or quotation (correctly punctuated).
- ○ Refer to both the poet's style (how the poem is written) as well as the themes (what the poet is writing about).
- ○ Select interesting phrases that give you an opportunity to discuss subject matter and use of language.
- ○ Avoid writing summaries.
- ○ Engage with the poem by responding genuinely to what the poet has written.

Prescribed Poetry (50 marks)

aims

- Identifying and understanding the key themes and writing styles of prescribed poets.
- Developing effective responses to examination questions.

There will be questions on four poets (from the eight prescribed) on the examination paper. You are required to **write about one poet only**. This means that you will need to **study at least five poets** to ensure that you will be prepared for this section.

exam focus

Examiners will reward your awareness of the poem's language – especially imagery, tone, sensuous qualities and suggestiveness.

Prescribed poets

Poets prescribed for Higher Level, to be examined in the following years:

2021	2022
Bishop, Elizabeth	Bishop, Elizabeth
Boland, Eavan	Dickinson, Emily
Durcan, Paul	Keats, John
Frost, Robert	Kennelly, Brendan
Heaney, Seamus	Lawrence, D. H.
Hopkins, Gerard Manley	Rich, Adrienne
Keats, John	Wordsworth, William
Plath, Sylvia	Yeats, W. B.

> **Elizabeth Bishop** and **John Keats** are prescribed poets for both the 2021 and 2022 Leaving Cert (Higher Level) examinations.

Exam overview

You are not expected to write about any set number of poems in the examination. Many candidates use the 50 minutes allocated for this question to focus on three or four poems; they usually write one or two well-developed paragraphs on each of the poems they have chosen for discussion.

When discussing recurring themes or features of style, appropriate cross-references to other poems may also be useful.

Analysing poetry

In preparing for the exam, study the following aspects of your chosen poems:

- Theme – what the poem is about (ideas or experiences the poets wish to share with readers).
- Title – what does it suggest?
- Imagery – visual images can be evocative and dramatic.
- Sound effects – these include rhyme, rhythm, repetition, alliteration and onomatopoeia.
- Tone – is there a dominant tone? Tones vary greatly: happy, excited, sad, angry, etc.
- Mood or atmosphere of the poems.
- Words and phrases that you find interesting.

> See list of poetic features on page 231.

- In answering exam questions, discuss the poet's key themes and distinctive style.
- Examine imagery, tone, sound effects, rhythm, etc. Comment on language use.
- When writing about interesting images or sounds, always discuss their effectiveness.

Revising Elizabeth Bishop (1911–1979)

Elizabeth Bishop was born in Worcester, Massachusetts, in 1911. She spent part of her childhood with her Canadian grandparents following her father's death and her mother's hospitalisation. She then lived with various relatives.

These unsettling events, along with the memories of her youth, inspired her to read poetry – and eventually to write it. After studying English at university, she travelled extensively and lived in New York, Florida and Brazil.

As a poet, she wrote sparingly, publishing only five slim volumes in 35 years. However, her poetry received high praise. 'I think geography comes first in my work,' she told an interviewer, 'and then animals. But I like people, too. I've written a few poems about people'.

Key themes	Poetic style
• The natural world	• Observational descriptive detail
• People's relationship with nature	• Vibrant visual imagery
• Childhood and coming-of-age	• Evocative sound effects
• Travel	• Dramatic settings
• The mystery of life	• Sympathetic/reflective tone

The 50-minute poetry question focuses essentially on the **poet's themes and style**. Study the wording of questions carefully to identify the key aspects of themes and style to be discussed.

Prescribed Elizabeth Bishop poems (2021 and 2022)

1. The Fish*

A narrative poem that describes catching 'a tremendous fish'. The experience focuses Bishop's thinking on the relationship between human beings and nature.

2. The Bight

Bishop's description of a small, untidy bight (bay) makes her reflect on the chaotic nature of everyday life.

3. At the Fishhouses
The poet returns to her childhood home in Nova Scotia and observes significant changes that have taken place.

4. The Prodigal*
Based on the bible story of the Prodigal Son, this poem explores the power of the human spirit to endure hardship and retain hope.

5. Questions of Travel
This reflective poem addresses themes of identity, self-understanding and the morality of tourism. Bishop challenges readers to consider the meaning of 'home'.

6. The Armadillo
The poet describes the beautiful – but dangerous – fire balloons lighting up the night sky during a religious festival in Rio de Janeiro.

7. Sestina
This tender account of a grandmother and a child living with loss explores poignant themes of grief and coming-of-age.

8. First Death in Nova Scotia
Bishop's intensely vivid memory of the death of her cousin Arthur leads to reflections on childhood bewilderment and innocence.

9. Filling Station*
Closely observed description of a run-down filling station where the nurturing influence of women is evident.

10. In the Waiting Room
Bishop recalls sitting in the dentist's waiting room when she was six years old. The dramatic scene highlights difficult aspects of childhood experience.

* Note: Poems marked with an asterisk are also prescribed for the Ordinary Level course.

Revision notes – 'The Fish'

Subject matter
In this deceptively simple poem, Bishop recalls catching a fish and observing it closely. As she scrutinises the fish, she begins to admire its courage and resilience.

Development of thought
Bishop's intimate first-person style immediately involves the reader: 'I caught a tremendous fish'. Short run-on lines suggest her excitement. As she observes the fish closely, the poet's sense of wonder increases. Its surface details are painstakingly and imaginatively described.

This mysterious creature has skin like wallpaper. The texture of its 'speckled' and 'infested' skin is detailed graphically as if magnified under a microscope. Bishop even imagines the fish's insides ('pink swim-bladder/like a big peony'). Such vivid images appeal to both our visual and tactile senses.

This fish has survived previous battles ('five big hooks/grown firmly in his mouth') and Bishop's sympathy is clear as she notes its 'aching jaw'. The poet's attention is then drawn to a small pool of oil in the boat, and the way it has spread into a rainbow.

In awe of the fish, she suddenly experiences a strange feeling of transcendence. For a moment, Bishop is overcome by the beauty of the scene and everything is transformed. In the end, the fish has won her respect and she returns it to the water.

Key quotes from 'The Fish'	
'He hung a grunting weight, battered and venerable'	The onomatopoeic effect of 'grunting' allows us to be part of this scene, as we hear the distressed noises from the exhausted fish. Bishop already feels that it is 'venerable', ancient and worthy of reverence.
'A green line, frayed at the end where he broke it'	This precise image emphasises the severity of the fish's previous encounters as it struggled to be free. Closely observed colour and texture recur throughout the poem.
'until everything/was rainbow, rainbow, rainbow!'	Bishop's relationship with the fish has changed. Her enthusiastic tone expresses a deep sense of joy which is symbolised in the beautiful image of a rainbow.

Writing a practice paragraph

Question

'Elizabeth Bishop's nature poems have a sense of energy and drama that reflect the poet's deep sense of wonder.'

Discuss this view, supporting your answer with particular reference to 'The Fish'.

Sample paragraph 1 (basic grade)

The fish is a very good nature poem in which Bishop remembers catching a fish. This big fish has plenty of energy and is hard work. We learn a lot nowadays about how fishing can be dangerous from shows on tv. Bishop makes a bit of a drama out of catching this fish. She says its grunting and she gets obsessed by it. Bishop finds a few rusty hooks stuck in its jaw and this gets her thinking about the way it must have escaped getting hooked in long ago. The best bit of drama in this nature poem is at the very end. She keeps staring at the poor fish who is like a brave soldier to her and she then feels sorry for catching it in the first place and then lets the fish go back to where it belongs in the water.

Improving the answer:
- Much more attention needs to be given to addressing the question directly by examining three key elements of the question (energy, drama and the poet's sense of wonder).
- The use of suitable and accurate quotations would provide a good basis for developing relevant points successfully.
- Various mechanical flaws include omission of some capital letters and punctuation marks.
- None of these errors are evident in the focused top-grade paragraph that follows.

Sample paragraph 2 (top grade)

The poem opens dramatically as Bishop reels in 'a tremendous fish'. Her excited tone reflects her fascination and sense of wonder. Bishop personifies the fish – 'He didn't fight' – and describes its appearance in great detail, 'He was speckled with barnacles'. In a strange way, she sees the fish and herself as characters in a tense confrontation, 'I looked into his eyes'. Vivid imagery suggests the power of the fish, 'the dramatic reds and blacks of his shiny entrails'. The fish's irises seem 'packed with tarnished tinfoil'. The sharp aural effects and alliterative 't' sound emphasise this striking image. Repetition of 'stared' reflects the poet's increasing involvement in the stand-off. As her respect for the 'venerable' fish intensifies, Bishop becomes mesmerised by this beautiful creature and its fight for life. The drama builds to a climax as she suddenly decides to 'let the fish go'.

Revision points

- Themes in 'The Fish' include endurance, and the relationship between people and nature.
- Observational details, vibrant language, personification, striking comparisons.
- Emotional intensity and varying tones – excited, admiring, celebratory.
- Memorable sound effects – assonance, alliteration, sibilance, repetition.
- Dramatic development ends in a moment of insight.

Revision notes – 'Filling Station'

Subject matter

Closely observed description of a run-down filling station where unexpected signs of beauty and the nurturing influence of women are evident.

Development of thought

Over the course of the poem, Bishop describes her initial reaction, and later feelings, about a shabby filling station. She immediately observes that everything seems to be covered in oil, including the father and his sons who work there. Images of dirt and grease are emphasised.

The poet's focus then moves away from the unappealing aspects of this grimy setting to some unexpected artistic touches. She wonders about the lives of the people who run the filling station. Certain objects suddenly attract her attention.

The begonia houseplant and embroidered doily seem to represent the human search for a little attractiveness in a world that is often grim. The family's lifestyle raises several questions (none of which are fully answered).

After seeing the care given to a few parts of the home, however, Bishop reaches the conclusion that there is usually 'Somebody' behind the scenes who lovingly manages everything, even if her work is not always obvious.

Key quotes from 'Filling Station'	
'several quick and saucy/and greasy sons assist him'	Bishop often uses aural effects to convey meaning. Sibilant 's' sounds highlight the easy fluid movements of the young workers.
'Embroidered in daisy stitch/with marguerites'	Precise detail is a recurring feature of the poet's familiar 'painterly style'. In this case, she detects the artistic feminine touch in contrast to the chaotic male world at the front of the filling station.
'Somebody loves us all'	The ending is usually interpreted as being reassuring. But could Bishop's tone be ironic? Is the world really so caring?

Writing a practice paragraph

Question

'Elizabeth Bishop's carefully crafted poems often explore aspects of ordinary life with great compassion.'

To what extent do you agree with this statement? Develop your answer with particular reference to 'Filling Station'.

Sample paragraph 1 (basic grade)

Bishop's poems are carefully crafted. Their crafted to explore aspects of ordinary life with great compassion. The woman in the car goes in for petrol and she is soon sorry the place is so dirty and 'oil drenched'. The whole outside is covered in oil and its dangerous if anyone struck a match. I think she's having second thoughts about staying but she sees a few comics and a lot of pot plants, so she thinks their is a family living round the back and they craft the plants and line up the oil cans in a row. She changes her mind about the station because it's not all bad and so she gets her fuel and stops giving off about how dirty the outside yard is. At the end the woman has a funny feeling about how the family all love each other to bits which is some change from how she felt when she first parked at the pumps.

Improving the answer:

- A more focused response would trace the development of thought. High-grade answers show how imagery, tone, sound, etc. establish the setting and the speaker's changing mood.
- Successful responses use apt reference and accurate quotation to address the main elements of the question (poet's craft, aspects of life and compassion).
- Mechanical flaws include awkward grammar and some spelling errors. None of these are evident in the focused top-grade paragraph that follows.

Sample paragraph 2 (top grade)

The poet begins by expressing her disgust over the state of 'this little filling station'. She notices the signs of a disorganised male world, 'oil permeated' and 'thoroughly dirty'. Her tone is critical at first – 'Oh, but it is dirty!' Each stanza takes a closer look around the station and detailed visual images build up a vivid picture. Bishop becomes fascinated, asking herself a series of carefully considered questions about the day-to-day lives of the people living there. She wonders about the strangeness of their presence and the evidence of items that are lovingly made and cared for. In complete contrast to the greasy outside space, there is some attractive furniture: a taboret, plus a begonia and a crocheted doily. Bishop understands that it's important not to judge on first impressions. Ordinary lives are not just about work. People are interested in beauty as well. The ending is much more compassionate, although she leaves it up to us to decide who exactly 'loves us all'.

Revision points

- Themes in 'Filling Station' include family life, nurturing femininity, appearance and reality.
- Vivid picture of homely petrol station through closely observed visual detail.
- Cinematic techniques: close-up images, cutaway scenes, dialogue, cast of characters.
- Conversational and colloquial language, flashes of humour.
- Contemptuous tone gives way to a concluding note of reassurance.
- Realisation that love and beauty can be found anywhere.

Sample essay

exam Q

Question

'Bishop makes effective use of a range of stylistic features to explore how human beings respond to the challenges and uncertainties of everyday life.'

Discuss this statement, developing your answer with reference to the poetry of Elizabeth Bishop on your course.

Sample answer

1   Elizabeth Bishop's poems are mostly based on personal experiences. Many of them go back to her own painful memories of her childhood. These lead to insights about life. Poems like 'The Prodigal', 'Sestina' and 'First Death in Nova Scotia' show her understanding of life's problems. She often explores the confusion of growing up and grief. Bishop is known for descriptive language, especially in her use of imagery and atmosphere.

2   'The Prodigal' is her version of a Bible story of a young man who sinks very low in society because of alchohol addiction. Bishop focuses on life's bleak side. The opening shows her skill at setting up the shameful farmyard scene in which he lives. The youth is with the pigs in dehumanised conditions. Effective images show the filthy atmosphere in 'the brown enormous odour'. Bishop gives a disturbing view of alchoholism and how it can ruin people. In the early morning, the situation is seen through a cloud of alchohol. The youth can even find the beauty in nature, 'the sunrise glazed over farmyard mud with red'. She shows him responding to his addiction and the truth about his life is beginning to be understood by him and he feels he may be able to 'go home'.

3   One of Bishop's best skills is detailed descriptions. This is seen in 'Sestina', one of her personal poems that is filled with unhappiness. She describes an ordinary everyday situation, with a grandmother sitting in the kitchen as rain falls outside and the light fades. She is making tea and reading to her granddaughter. But this cosy scene changes in tone as there is a strange feeling of uncertainty to do with the passing of time.

4   Bishop shows her writing skill in this poem. Everything takes place in the kitchen. The atmosphere has mystery and magic. It's also very dark and secretive like a fairytale. In the end, a very surprising thing happens. The buttons in the child's drawing seem to be 'little moons that fall down like tears ... into the flower bed' in the drawing. The attention is on the tears as if Bishop is saying that life will bring about pain and sadness to everyone, both old and young. Bishop offers an awareness into the disappointments and challenges of life. People often worry about the whole mystery of life and are afraid of getting old.

5   'First Death in Nova Scotia' is from the view of a child experiencing death for the first time. Her mother has brought her to see the body of her cousin Arthur. The child observes the portraits of a royal family hanging around

the body. These are all 'warm in red'. This gets her to imagine that they have called him to be a page boy in court Bishop creates very disturbing images. Near the body is a stuffed loon bird on a 'marble topped table'. The dead body appears 'white, like a doll' and 'Jack Frost had started to paint him'. The images are quite weird. She contrasts Arthur with the royal couples in their ermine fur. The young girl is confused about death and wonders how Arthur could get to the royal court 'with his eyes shut up so tight and the roads deep in snow'. This is suggesting that the child and perhaps Bishop herself as an adult is questioning the existence of an afterlife. Once again, this is a topic that affects a lot of people who are concerned about death and their religous faith.

6   Bishop's comparisons are also very effective. She uses these stylistic features to show an awareness of the suffering of animals in 'The Fish'. Her description of the 'tremendous fish' is very detailed. Its 'brown skin hung down in strips like old wallpaper'. Bishop shows the fish's blotched skin 'like full-blown roses' and gives a close-up cinematic picture of the vivid colours, 'dramatic blacks and reds'. Bishop is facing a challenge of what to do with the fish. The fish represents nature and people everywhere have to deal with nature as to respecting it or not. She sees how the fish has suffered so much with 'five hooks' still stuck in its sore jaws. Another powerful image shows its 'sullen face'. Bishop begins to admire the fish for its beauty and for putting up a fight. This leads to her showing respect for nature, so she acts. 'I then let the fish go'. Again, we all live in a world where we are in danger of destroying nature. So, this is another challenge of everyday life that Bishop explores effectively.

7   Bishop shows a wide variety of stylistic features to communicate ideas about life. The stories and people in her poems are often associated with loss, suffering or asking questions about the uncertain aspects of life. Many of the poems show her facing life's realities and her themes of death, pain and loss of innocence are timeless.

(825 words)

EXAMINER'S COMMENT

The essay includes some reasonably authentic engagement with the question, with discussion rooted in the texts of the poems. Paragraphs 5 and 6 contain good commentary on the poet's style. The analysis could have been clearer and more developed at times. Despite misquotes, repetitive functional expression and mechanical errors (e.g. 'would of', 'in which', 'alchohol', 'religous'), this is a solid mid-grade response that interacted quite well with Bishop's themes and style.

GRADE H3

P = 11/15

C = 11/15

L = 10/15

M = 4/5

Total = 36/50

Revising John Keats (1795–1821)

John Keats is one of the most widely recognised English poets. He is best known for his series of odes, filled with rich images of nature. Many of his poems reflect his intense inner conflicts and are noted for their strength of feeling.

Time and the mortality of human existence are recurring subjects. Keats often associated love with pain – both in his personal life and in his poetry.

While Keats's style is characterised by sensual language and other poetic devices, all of these contribute to the rhythm and music in his work. His images range across all our physical sensations: sight, hearing, taste, touch and smell.

A passionate believer in the power of the imagination, Keats often contrasted the real-world human experience with an ideal world of permanence. In his view, poetry made life permanent.

Key themes	Poetic style
• Love	• Vivid imagery
• Nature	• Sensual sounds
• Beauty	• Personification
• Imagination	• Contrasts and tension
• Art and literature	• Rich symbolism
• Human mortality	• Evocative tones

Prescribed John Keats poems (2021 and 2022)

1. To One Who Has Been Long in City Pent
Evocative sonnet describing the delights of the countryside and reflecting tenderly on the passing of time.

2. Ode to a Nightingale
In this highly passionate poem, Keats tries to escape from reality through the haunting beauty of the nightingale's song.

3. On First Looking into Chapman's Homer *
After reading the translated works of Homer, the poet expresses his excitement and delight in this dramatic sonnet.

4. Ode on a Grecian Urn
Keats's famous ode explores the relationship between the permanent world of art and the transience of real life.

5. When I Have Fears That I May Cease to Be
This carefully crafted sonnet expresses Keats's anxiety about dying before he has time to fulfil his potential as a poet.

6. La Belle Dame Sans Merci *
Medieval ballad telling the tragic story of a lovesick knight and his 'beautiful lady without mercy'.

7. To Autumn
The poem highlights nature's beauty by contrasting the pleasures and rich abundance of the season with human transience.

8. Bright Star, Would I Were Steadfast as Thou Art
Keats is fascinated by the prospect of a beautiful unchanging world, but is forced to accept that his dream is impossible.

* Note: Poems marked with an asterisk are also prescribed for the Ordinary Level course.

Revision notes – 'On First Looking into Chapman's Homer'

Subject matter
In this beautiful sonnet, Keats describes the astonishing effect of discovering great works of literature.

Development of thought
In the opening lines, Keats expresses his personal love of classic poetry, which he sees as a breath-taking adventure. He compares himself to a traveller who delights in exploring exciting new places, 'realms of gold'. This metaphor of discovery is extended throughout the poem.

Keats had only heard about the imaginative world of the Greek poet Homer, but everything changed when he read the translations of Homer's work by George Chapman. The impact was 'loud and bold'.

The sense of astonishment is conveyed through powerful run-on lines and two dramatic similes. Keats suddenly felt like an astronomer witnessing 'a new planet' among the stars. He also likens the experience to the kind of wonder felt by the Spanish explorer Cortez when he first set eyes on a new ocean.

By the end of the poem, Keats is completely 'silent', overwhelmed by the power of literature. Homer's poetry has invited him into what appears to be an exhilarating new world.

Key quotes from 'On First Looking into Chapman's Homer'

'Much have I travell'd in the realms of gold'	Keats uses a striking travel metaphor to show his love of literature, comparing himself to an explorer who has discovered wonderful poetic treasures.
'Then felt I like some watcher of the skies'	The poet's forceful simile highlights the stunning experience of reading Homer's poetry. Keats felt like an astronomer witnessing a new planet.
'all his men/Looked at each other with a wild surmise'	In a final dramatic comparison, Keats imagines how the first European explorers reacted to seeing the vast Pacific Ocean when they observed it from a mountain peak in the Darien region of Panama.

Writing a practice paragraph

Question

'Keats makes effective use of a variety of stylistic features to express his intense awareness of human experience.'

Discuss this view, supporting your answer with particular reference to 'On First Looking into Chapman's Homer'.

Sample paragraph 1 (basic grade)

Keats has an effective use of stylistic features to express his intense human awareness of experience in his poem intitled First looking into chapmans Homer. The poem is all about his experience of reading about a greek poet and it protrays a love of travelling and Keats talks about sailing into a western island which really stands for the greek writer. The writing of Homer was translated so that made it easy for Keats to discover it. He was really shocked to read greek litrature as protrayed in english. Keats uses a variety of very good images to talk about the effect of all this on his mind. It was as if he was sailing in the old days and finding a new western island or even hiking across a mountain peak where there was nothing but new sights and sounds to be discovered. So, this is how Keats uses stylistic features to express an intense awareness of human experience.

Improving the answer:

- Much greater focus is needed on the poet's use of comparative language (metaphors and similes) to express his feelings.
- Mechanical errors ('intitled', 'protray', 'litrature') and lack of capital letters ('greek', 'english') weaken the response.
- A successful answer would discuss how Keats conveys his sense of wonder through vivid imagery, enthusiastic tone, run-on lines and insistent rhythms.

Sample paragraph 2 (top grade)

The opening lines of the sonnet 'On First Looking into Chapman's Homer' describe Keats's travels in the 'realms of gold'. The metaphor refers to his imagination. Keats develops the image of discovery in a series of images – 'states and kingdoms', 'islands', 'the Pacific'. He associates himself with the explorers of the past, giving his journeys into literature a similar sense of adventure. In the sestet, Keats reveals his delight in reading Homer's poetry, using a tone of breathless excitement – 'Then felt I like some watcher of the skies/When a new planet swims into his ken'. The poem builds to a dramatic climax with the vivid image of Cortez staring in awestruck silence at the sight of the Pacific. The alliteration of the phrase describing his 'eagle eyes' emphasises the power of both the vast ocean and great poetry. This final symbol leaves me with an understanding of Keats's own feelings of wonder at discovering 'deep-browed Homer'.

Revision points

- Sonnet celebrates the imaginative vision of great literature.
- Archaic language in keeping with Keats's regard for Homer's epic poetry.
- Run-on lines add to the poem's powerful rhythm.
- Sustained metaphor of exploration.

Revision notes – 'When I Have Fears That I May Cease to Be'

Subject matter

Keats expresses his anxiety about the transience of human existence and reflects on his poetic achievement and reputation.

Development of thought

Keats reflects on the inevitable passing of time and the possibility that he might die before he has achieved his creative potential. He views his poetic imagination as a landscape ready to be harvested. Images of fertility – 'gleaned', 'garners', 'full ripen'd grain' – reinforce this idea.

exam focus

- Avoid starting poetry essays with prepared biographical sketches.
- Focus on the actual question and discuss key poems.

Observing the starry night sky, a vital source of romantic inspiration, the poet wonders if he will ever get the chance to understand nature's wonders – 'cloudy symbols of a high romance'.

But as well as being anxious about not being able to fulfil himself as an artist, Keats is also fearful of not experiencing human intimacy as a lover.

In the concluding couplet, Keats sees himself as isolated, cut off from all human contact; he is a lone figure on a forsaken shore. He appears to have reached a stage beyond fear and yearning. The fatalistic tone and the slow rhythm seem to reflect his stark realisation that mortality turns everything to 'nothingness' – including love and poetry.

Key quotes from 'When I Have Fears That I May Cease to Be'	
'Before my pen has gleaned my teeming brain'	The farming metaphor suggests that Keats hopes to write many more poems and to harvest the fruits of his lively imagination.
'Never have relish in the faery power/Of unreflecting love'	Keats fears that he may never fully enjoy the pleasures of a romantic relationship that will allow him to abandon himself to pure feeling.
'... I stand alone, and think/Till love and fame to nothingness do sink'	When measured against the scope of the 'wide world', Keats realises that all his earlier concerns are insignificant. Assonant sounds emphasise his deep sense of despair.

Writing a practice paragraph

Question

'Keats's poems are often defined by sensuous imagery, personal tensions and a preoccupation with mortality.'

Discuss this view, supporting your answer with particular reference to 'When I Have Fears That I May Cease to Be'.

Sample paragraph 1 (basic grade)

John Keats wrote a lot about dying and he had fears of dying in When I Have Fears, his famous poem. He's just young in which his whole life lay ahead of him and he didn't think it was fair that he was seriously ill so that he would not have enough time to write great poems that would make him famous. This is nearly a preoccupation of his in which he has a whole bucket list of plans ahead. John also wants to be with his girlfriend because she's a fair creature who has a hold on him. But it's not going to happen because he's facing into a death sentence that defines him. The sensual imagery is there when John walks along the sea front and is feeling sort of down because he knows the game is up and he is sinking into nothing. A lot of the sensual image defines him sinking into the sand as he walks along the beach.

Improving the answer:

- A much more successful response would focus on the other key aspects of sensual language and tensions as well as the theme of mortality.
- Discussion of the harvest and sky images, sensual sound effects and the poem's poignant ending would improve the standard.
- Expression could be more carefully controlled – particularly by avoiding slang and repetition. In addition, it is not usual to refer to poets by their first name.

Sample paragraph 2 (top grade)

'When I Have Fears That I May Cease to Be' expresses Keats's tragic character and the personal turmoil in his life. The fact that he won't have time to make his mark on the world is captured by the urgency of the opening of the sonnet. His anxiety is seen in the dramatic tone as he worries about his efforts to write new poems, 'the full ripen'd grain'. Deep down, he wonders if he will reach his full creative potential before his pen has even 'gleaned' his 'teeming brain'. The imagery is rich and sensuous, Keats is like a farmer harvesting the fruits of his fertile imagination. The conclusion is particularly dramatic, set on the 'wide world' of the shore. In a strange way, the tension eases as Keats accepts the fact he will die and never achieve his goals. Poetry and love will not matter in the end when there will only be 'nothingness'.

exam focus

In preparing for the prescribed poetry question, it makes sense to have studied as many poems as possible by each of your chosen poets. This will give you more choice in selecting poems that directly relate to the elements of the examination question. Aim for at least four or five poems by your chosen poets.

Revision points

- Explores familiar themes: transience, love, reputation, death.
- Concise sonnet form intensifies the poet's feelings.
- Effective use of vivid imagery – extended harvest metaphor.
- Evocative sound effects, personification, contrasting tones.

Sample essay

Question

'Keats's frequent desire to escape from reality is expressed through his effective use of sensual language and dramatic moments.'

Discuss this statement, supporting your answer with reference to the poetry of John Keats on your course.

Sample answer

1   John Keats keeps longing for an imaginary world. He has a deep desire to escape from life's realities, especially suffering, transience and the fear of death. At other times, he even wants to escape through dying. Keats creates powerful poetry using sensuous language. The poems are often dramatic. From the ones we have studied, I believe that even though he has fantasies about leaving the real world, he usually accepts reality despite all its challenges and disappointments.

2   The world of nature seems to represent a kind of paradise in John Keats's imagination. His wish to find happiness always suggests that his own life's existence was filled with pain. His poetry is characterised by intense feelings – often reflecting inner tensions. But strangely, Keats never fully escapes into this ideal world of beauty and perfection.

3   In 'Ode to a Nightingale' Keats is caught between different forces. He wants to end the suffering of this world, especially illness. This is portrayed in the sensual image of a young man 'pale, and spectre-thin'. But Keats also wishes for an ideal dream world. His sensual language remembers the real world's pleasures, such as the drinking of wine, 'a beaker full of the warm South … With beaded bubbles winking at the brim'. He also creates the dramatic setting of warm summer nights, using assonance, 'murmurous haunting flies'. Keats feels he would be deprived of the natural world's beauty, unable to see the flowers if he escaped into death. He would no longer hear the nightingale's song, 'Still wouldst thou sing, but I have ears in vain'. The 's' sounds add to the mysterious dramatic atmosphere.

4   Keats includes many dramatic images associated with death as a theme, such as 'embalmed' and 'requiem'. But dying has positives. Keats sees it as 'easeful', freeing him into an eternity of which there is no more suffering. But at the end, he wakes up from his dream to face life head on. He discovers that the imagined world created in his poetry is not lasting. So, he abandons this fantasy of escaping and admits that the dream is only temporary, 'cannot cheat so well/As she is fam'd to do'.

5   'La Belle Dame Sans Merci' is a dramatic poem about unhappy love between a medieval knight and a beautiful woman, 'a lady in the meads'. The knight is hoping for eternal romance. Keats describes the lady using sensual language, 'her hair was long, her foot was light'. The couple have a passionate affair, 'I shut her wild wild eyes/With kisses …'. However, she

soon rejects him and their relationship does not last. He sees other men she has rejected, 'pale kings and princes'. The image creates a haunting scene and a very dramatic atmosphere. The horrific sight of their 'starved lips' shows the consequences of falling in love with this merciless woman who eventually breaks all their hearts. Seeking perfect love is seen as an impossible dream that only causes tragedy.

6   'On First Looking into Chapman's Homer' is another poem that deals with escape. In this case, an escape into great literature. Keats creates a dramatic scene of discovery using a metaphor of exploring new seas. This suggests the moment when he first read Chapman's translation of Homer's epic poetry, 'Then felt I like a watcher of the skies'. The graphic image of the famous Spanish explorer, 'stout Cortez' staring at the Pacific Ocean 'with eagle eyes', really symbolises reaching perfection.

7   Keats compares himself to an astronomer struggling with his new discovery when an unnamed planet 'swims into his ken'. Once again, he uses sensual language to show his astonishment, 'wild', 'surmise'. At the end of the poem, he describes the sailors who travelled with Cortez as they reached the mountain top overlooking the great new expanse of sea, 'silent upon a peak in Darien'. People long to escape but often struggle to understand these new places. This is very similar to the conclusion in 'When I Have Fears That I May Cease to Be' when the poet stands 'on the shore/Of the wide world' alone and thinks 'Till love and fame to nothingness do sink'.

8   There is always tension between what Keats imagines and everyday reality. In 'When I Have Fears', he is afraid to die before he writes the poems he wants to. In this case, he does not wish to escape life. Instead, he is keen on escaping death for as long as possible. In the second section of the sonnet, he is filled with regret that he will not reach this 'high romance'. Keats uses natural images to describe his 'teeming brain'. The language is intense, filled with references to harvesting the fields to produce 'full ripen'd grain'.

9   So many of Keats's poems show him as a dreamer whose imagination allows us to share his desire to escape reality. Yet, in all of these visionary poems, he comes to accept and value the real world, with all its wonder.

(828 words)

EXAMINER'S COMMENT

A good essay, generally focused on the main elements of the question (escape, sensual language, drama). The stance set out in the introductory paragraph is followed by some perceptive critical discussion – particularly in paragraphs 3, 4 and 5 where aspects of style are highlighted. However, more development of main points would have been welcome. Expression is functional and reasonably well-managed, although there is occasional awkwardness (e.g. in paragraph 4). Effective use of accurate quotations throughout, often well-integrated into the commentary.

GRADE H2

P = 12/15

C = 12/15

L = 11/15

M = 5/5

Total = 40/50

Revising Eavan Boland (Prescribed for 2021 only)

Key themes	Poetic style
• The marginalised and excluded	• Dramatic features
• Love and family relationships	• Evocative atmospheres
• Oppression of women	• Striking observational details
• Irish history and tradition	• Precise vivid images
• Mystery and beauty of nature	• Mythical references

Sample essay

Question

'From the poetry of Eavan Boland that you have studied, select the poems that, in your opinion, best demonstrate her skilful use of language and imagery to explore aspects of identity and exclusion.'

Justify your selection by demonstrating Boland's skilful use of language and imagery to explore aspects of identity and exclusion in the poems you have chosen.

Sample answer

1   Eavan Boland's poems range over many topics, sometimes celebrating the importance of family and at other times being very critical of society – particularly the treatment of outsiders. She often uses personal experience to reflect on issues of universal importance, as in 'The Shadow Doll' and 'Child of Our Time'. Boland also addresses the realities of women's experiences. Her low-key poetic style is known for its precise imagery and variety of compelling tomes.

2   In my opinion, Boland explores women's issues most interestingly in 'The Shadow Doll'. The poem opens with a description of a porcelain doll. There are close-up details of the doll's 'stitched' dress with its fine 'ivory tulle' and 'hoops for the crinoline'. The doll is modelling the wedding dress that was sent to a young bride in Victorian times. Boland cleverly uses the doll image as a striking symbol of restriction. It is 'neatly sewn' and confined inside the 'airless glamour' of a small glass dome. The doll represents the way women are expected to fit a passive role in life, in this case, the bride. It is kept 'under wraps', excluded from expressing desires – 'quickenings and lusts'.

3   Boland goes on to reflect on the feelings she had the evening before she herself got married, 'the vows I kept repeating'. There is a sense that she remembers being scared as she sat 'astray among the cards and wedding gifts'. The final lines convey a dramatic image of herself 'pressing down' on her 'battered' suitcase. The adjective suggests the abuse that has often been experienced by unfortunate women who have had to endure violence in their relationships. Boland seems to be also hinting at the loss of individual identity that can occur through marriage.

4 'Child of Our Time' addresses the effects of violence more directly. It was written in response to a photograph of a fire fighter carrying an innocent child victim during the chaos of the Dublin bombings In 1974. The poem is typical of where Boland speaks up for victims and reminds Irish people of their responsibility because of our common identity. The tone gradually changes from sympathy for the child, 'Yesterday I knew no lullaby' to indignation and resentment, 'our times have robbed your cradle'.

5 Boland condemns Irish society that allowed this to happen and 'must learn from you dead'. Once again, her language is precise. The poem moves from the use of the pronoun 'I' in the first stanza to 'our' in the final section. It is 'our idle/Talk' that has cost the life of this child. The run-through line and assonance reflect the poignant subject of this poem. Boland mourns the 'unreasoned end' and challenges every Irish person to find 'a new language' to bring about a peaceful future.

6 A sharp awareness of Irish identity is found in 'The Famine Road'. Boland uses multiple narrative voices to link the mistreatment of impoverished Irish people during the Great Famine and the experience of a modern woman who is disrespected by her doctor. The sense of Irish identity that comes across is relatable because it is all about victimisation. Being downtrodden and living pointless lives. The excluded peasants were abused by the English who forced them to build roads just to tire them out. Boland links this to a modern woman who is unable to get pregnant, 'never to know the load of his child in you'. Her doctor shows no compassion. But just tells her to accept the bad news. This is how the woman sees her own life. Again, the symbol of a famine road going nowhere gets the theme across.

7 Boland often speaks for forgotten people who are discarded to the margins of society. The very title of 'Outside History' shows her interest in the excluded. 'The War Horse' explores middle-class attitudes to the vicious conflict that went on in the Northern Troubles and in the earlier Irish Civil War. Using the symbol of a runaway horse that is ignored by the local residents, the poet challenges us to think about how we respond to warfare. The noise of the 'loosed' animal is described through the onomatopoeic sound effects, the 'clip clop' of the horse's hooves which are out of place in the suburbs where residents wish to protect their lawns. Boland's images are forceful, 'stamps death', 'breath hissing'. The most disturbing image is of the crushed crocus. She describes its 'bulbous head' as 'one of the screamless dead'.

8 Boland is quietly critical in her poems. In 'The War Horse', she accuses Irish people of looking out for themselves and not being interested in the 'screamless dead' who suffered in past conflicts. This is typical of her compassion for the excluded. In exploring themes of power and powerlessness, her poetic style is always engaging. The use of vivid images and symbols as well as changes in tone and atmosphere define Boland as a skilful and thought-provoking poet.

(820 words)

EXAMINER'S COMMENT

Focused discussion on recurring themes and key aspects of the poet's style sustained throughout in the three chosen poems. However, the cross-reference to 'Outside History' in paragraph 7 deserved some development. Overall, good use of embedded quotes to illustrate main points. Expression was generally clear, apart from some repetition and awkwardness in paragraph 6.

GRADE H2
P = 14/15
C = 12/15
L = 12/15
M = 5/5
Total = 43/50

key point

You need to study at least five prescribed poets to be prepared for this section of the examination.

Revising Seamus Heaney (Prescribed for 2021 only)

Key themes	Poetic style
• Childhood in Co. Derry	• Colloquial speech
• Family relationships	• Striking figurative language
• Love, sorrow and yearning	• Sensuous sound effects
• Rural landscape and tradition	• Precise vivid images
• The natural world	• Contrasting moods

Sample essay

exam Q

Question

'Seamus Heaney's reflective poems explore love and loss, using language that is both precise and understated.'

Discuss this statement, supporting your answer with reference to the poems of Heaney on our course.

Sample answer

1   The poetry by Seamus Heaney on our course mostly took a personal narrative approach and included his nostalgic memories of growing up in Northern Ireland. Some poems reflected on relationships and rural life. Heaney has a deceptively simple style, evident in poems such as 'The Forge', 'Mossbawn: Sunlight' and 'The Skunk'. His style is known for his precise imagery and sound effects, but I have always found him to be a subtle poet whose poetry is highly emotive and filled with hidden meaning.

2 'The Forge' gives a vivid picture of the life of a traditional blacksmith who used to be one of the most important people serving the farming community, making iron implements and horseshoes. Heaney thinks back on his youth and describes the outside of the mysterious forge building in detail, with its 'old axles and iron hoops rusting'. The rust on these objects suggests time passing since the blacksmith began doing his traditional ironwork craft. The precise 'ring' of his anvil against the iron along with sparks flying and the hiss of water cooling a horseshoe sums up the magical process. The noisy activity is made real by Heaney's use of sibilance. The 's' sounds in 'hiss' made by the red-hot horseshoe cooling in water conveys the work going on inside the busy forge.

3 The exact description in this sonnet is carefully crafted – just like the blacksmith's work itself. The poem is reflective and can be interpreted as an elegy to the past. Heaney's tone is quite sad, suggesting that he is lamenting the lost tradition of the country blacksmith. I liked the way he compares the blacksmith to a priest by using a precise image. The anvil block where the blacksmith works is shaped like 'an altar' and the blacksmith is beating out 'real iron'. But even then, the modern world was beginning to change with tractors replacing ploughs. Instead, tractors were 'flashing in rows'. Reading 'The Forge' gave me an insight into how much Heaney loved the past and how he regretted the loss of traditional Irish crafts.

4 'The Skunk' focuses on Heaney's love for his wife. He reminisces about when he was separated from her while working in America. The opening lines are based on memories of the 'black striped' skunk appearing in the back garden of his house. This reminded Heaney of his wife back home. His sense of longing for her is evident. The setting in 'The Skunk' included detailed description of the exotic West Coast of Califronia, 'oranges loomed in the orange tree'. He really wasn't at home there. He is fascinated by the exotic animal. Just as he finds his wife extraordinary and precious. This is evident by the comparison where he thinks of her as a 'stored cask' treasured by the poet.

5 The images are sensuous and romantic. Heaney's language sums up a lot of smells, sights and sounds of California, all celebrating the primative nature of longing and desire. In the last stanza, he has a more recent vivid memory of waiting in bed for his wife as she changed into her 'plunge line nightdress'. Once again, he uses sibilant 's' sounds, 'stirred by the sootfall' and these are very atmospheric. I imagined the warm nights and the unusual scent – 'tang of eucaliptus spelt your absence'. Heaney often uses assonance to highlight sensations.

6 Conversational language is found throughout 'Mossbawn: Sunlight'. In this emotive poem, Heaney reflects on the heartfelt love he felt for his aunt and his longing for a childlike sense of security. The poem starts with a description of the silence he remembers when growing up in Mossbawn. Outside in the yard, the water pump is warmed by the sun. Another vivid image describes the 'slung bucket' of water as 'honeyed'. There is a feeling of time standing still. Heaney recalls the sunlight standing like a 'griddle cooling against the wall'. As she bakes bread in the kitchen, his aunt's hands are 'scuffled'.

7 The cinematic setting and close-up details really bring the scene to life. For me, this excilerating poem captures a special magical occurrence in Heaney's childhood. It sums up the love he felt for his aunt while also mourning the transcience of time. Picturing those minutes on a long afternoon, the poet freezes an image of family life into a timeless picture of love and security. The reference to the 'tick of two clocks' sums up the past and present very effectively. Heaney's alliteration quietly emphasises the cycle of life. It suggests the love that is now lost in a gentle understated way.

8 Heaney's poems often reflect on childhood and family themes. Not all of them are nostalgic, but many explore memory and the intense experiences of the past. Family memories have inspired very emotional poems, such as 'The Harvest Bow' and 'A Call' where the poet recalls his close relationship with his parents. The conversational language Heaney uses and the precision of sound and visual images really help to re-create the settings in such poems. Heaney's poems are carefully crafted and filled with subtle and underlying meanings.

(845 words)

EXAMINER'S COMMENT

This focused essay addresses all the main elements of the question and displays a good solid knowledge of the selected poems. Most discussion points are reasonably well-supported with apt quotation. Some weaknesses in expression (e.g. in the note-like paragraph 4). Both 'evident' and 'sums up' are overused, and there are several spelling errors ('primative', eucalyptus', 'excilerating', 'occurrence' and 'transcience').

GRADE H2

P = 13/15

C = 13/15

L = 12/15

M = 4/5

Total = 42/50

exam focus

You are unlikely to be rewarded for just pointing out features of the poems, such as images or other devices that are used. Aim to comment on the effects of such techniques, how they are linked to the ideas in the poems, and why you think they have been used.

Revising Brendan Kennelly (Prescribed for 2022 only)

Key themes	Poetic style
• Innocence and the wonder of life	• Contrasting tones – reflection, joy, anger
• The beauty and mystery of nature	• Distinctive rhyme and rhythmic patterns
• Family relationships and marriage	• Various forms – ballads, sonnets, letters
• Ireland's history and culture	• Striking visual and aural imagery
• Artistic creativity, love and loneliness	• Personification, range of narrative 'voices'

Sample essay

Question

'Brendan Kennelly uses language in skilful and innovative ways to explore a variety of contrasting emotional experiences.'

Discuss this view, supporting your answer with suitable reference to the poems by Kennelly on your course.

Sample answer

1   Brendan Kennelly's poems vary greatly. At times, he touches on troubling experiences, such as in 'Oliver to His Brother' where he presents Cromwell in a surprising way as a loving father and uncle. 'Fragments' is a reflective poem about how relationships change over time and couples fall out of love. 'A Cry for Art O'Leary' is a dramatic story of grief and love and anger. In complete contrast, Kennelly celebrates the joy and innocence of everyday life in his upbeat poem 'Begin'.

2   Kennelly's writing style also varies as much as the subjects he writes about. His inventive language is seen in 'Oliver to His Brother'. Cromwell is usually protrayed as a hateful figure in Ireland, but Kennelly presents another view – the loving concerned father and the polite brother. In presenting such a complex character, Kennelly imaginatively uses the actual words of Cromwell from a letter he once wrote. This makes the poem more authentic and truer to reality. The polite brother begins with a gentle address, 'Loving brother', and includes warm wishes at the end, 'I send my affection to all your family'. This tone shows a stark contrast to the usual image of Cromwell as the cruel hate figure who masacred thousands of Irish people.

3   Although Kennelly shows Cromwell's tender nature, he also creates a picture of a complex military commander who has a harsh side to his character, 'I have things to do, all in my own way.' He makes a disturbing comment after the execution of the three Irish soldiers, 'Men die their different ways'. This is a matter-of-fact tone, but it's realistic. The poem ends with the unsettling line, 'I have work to do in Ireland'. Kennelly is suggesting we look at a historical figure who combined good and evil. There are two Cromwells in the poem: a caring family man and the heartless army officer.

4   Kennelly uses many different types of poetry, one of which is the sonnet form. These short poems are often intense and dramatic. In 'Fragments', a series of rhetorical questions engage readers. The speaker is a man who is looking back on a failed relationship or an unhappy marriage. Kennelly depicts tragedy. The man has nothing left 'to say' to the woman he once loved, 'What had he to say to her now?' As she leaves him, it's clear that he no longer really knows her, 'Who was this stranger with the graven

face?' The man now questions everything, 'What led to the dreaming-up of a home?' He has even forgotten who he is because he has shared himself with another person for so long: 'And what was he, at sixty?'

5 The future is hopeless, 'quietly dying'. This man thinks of himself as no more than a series of 'scattered, black fragments, crying' like the plover flying off in the distance. Kennelly's bleak tone adds to the great sense of tragedy. This vivid image of the plover as 'black fragments' suggests that couples can eventually lose love and must accept loss and depression.

6 'A Cry for Art O'Leary' is a translation of an old traditional Irish ballad. Kennelly describes the feelings that a heartbroken wife goes through. Art's widow's feelings are seen through the tone she uses in expressing grief in the rhetorical questions she uses, 'What else could I do?' She uses a metaphor, 'My heart is a lump of grief' to suggest the weight of her sorrow. The poem includes contrasts of love and hatred. Art's widow despises her husband's killer, and is full of vengeance. Yet the poem ends with great dignity. When a woman is faced with loss and sorrow, often caused by a disappointing man, she still has to carry on.

7 'Begin' shows Kennelly at his happiest. A cheerful opening suggests the wonder of a spring morning. He uses a childlike half-rhyme, 'Begin again' and 'i' assonance 'sight of light at the window' to suggest his optimistic mood. I found this poem to be inspirational as it contains a message of hope in the midst of loss, 'old friends passing though with us still'. We are being reassured that we never really lose those we love because they live on in our memory.

8 Through bright imagery and lively sound effects, the poet lets us see 'branches stark in the willing sunlight'. The broad vowel sounds slow down the pace as Kennelly describes the beauty of tree branches silhouetted in the morning sunshine. His conclusion is positive. This world is not only about sadness, but about keeping going and being hopeful, 'something that will not acknowledge conclusion insists that we forever begin'.

9 Kennelly's poems look at the best and worst of human life, suggesting that good and evil can often exist together. Through his great skills with language – especially sound effects, seperate poetic forms, vivid imagery and tones, Kennelly explores many different emotional experiences and often surprises readers with 'a sense of wonder'.

(825 words)

EXAMINER'S COMMENT

In general, this focused response shows some engagement with Kennelly's poetry. Discussion points are well-supported with accurate quotations throughout. The opening provides a useful overview of the ranging emotions in the poems. Critical analysis includes developed commentary on interesting aspects of style, particularly tone, rhetorical questions and sound effects. Expression is functional, but note-like at times, and 'suggests' is overused. Mechanical errors include several misspellings ('protrayed', 'masacred', 'dissapointed', 'seperate'). Overall, a solid high-grade essay.

GRADE H2

P = 13/15

C = 12/15

L = 11/15

M = 4/5

Total = 40/50

Revising D. H. Lawrence (Prescribed for 2022 only)

D. H. Lawrence wrote over 800 poems. Among his most memorable are 'Piano', 'Snake' and 'Bavarian Gentians'. Some of his best-loved poems address the physical and inner life of plants and animals.

Others are bitterly satirical and express outrage. He was particularly critical of the dehumanising effects of industrialisation and the modern world.

Lawrence often confronted issues relating to emotional health and happiness, spontaneity, human sexuality and instinct. He was a fierce critic of the hypocrisy of conventional society.

Lawrence believed that poems should be personal sentiments, with a deep a sense of spontaneity. In much of his later work, he attempted to capture emotion through free verse.

Key themes	Poetic style
• The natural world	• Free verse
• People's relationship with nature	• Vibrant visual imagery
• Death, sorrow and loss	• Evocative sound effects
• Dehumanising effects of modernity	• Rhetorical devices
• Self-fulfilment	• Personification

Sample essay

Question

'D. H. Lawrence uses sensual language and imagery to explore compelling themes with sympathy but without sentimentality.'

To what extent do you agree with this view? Support your answer with reference to the poems by D. H. Lawrence on your course.

Sample answer

1 Three common themes in the poetry of Lawrence are memory, relationships and nature. Lawrence is known for honest and strong emotions, but he is not sentimental. He uses sensual language to express feelings in a realistic way. In poems such as 'Piano', he even stops himself from becoming sentimental. His attitude towards nature is also cautious. In 'Snake', he describes the natural world both as a beautiful and frightening thing. Lawrence sees nature as a wonderful thing, but something that we should respect.

2   In 'Piano', Lawrence talks about how the memory of his mother brings him uncontrollable feelings of nostalgia. This nostalgia, however, may bring both joy and suffering. The sound of the piano 'betrays' him back into the past, and he is forced to revisit a time in his life he had so far buried in his mind. 'Piano' has a sorrowful tone, and it is clear he wants to avoid the sadness that comes with revisiting the past.

3   The piano is a symbol of childhood. The mood is calm and peaceful. Lawrence is listening to a woman singing, which reminded him of his mother and of the past. 'Taking me far back down a long vista of years.' This means he is taken into his memories; he recalls sitting at the piano, 'pressing the small, poised feet of a mother who smiles as she sings.' The sensuous language is gentle. With the sibilant 's' alliteration. We can understand the love between Lawrence and his mother. 'In spite of myself, the insidious song betrays me back.' These soft sounds and images add to the gentle mood without being sentimental or false. But Lawrence doesn't want to forget his mother or her memories. His 'heart weeps to belong'.

4   Lawrence uses shorter lines when he is in the present, but uses longer lines when he is in the past. This shows just how many more memories he has of the past with his mother. In the last part: 'So now it is all in vain' means that now it is pointless. This shows how Lawrence believes it is pointless for the singer to play the piano passionately. Because he is not listening anymore. 'The glamour of childhood is upon me, I weep like a child for the past' is the conclusion of the poem, and it portrays many things. It shows how he was wrapped up in the glamour of the memories.

5   In the nature poem, 'Snake', Lawrence describes a scene that is set in Sicily. He uses sensuous description to portray the snake at his water trough, 'in the deep strange-scented shade'. He uses sibilance to show the snake's colour, 'yellow-brown slackness soft-bellied'. Lawrence has conflicted feelings and this is why his theme regarding the attitude people have to nature is so compelling. Humans believe that the snake 'must be killed', but the poet respects the snake. 'I confess how much I liked him'. Once more, Lawrence is balancing his emotions and thoughts, his heart and head. He debates what he should do without becoming sentimental.

6   The poem is filled with details of the stand-off between Lawrence and the snake. This is very dramatic and emphasises the theme – about how we humans treat nature. Lawrence uses sensual imagery to show the snake's dignity, 'slowly turned his head, and slowly very slowly, as if thrice in a dream'. This contrasts with the poet who throws a stick at the animal, 'I threw it at the water trough with a clatter'. Lawrence leaves the readers to make up their own minds. His account of the way he treated the snake is realistic. Completely without any sentimentality.

7   In 'Mosquito' Lawrence also treats nature without any false feeling. To him, the insect just spreads diseases, so he does not hide his feelings. It is a 'ghoul on wings'. He describes the tiny mosquito in great detail, 'you stalk and prowl the air'. He shows the insect as a small but deadly physical body,

'on thin long shanks'. He hears it up close, 'your small hateful bugle in my ear'. After the mosquito bites him, the language becomes more sensuous, 'Sucking live blood'. The poet is left in a total rage as he kills the mosquito, 'what a dim dark smudge you have now disappeared into'. The alliteration shows disgust for this 'hateful' insect. As in the other poems, Lawrence shows strong feelings but absolutely no sentimentality. Nature is not glorified in this poem.

8   From the poems I've studied, it is clear that Lawrence is keen on sensual language and imagery to explore compelling themes without sentimentality. He presents his views on such topics as memory, nature and relationships in a balanced and realistic way. He is honest in what he says and allows us to make up our own minds about such subjects.

(807 words)

EXAMINER'S COMMENT

This response remains reasonably focused on the three key elements of the question (sensuous language, compelling themes, lack of sentimentality). There is some good, developed discussion of three poems. Supportive quotations are well-integrated into the discussion – but some of these quotes contain inaccuracies. Expression is reasonably controlled, but repetitive and functional at times, e.g. paragraph 4. A solid mid-grade essay.

GRADE H3

P = 11/15

C = 11/15

L = 10/15

M = 5/5

Total = 37/50

You are unlikely to be rewarded for simply pointing out features of the poems, such as images, sounds or other devices that are used. Aim to comment on the effects of such techniques, discussing how they are linked to the ideas in the poems, and why you think they have been used.

Practising SEC Past Paper questions can be a useful revision exercise.

● Study the wording closely to identify the main elements of the question.
● Work within a realistic time frame. (Allow 45–50 minutes per essay.)
● Organise key points into paragraphs.
● Use suitable textual support when appropriate.
● Write clearly and carefully at all times.

Checklist

- ○ Study at least five or six of the prescribed poets.
- ○ Focus on key themes and poetic style.
- ○ Learn to use the language of critical literacy.
- ○ Become familiar with stylistic features – imagery, sounds, tone, etc.
- ○ Identify all the key elements in examination questions.
- ○ Practise making outline plans for focused responses.

Poetry – stylistic features

Alliteration: The use of the same letter or sound at the beginning of each word in a phrase, e.g. *'Season of mists and mellow fruitfulness'* ('To Autumn'). Alliteration often adds emphasis and is just one of many sound effects found in poetry.

Assonance: Another common sound (or aural) effect involving the use of the same vowel sound within a group of words, e.g. *'The enormous odour he lived by/was too close'* ('The Prodigal').

Ballad: Narrative poem similar to a traditional folk-tale with one or more characters and usually constructed in verses, e.g. John Keats's 'La Belle Dame Sans Merci'.

Elegy: A mournful poem, usually lamenting the dead, e.g. 'First Death in Nova Scotia'.

Emotive language: Language designed to arouse an emotional response in the reader, e.g. *'"Beauty is truth, truth beauty" – that is all/Ye know on earth, and all ye need to know'* ('Ode on a Grecian Urn').

Enjambment: The continuation of a sentence without a pause beyond the end of a line or stanza.

Epiphany: A moment of insight or understanding, e.g. *'Somebody loves us all'* ('Filling Station').

Free verse: Unrhymed and unmetred poetry, often used by modern poets, e.g. Elizabeth Bishop's 'The Fish'.

Imagery: Descriptive language or word-pictures, especially appealing to the senses, e.g. *'night's starr'd face'* in 'When I Have Fears'. Here the imagery vividly suggests Keats's alarm about losing creativity.

Irony: The contrast or incongruity between expectations and reality, e.g. the speaker in 'Filling Station', concludes that aesthetic beauty can be found in the most unlikely places.

Lyric: A short musical poem expressing feeling.

Metaphor: Image that compares two things without using the words 'like' or 'as', e.g. *'Much have I travell'd in the realms of gold'* ('On First Looking into Chapman's Homer').

Ode:	A lyrical poem, often in praise of something, such as Keats's 'Ode on a Grecian Urn'.
Onomatopoeia:	The sound of the words imitates or echoes the actual sound being described, e.g. *'in a wailful choir the small gnats mourn'* ('To Autumn').
Personification:	Where the characteristics of an animate or living being are given to something inanimate, e.g. *'He hadn't fought at all'* ('The Fish').
Rhyme:	Identical sound of words, usually at the end of lines of verse, often adding emphasis.
Rhythm:	The beat or pace of words in poetry. Rhythm usually reflects the mood and can vary – fast, slow, regular, irregular, etc.
Sibilance:	Subtle hissing 's' sound, e.g. *'a drowsy numbness pains/My sense'* ('Ode to a Nightingale').
Simile:	A comparison using 'like' or 'as', e.g. *'His brown skin hung like wallpaper'* ('The Fish').
Sonnet:	A 14-line poem. The Petrarchan or Italian sonnet is divided into eight lines (octave), presenting a problem or situation and six final lines (sestet) resolving it. The Shakespearean sonnet is divided into three quatrains (4-line sections) and concludes with a rhyming couplet.
Stanza:	A group of lines, sometimes referred to as a verse (if the lines rhyme). The word 'stanza' derives from the Italian for 'room'.
Symbol:	An object, place, action, etc. that suggests more than its literal meaning, e.g. the urn in 'Ode on a Grecian Urn' symbolises immortality because of its endurance over time.
Theme:	The central idea or message in a poem.
Tone:	The type of voice or attitude used by the poet towards his or her subject, e.g. *'on the shore/Of the wide world I stand alone'*. This reflects Keats's anxiety in 'When I Have Fears That I May Cease to Be'.

Mechanics Revision

Mechanics: Marks for correct spelling and grammar are awarded in the M part of the PCLM marking scheme. They are independent of Purpose (P), Coherence (C) and Language (L).

Common errors

accept	verb – agree/receive	= I accept your invitation.
except	preposition – with the exclusion of	= Everyone except Conor went to the disco.
advice	noun – opinion/guidance	= My teacher gave me good advice.
advise	verb – make a suggestion	= I advise you to go home right now.
affect	verb – influence	= Regular exercise affects your mood positively.
effect	noun – result of an action	= Poor spelling had an adverse effect on Zoe's grades.
allowed	verb – permitted	= We were not allowed outside.
aloud	adjective – out loud	= She read the poem aloud to the listeners.
its	possession – belong to it	= The dog licked its sore paw.
it's	short form – it is	= Oh no! It's raining again.
loose	adjective – not fastened	= The car wheel suddenly became loose.
lose	verb – not win	= Let's hope we won't lose the match next Sunday.
passed	past tense of verb 'pass'	= Laura passed her exams with top honours.
past	noun – an earlier time	= The past cannot be lived again.
practise	verb – prepare	= Sheila needs to practise her scales.
practice	noun – preparation	= Practice is needed to become good at sport.
principal	noun – chief	= The school's principal spoke at assembly.
principle	noun – basic idea	= The principle of equality is important.
quite	adverb – not completely	= I am quite fit these days.
quiet	adjective – not noisy	= Liam and Rory are both quiet little boys.

stationary	adjective – stopped	= Always wait until the bus is stationary before you get off.
stationery	noun – writing materials	= The office ran out of stationery.
there	noun – place	= Let's sit over there and have lunch.
there	pronoun introducing noun or sentence	= There is supposed to be sun tomorrow.
their	possessive adjective – stopped	= Their new cat Jolie is really awesome.
they're	short form – they are	= They're getting tired of all this study.
whether	conjunction – alternative	= We do not know whether to go right or left.
weather	noun – state of atmosphere	= The weather is wonderful today.
your	pronoun – belonging to you	= Your car is fixed at last.
you're	short form – you are	= Oh dear! You're going nowhere fast.

Two separate words

A lot, as well, no one, thank you, each other, in fact …

Avoid!

Majorly, relatable, must of, could of, would of, might of, should of, sort of, you know, like …

Finally, a reminder that careful punctuation will help you side-step embarrassing errors, such as these familiar ones:

- I love my parents, Lady Gaga and Peter Rabbit.
- We make great burgers here – and the secret ingredient is our people.
- Lost: Pony belonging to young girl with a silver mane and tail.
- I always take time out for baking my family and my dog.
- The panda giant usually eats shoots and leaves.
- Thank you. Your donation has helped someone. Get a job.
- Today, we will learn how to cut and paste kids.
- Try our bananas. None like them.
- Yesterday I saw my two cousins, a tortoiseshell cat and a gerbil.
- Have you eaten Grandad?

Acknowledgements

The authors and publisher are grateful to the following for permission to reproduce copyrighted material:

'Patricia Cornwell: how extreme sports changed my life' in *The Guardian*, by Patricia Cornwell. © Guardian News & Media Ltd 2020.

The Red Door: The Complete English Short Stories, 1949-76 by Iain Crichton Smith, Birlinn Ltd, 2001. Copyright © the estate of Iain Crichton Smith, 1949-76. Reproduced with permission of Birlinn Ltd via PLS Clear.

Excerpt from pp. 1–2, book cover from *Desert Flower* by Waris Dirie and Cathleen Miller. Copyright © 1998 by Waris Dirie. Published by HarperCollins Publishers.

Extract from 'Parents rise up! We CAN tame today's spoilt little terrors ... and in a new book, an expert in good old-fashioned discipline shows you how' by Liat Hughes Joshi, *The Daily Mail Online*, 2015. Reproduced by kind permission of Liat Hughes Joshi.

'November Night, Edinburgh' by Norman MacCaig, taken from *The Poems of Norman MacCaig*, Polygon Books, 2009. Copyright © Norman MacCaig. Reproduced with permission of Birlinn Ltd via PLS Clear.

Let the Great World Spin by Colum McCann. Copyright © Colum McCann, 2009, *Let the Great World Spin*, Bloomsbury Publishing Plc.

Nothing on Earth by Conor O'Callaghan. Copyright © Conor O'Callaghan, 2016. Published by Doubleday Ireland.

'First Love' from *Collected Poems* by Brian Patten. Published by HarperCollins, 2006. Copyright © Brian Patten. Reproduced by permission of the author c/o Rogers, Coleridge & White Ltd., 20 Powis Mews, London W11 1JN.

Resistance by Owen Sheers. Copyright © Owen Sheers, 2007. Published by Faber and Faber Ltd.